# The Politics of Intervention

A PUBLICATION OF
THE MERSHON CENTER FOR EDUCATION
IN NATIONAL SECURITY

# The Politics of Intervention

## THE MILITARY OCCUPATION
## OF CUBA, 1906-1909

BY ALLAN REED MILLETT

OHIO STATE UNIVERSITY PRESS

# *Preface*

I N THE YEARS immediately following the Spanish-American War, the realities of Cuban independence weighed heavily on the United States. In September, 1906, as the result of an insurrection in Cuba, Theodore Roosevelt, citing his responsibilities to Cuba under the Platt Amendment, intervened to end the war and reluctantly assumed direct control of the Cuban government. Five thousand American troops occupied the island. Until the occupation ended in 1909, the American government attempted to restore the pre-revolt political alignment, although the intervention and occupation had made such a restoration impossible. This policy was determined by some factors that had little relation to Cuban political life: recent civil and military experiences in the Philippines and the public reaction to them, the American presumption that the occupation was temporary, American assumptions about the efficacy of political parties as a mode of political expression, and the Roosevelt administration's conclusion that popular elections were essential to stable and legitimate government.

Political and economic influence in one form or another was the historic state of relations between the United States and Cuba. Constitutionalized as the right of intervention after 1898, this relationship became the promise of active political and administrative control of Cuba by the United States under certain conditions which might threaten Cuba's independence. It was assumed that the United States would be the initiator of such action. The possibility of intervention, however, as pledged in the organic law of both countries was a constant

factor in the plans, fears, and aspirations of Cuba's political
leaders as they sought to turn American policy to their
personal advantage.

Yet United States policy-makers were only half-aware of
the implications of their relationship with Cuba. They assumed
that the orderly transfer of power in a system of government
was the irreducible condition of stability, in American usage,
for it represented the violence-free accommodation of competing interest groups within the body politic. In terms of
day-to-day conditions, the absence of politically significant
violence was the gauge by which stability was measured. In
all, stability was a rather mysterious but prized condition.
When applied to Cuba, this definition was a narrow measure
of that nation's capacity for peaceful internal change. But
in American diplomatic usage, the maintenance of peace
rather than the substance of internal change was the criterion
for non-intervention.

Although this book is a political history, it stresses the use
of American armed forces in the Cuban crisis of 1906 and
the occupation that followed. It emphasizes the role of officers
of the United States Army in the policy-making process and
their relations with their civil superiors in determining both
the character of the Cuban intervention and the programs of
the occupation.

In terms of policy the Army officers serving in Cuba during
the Second Intervention (as differentiated from the one of
1898) influenced the decisions made within the Provisional
Government. More importantly, they favored alternatives to
American policy, which were rejected. They differed with
the United States political leaders by believing American
policy would be best served if basic changes were encouraged
in Cuba's domestic institutions. Unenthusiastic about dealing
with Cuba's professional politicians and placing little faith in
the reforming potential of Cuba's political parties, the officers
realized that supervised elections were essential to the grace-
ful liquidation of the occupation, but doubted the wisdom of
both elections and withdrawal. They believed that continued,

reformist American occupation would best serve the Cuban people and the interests of the United States.

In addition to describing American civil-military relations in the Cuban occupation, this study is a history of the use of American forces as an instrument of national policy and the political implications of their use in a specific historic situation. Essentially it deals with the constraints upon the Roosevelt administration as it worked to resolve the Cuban crisis without using force. It examines why Roosevelt tried to avoid employing troops and why the decision to occupy Cuba was taken largely from his hands by events over which he had little control, but for which he bore some responsibility.

Although the Second Intervention in Cuba involved two sovereign states, it was, militarily, a problem in applying the political, economic, psychological techniques of maintaining internal security. The management of internal security affairs in Cuba was an Army function, performed by the officers in the Provisional Government of Charles E. Magoon, the advisers to Cuba's constabulary, and the Army of Cuban Pacification. As an internal security operation, the occupation had its antecedents in the Army's experiences in Cuba after the Spanish-American War and in the Philippine Insurrection. Because of the domestic political reaction to these earlier military occupations, the Army's activities from 1906 to 1909 were restricted to the minimum tasks required to establish public order. As this study demonstrates, the Army was the guarantor of stability, and its officers were the major architects and critics of the work of the Provisional Government.

# Acknowledgments

I T IS NO NEWS to writers and readers of history that even though a title page bears the name of a single author, the work is inherently collaborative. This study is no different, for whatever the old cliché about "too many cooks," a history is much richer fare for the collaboration. Since this is my first work, I want to thank specifically all those who have assisted me and upon whom I am likely to rely again.

My thanks, first, to the archivists and manuscript librarians whose help was crucial, to the staffs of the National Archives of the United States; the Manuscript Division of the Library of Congress; the Western Historical Manuscript Collection, University of Missouri Library; the Manuscripts Division, University of Virginia Library; the Southern Historical Collection, the University of North Carolina Library, Chapel Hill; and the Division of Archives and Manuscripts, the State Historical Society of Wisconsin. I particularly want to thank Mr. Sherrod East, Mr. John E. Taylor, Mrs. Sarah D. Jackson, Mr. Milton Chamberlain, and Mrs. Miriam J. Stockwell of the National Archives for their invaluable assistance.

Of no less assistance were the staffs of the Ohio State University Library; the Columbus Memorial Library, Pan American Union; the University of North Carolina Library; the Library of Congress; the Duke University Library, the United States Military Academy Library; the Marine Corps Museum, Quantico, Virginia; and the Historical Reference Section, Headquarters Marine Corps.

I would also like to thank my adviser, Professor Harry L. Coles of the Department of History, Ohio State University, for his wise counsel and for collecting documents for me at the Public Record Office, London, England. I want to express my appreciation for the suggestions of all those who read the manuscript: the late Professor Edgar S. Furniss, Jr., and Professor Marvin Zahniser of the Ohio State University; and Professor Richard L. Millett, Southern Illinois University. I am also indebted to Dr. David A. Lockmiller, whose *Magoon in Cuba* is the pioneer study of the Second Intervention, and to Mr. Frank Steinhart, Jr., for their advice.

I would be derelict if I failed to mention the financial assistance that made this work possible: my thanks to the Woodrow Wilson National Fellowship Foundation, the Graduate School and the Mershon Center for Education in National Security at the Ohio State University, the Research Council of the University of Missouri, and my parents.

My sincere thanks to my friends Mr. and Mrs. A. A. Graham II of Washington, D. C., who run a most congenial hostel for itinerant scholars.

Lastly, but no less importantly, I wish to express my thanks and admiration to my wife Sally for her patience, understanding, interest, and constructive criticism.

ALLAN R. MILLETT

*Columbia, Missouri*
*June, 1967*

# Contents

# THE UNITED STATES ARMY AND THE
# BURDENS OF WORLD POWER

IN THE YEARS BETWEEN 1898 and 1917 the United States Army assumed the military responsibilities of a major world power with overseas possessions. By 1906 the Army was settled in its role as colonial administrator and defender with some fifteen thousand soldiers serving in the insular possessions. The Army was twice as large as it had been before 1898: 58,368 officers and men. Still it was four thousand men short of its authorized strength, Army life being underpaid and unattractive in comparison with civilian life.

If better-managed and supplied, the "semicloistered" Army remained outside the main stream of civil life.[1] Its expanded officer corps, becoming more specialized, suffered from branch parochialism. Service overseas was commonplace and came too often to suit the family men. Privates, who enlisted for a minimum of five years, received $15 monthly. Most of the soldiers were disenfranchised, there being no provisions for absentee voting. Businesses displayed signs reading "No Uniforms Wanted." Rank very much had its privileges as well as its responsibilities; the line between officers and men was clearly drawn. It was an Army unwavering in its views on discipline, spit-and-polish, minute accounting procedures, small unit tactics, individual marksmanship, and the superiority of its value system over that of American civil society.

The expansion of the Army during the war with Spain and the fortunes of active service catapulted new men into the Army's highest ranks. In 1906 only one of the thirty-four general officers on active service had worn stars before 1898, and the hardships of tropical service and a presidential decision to give some preference to ability over seniority brought officers of most unconventional accomplishments to important commands.

Perhaps the most stunning military career after 1898 was that of Leonard Wood. Born in 1860 of an old New England family of slight means and stern convictions, Wood took a medical degree at Harvard and, in 1885, joined the Army as a contract surgeon.[2] Commissioned and later awarded the Medal of Honor for his endurance in the pursuit of Geronimo, Wood became family physician to Presidents Cleveland and McKinley. During his years in Washington, he won highly placed friends, including Theodore Roosevelt. At the outbreak of the war with Spain, Colonel Wood and Lieutenant Colonel Roosevelt raised the First Volunteer Cavalry and campaigned gloriously in Cuba. Roosevelt, admirer and patron of the ambitious doctor-soldier, wrote of Wood in 1899:

> He combined, in a very high degree, the qualities of entire manliness with entire uprightness and cleanliness of character. It was a pleasure to deal with a man of high ideals, who scorned everything mean and base, and who also possessed those robust and hardy qualities of body and mind, for which no merely negative virtue can ever atone. He was by nature a soldier of the highest type.[3]

Wood had his enemies in the Army and in Washington, for he was outspoken, incorruptible, politically astute, a born publicist, and endlessly confident in his principles and abilities. He had risen quickly past more senior and (in their view) deserving officers, and his critics never missed a chance to attack him. He was a commander who often won unswerving loyalty from his subordinates. In all, Leonard Wood was one of America's greatest and most controversial soldier-administrators.

Roosevelt considered Brigadier General James Franklin Bell to be as able a soldier as Leonard Wood.[4] After his graduation from West Point in 1878, Bell served a long apprenticeship on the plains. In 1899 he was still just another graying captain of cavalry. As the colonel of a volunteer regiment, however, he won a Medal of Honor in 1899 in the Philippines. He then served as a provost marshal and district commander on Luzon from 1900 to 1903. In 1901, he became a brigadier general in the Regular Army, an advancement of four grades. Promoted by McKinley and admired by Roosevelt, Bell was appointed Chief of Staff in 1906 at the age of fifty.

Another of the new brigadiers, Thomas H. Barry, was a contemporary of Bell's at West Point. He joined the Seventh Cavalry on the frontier in 1877 (the Sioux and Nez Percés had created some openings) and built a reputation as a blunt, hard-working, and particularly effective staff officer. He was "fair and square . . . the best known Catholic officer in the service." As an assistant adjutant-general, Barry served in the Philippines and China from 1898 to 1901. Returning to the United States, he joined the new General Staff and, in the summer of 1906, was touring Europe to observe maneuvers. Barry appears in news photos as a stiff, white-haired, dark-browed model of a modern brigadier; the panoply of epaulettes, aiguellettes, sash, medals, and braid draw attention from his oversize ears.

However rapid the advancement of Wood, Bell, and Barry after 1898, the career of Brigadier General Frederick Funston was by comparison meteoric and far more controversial. He was incomparably the most colorful of the new generals, enjoyed wide public recognition, and was strictly not Old Army. The son of a Kansas congressman, Funston attended the University of Kansas for two years (1886–88). A fraternity brother, editor William Allen White, described his friend:

Fred Funston was . . . at that time . . . a pudgy, applecheeked young fellow, just under five feet five, who seemed to have decided in his cradle to overcome his runty size by laughing at himself. . . . He walked swiftly but not too steadily, indulged in no athletic sports whatever, was a good rifle shot, had absolutely no sense of fear, physical or spiritual, was a poor but passable student, read widely, had vast areas of curious information, loved good clothes which he could not afford to buy, was methodical and rather meticulous in his habits, affectionate by nature: everyone . . . loved him. . . .[5]

Quitting Kansas for more adventurous frontiers, Funston explored Alaska and Death Valley as a Department of Agriculture botanist. Returning to New York in 1896 from an unsuccessful business venture in Central America, he joined the Cuban insurgent army out of curiosity. After running the blockade, he subsequently commanded Máximo Gómez' artillery (three guns) in two years of fighting. In 1898, sick, wounded, and exhausted, Funston reached the American legation in Havana and returned to Kansas before the outbreak of war. On the strength of his Cuban service he became colonel of the Twentieth Kansas and led his regiment in thirty-five engagements against the Filipinos. For swimming the Rio Grande under fire at Calumpit, Luzon, and organizing a bridgehead which flanked the insurgents in a bitter skirmish, he won the Medal of Honor and promotion to Brigadier General, Volunteers. In 1901, as a district commander on Luzon, Funston engineered the most daring coup of the insurrection. Using loyal Macabebe scouts as a screen, he and a handful of Americans, posing as captives, bluffed their way to Aguinaldo's heavily-guarded headquarters and seized the general-president. Elihu Root in his report for 1901 called the feat "the most important single military event of the year."

In April, 1901, Funston, at the age of thirty-six and without a day's service as a Regular, became a Brigadier General, United States Army. His unorthodox career and sudden promotion led Adjutant General Henry C. Corbin to comment: "I am making lieutenants of better stuff than Funston every day. Funston is a boss-scout—that's all!"[6] In 1906, Funston again made headlines when an earthquake devastated San Francisco. As the senior officer present in the Bay area, he directed the soldiers who fought fires, rescued survivors, halted epidemics, stopped looting, treated the injured, and recaptured zoo animals. Yet these heroics did not obscure the fact that Frederick Funston knew Cubans and he knew guerrilla warfare, and in 1906 these were qualities the Army could ill-afford to ignore.

Whatever the accomplishments of individual officers, the Army by 1906 was no longer a haven for sword-waving romantics. From the end of the Civil War, the major trend in the Army's officer corps had been professionalization: the systematic study of war and the creation of organizational forms and attitudes best suited for the scientific conduct of war.[7] The Army's concerted effort to systematize itself for the most effective application of force contributed to its isolation from civil society. While the intellectual, political, and social elite of late nineteenth century America saw war as a moral evil, materially wasteful, and an unnatural disruption of human progress, the Army officers viewed it as a historical fact and a timeless expression of man's nature. To civilians, the military virtues were anachronistic, military society authoritarian, and the Army an economic burden. To soldiers, American society, dominated by materialism, self-indulgence, and license, was distasteful. Politicians who pandered to these values to gain personal power were morally suspect. The officer corps, due largely to its indoctrination, defined its major problem to be reconciling the United States military policy to the whims of the nation's foreign policymakers and to the niggardliness of Congress.[8]

## Years of Trial and Experience

Looking back to the halcyon days in the summer of 1898 when the United States was saving people it barely knew from Spanish oppression, General Hugh L. Scott remembered the war as the first time since 1865 that Americans discovered they had a regular army. He and his fellow officers knew "our army was organized for peace and not war," but the Army's low status in the United States was too great to overcome. Instead, inflamed by the news from Cuba, "the people . . . took the bit in their teeth and ran away." Although soldiers were blamed for inciting wars for their own ends, Scott believed the United States had gone to war with Spain "without the soldiers exerting the slightest influence toward that end. It is the people and the politician that make war and the soldier who makes peace."[9]

In 1898, when forced by "the People" to fight its first foreign war in fifty years, the Army, a meager twenty-eight thousand, found the task beyond its resources. There were too few hands and too little experience to draw upon, from the Secretary of War down to the newest lieutenant. At Las Guásimas, General Joe Wheeler may have thought the Spaniards were Yankees; the rest of the Army conducted the war as if it were fighting the Sioux.

Soon enough the Army and the American public were made aware by foreign military observers, a legion of correspondents, and the Dodge Commission that little was right with the American military system. Even so, Elihu Root, upon becoming Secretary of War in July, 1899, found it difficult to make the reforms to correct the moribund organization of 1898. Nonetheless, the Root reforms did begin to reorient the Army to the demands of the twentieth century. By 1903 legislation had created an embryonic General Staff with planning and supervisory responsibilities over the Army bureaus, replaced the commanding general with a chief of staff of limited tenure, established the Army War College, and reorganized the National Guard. For the first time the United States Army was placed on an organizational par with European armies.

The reforms had little immediate applicability to the Army's most pressing problem, that of pacifying and administering America's new colonial possessions. The only change that helped was the enlargement of the Army. Whether Root was most influenced by the new problems of world politics or by the belief that his reforms had universal appropriateness in terms of managerial efficiency, he directed American military thinking toward the problems of defending the United States from the organized armed forces of other industrialized nations. This is not to say that Root slighted colonial problems. Much of his work as Secretary of War (indeed the rationale for his appointment) was to administer the insular possessions.[10] Although he might have chosen to thrash out publicly the policy with which the United States should govern culturally and racially different peoples, he did not.

The determining factor was the quick cooling of the evangelistic fervor that had helped sweep Americans into war in 1898.

Although the war with Spain reshaped the United States Army, it was the Philippine Insurrection that was the Army's major experience between the Indian wars and World War I. In crushing Philippine resistance to American tutelage, the Army lost ten times as many battlefield casualties as it suffered in Cuba. The insurrection was a costly, unpopular war, long on hardship and short on measurable victory. It was fought, in the view of many educated Americans, in a distasteful manner for confused goals. The Philippine Insurrection brought public censure to the Army, and it also put the Army into the business of colonial government, for which its frontier service provided only partial education.[11]

Because the Army had to draw upon its own resources and experiences in pacifying the Philippines and because its past was most closely linked with its constabulary service on the Great Plains, the Army was guided by some definite assumptions about controlling rebellious subject peoples. The Army, dealing with the Plains Indians, had used a simple code of justice: good behavior was rewarded and breaches of the peace were punished as quickly as possible. There was little room for negotiation and compromise. There was, however, some humane concern for the Indians, but the Army's approach was distinctly paternalistic. In all, the Army found force or the threat of force the best method of subduing the Indians, and it received little meaningful education in governing complex and alien societies. An interesting insight into the residual effects of this experience is the respect the American officers felt for the Moros, a savage, primitive Moslem people who inhabited the southernmost Philippines. American officers, on the other hand, could scarcely hide their distaste for the Hispanized, Christian Filipinos of Luzon.

The outbreak of the Philippine Insurrection in 1899 produced shock in the United States. Even so, there was little criticism of the subsequent Luzon campaigns, which shattered conventional resistance by the end of that year. But the fighting continued, despite staggering losses to the insurgents. The Army's problems were not easily solved. In the Philippines the Army faced millions of inhabitants, urban and rural, living in both complex and simple societies. It was confronted with ancient social, tribal, religious, and economic rivalries and a subwar between the Filipinos themselves. It was matched against political organization and nationalism.

In 1899 the Army needed sixty thousand men just to hold the major towns and break up the organized insurgent army. In the meantime, the rebel shadow government continued to function; taxes were collected for the rebels even inside occupied Manila. The population supplied the insurgents with arms, food, recruits, and information. Native policemen, local officials, and American sympathizers were kidnaped, tortured, and murdered. Nationalist propaganda, much of it publicizing American anti-imperialist sentiment, reached many *barrios*. The strength of the resistance, built on a foundation of popular support, was admitted by Major General Arthur MacArthur— in 1900 the senior Army commander in the islands: " . . . the real effective opposition to pacification comes from towns. The 'skulking bands of Guerrilla' . . . are mere expressions of the loyalty of the towns. They could not exist for a month without urban support."[12]

The American response was to increase the number of occupying troops to seventy-three thousand in 1900 and to step up its efforts to control the population. Appalled by the cruelty of the insurgents to their own countrymen and outraged by what it considered to be guerrilla treachery and brutality, the Army showed little sympathy for suspected insurgents. Although policy until 1900 had been to leave civilian sympathizers alone, this act of generosity, according to Secretary Root, was interpreted as a sign of weakness. A Filipino officer-historian writes, however, that "the violent repressive measures adopted by the Americans in subduing the guerrillas proved ineffective because, instead of winning the sympathy of the Filipino civilians, they brought about more indignation and defiance against the Americans."[13]

Even the effectiveness of the American soldiers in skirmishes with guerrilla bands turned against them. By virtue of better marksmanship, leadership, and tactics, the Americans killed twenty-five insurgents for every soldier lost. This kill ratio and the relatively few numbers of wounded captured seemed implicit proof of wanton slaughter, despite General MacArthur's patient explanations to Congressional investigators.[14] In any event, General MacArthur, according to an Army historian, "saw the profitlessness of treating captured insurgents with consideration. They always responded with cruelty and treachery. Leniency seemed merely to cause more blood to be spilled."[15]

The American public, on the other hand, saw its soldiers behaving in what some considered a dishonorable, unchristian, and inhumane manner. As one journal put it: "There have been more wicked wars than this on the liberties of the Filipinos, but never a more shabby war." While Funston was praised by many for his capture of Aguinaldo, he was also memorialized in a ditty of the day:

> Sing a song of Funston
> How his treachery
> Captured Aguinaldo;
> Macabaeus by.
> Forgery and lying
> That's the modern thing. . . .[16]

Funston also won the attention of Mark Twain's *North American Review*. A staunch anti-imperialist, Twain condemned Funston for using a ruse to enter Aguinaldo's camp. Funston had defiled the "holy custom" of respecting the safety of these who fed the distressed. By feigning hunger, Funston, instead, had captured his host. Funston, in Twain's eyes, represented a new man, an amoral agent of imperialism, the irresponsible hero of a nation run amok.[17]

One especially controversial tactic was the resettlement of rural noncombatants and the destruction of their property: reconcentration. For the American newspaper reader in 1900, reconcentration conjured up all manner of horrors: "Butcher" Weyler herding Cuban men, women, and children into crumbling towns to die by the thousands of typhoid and starvation. Across the Atlantic, so the papers said, the British Army was penning thousands of suffering Boers behind barbed wire. This was the kind of military barbarism Americans had gone to war to end in 1898. Yet suddenly from the Philippines came news that reconcentration was part of the price of bringing freedom to the Filipinos. This revelation was a shock, and provided an explosive political issue.

The Army officers in the Philippines knew the necessity of reconcentration in ending the insurrection, but the shortage of troops and logistical support, plus their awareness of the probable American reaction, restrained them. In December, 1900, however, continued resistance in the provinces of Batangas and Tayabas, Luzon, forced General J. Franklin Bell, the local commander, to round up the rural population and resettle them in closely guarded camps. An estimated ten thousand active supporters of the revolt were thus segregated from the insurgents.[18] On Samar in 1901, as Brigadier General Robert P. Hughes testified in Senate hearings, some one hundred and fifty thousand natives were forcibly resettled.[19] In both instances the Army made an effort to keep individual deprivation to a minimum, but there were the inevitable deaths from disease. The Army indeed provided security for the Filipinos, but reconcentration was not the kind of freedom Americans understood.

With the political stakes high and a sincere desire to provide the Filipinos something more than war, and with the Army apparently unable to make headway in pacification, President McKinley sent the Second Philippine Commission in 1900 to begin the political and economic development of the islands.[20] The Commission's president, William Howard Taft, became the civil governor with complete authority over the pacified third of the Philippine provinces; and Taft, as his control gradually replaced Army rule throughout the islands, did much to conciliate the Filipinos. He worked hard to introduce education and health programs, to stimulate the economy, revise the legal system and provide local law and order. Throughout his governorship the genial, sympathetic former Federal Judge from Ohio sought to cultivate the friendship and loyalty of the Filipinos, particularly those "as orthodox in matters of [economic and legal] importance as we are."[21] Still the Army had to take to the bush after the remaining insurgents, and its general attitude toward the Civil Governor is preserved in a popular marching song:

I'm only a common soldier man in the blasted Philippines.
They say I've got Brown Brothers here, but I dunno what it means.
I like the word Fraternity, but I still draw the line.
He may be a brother of Big Bill Taft, but he ain't no brother of mine.
Damn, damn, damn the insurrecto
Pock marked, khakiac ladrone.
Underneath the starry flag
Civilize 'em with a Krag
And return us to our own beloved homes.

The administration, sensitive to the criticism of American policy articulated as condemnation of the Army, attempted to scotch the atrocity charges and vindicate the policy. In public speeches and in his annual reports, Elihu Root repeated his message: the American soldiers were as innocent and humane as one could expect under the circumstances, and, in any case, America's civilizing mission was noble enough to push forward at the going cost.[22]

All this verbiage may have been a tonic for the Army's nerves, but its officers did not forget that they would have to answer for what were portrayed to American readers as atrocities. In February, 1906, at Bud Dajo, Sulu, a punitive column of soldiers, sailors, and Philippine constabulary attacked and killed six hundred renegade Moros, men, women, and children. The Moros would not surrender; the women fought along side the warriors, and both used children for shields. Ninety-four of the assaulting force of four hundred were casualties. Yet in the United States the *Washington Post* and the New York *World* described the fight as a massacre and compared Leonard Wood, the local commander, with Cortez and Pizarro. On the floor of the House, John Sharp Williams recited a parody to the vast amusement of the Democratic members:

> Chased them from everywhere
> Chased them all onward
> Into the crater of death,
> Drove them—six hundred!
> "Forward, the Wood Brigade!
> Spare not a one," he said.
> "Shoot all six hundred."[23]

Although the administration quieted the clamor by publishing the after-action reports of the Bud Dajo fight, Secretary of War Taft felt the need to caution Wood against the wanton killing of women and children.[24] When it came to putting down insurrections, the officers of the United States Army could see that pacification was not a popular instrument of public policy.

### Military Pacification

In the first decade of the twentieth century, the U.S. Army mastered a difficult kind of warfare: the military pacification of a rebellious civil population by military, psychological, and economic methods. Its leaders knew that pacification was full of political and social impications at home and abroad that could threaten the Army's reputation and its ability to defend the nation. Its officers did not always agree on the Army's tactics in pacification operations or to what extent it should function in areas reserved to civil government in the United States. Yet, the Army was well aware that America's expanding interest in the Caribbean, as well as the Pacific, could once more put it in the business of administering a foreign land.

The United States Army's approach to colonial policy was in step with its own institutional history and its view of human behavior.[25] Basically, the Army's philosophy of human nature was based on its nineteenth century experiences: the policing of the frontier, the absorption of immigrants into its own ranks, and, as in the Civil War and in 1898, the necessity of disciplining and organizing mass armies of civilians. Man, in the Army's view, was by nature undisciplined, emotional, and potentially violent, but he was also weak-willed, malleable, and always yearning for a secure place in a human community more permanent than himself.

In an institution like the Army, man's adjustment was accomplished by constant training in co-operative ventures and by imposed and self-discipline. Through the paternal guidance of one's superiors (those responsible for the adjustment process), one learned to equate his personal well-being and goals with those of the institution. In the process of socialization, happiness (the sense of belonging) lay within every man's grasp, however limited his talents or humble his origin. Of course, the practical purpose of this process was to produce men who were willing to follow orders and die in combat rather than disgrace themselves, their comrades, and the honor of the regiment. In personal terms, the Army's view of human nature put a high premium on such qualities as honor, truthfulness, obedience, self-sacrifice, justice, and loyalty, all qualities which could be inculcated in time. In social terms, the Army emphasized order through social harmony, co-operation, and education.

The Army's view of human adjustment became doctrine when it was applied to the peoples of the Philippine and Caribbean. Paternalistic guidance and long tutelage were the Army's cures for the anarchy, corruption, and exaggerated individuality which, as the Army saw it, were the inherited ills of Spain's former colonies. The Army's colonial policy, by both circumstance and conviction, was to substitute a beneficent military government for the exploitative, chaotic governments of Spain or the indigenous political elite. The goal of Army policy was to inculcate a sense of community and order in the governed.

In the Army's colonial policy there was some appreciation of the effects of poverty on human behavior and the importance of economic development on internal peace, but the officers of that era accepted the dogma of industrial capitalism without serious question. They may have suspected the personal values of the business world, but they deferred to the businessmen's expertise in economic matters. Consequently, the Army assumed that government did not bear the major responsibility for the economic well-being of the dependencies. In the area of political organization the Army was less committed to spreading democratic institutions than America's political leaders. The road to democracy meant encouraging political parties and holding elections in backward societies, and the Army saw such activities as a source of violence and injustice.

The Army's Philippine experience, shared by most of the officers of the combat arms, produced a group of military measures for the response to a popular uprising which had unquestionable political implications. A lucid commentary on the tactics of pacification may be found in Captain John W. Furlong's "Notes on Field Service in Cuba."[26] Furlong, basing his analysis on Spanish military operations and his own four years of service in the Philippines and Cuba, stressed that the three major tasks in operations against insurgents were identifying them, depriving them of popular support, and eliminating them by aggressive, continuous operations. To identify the insurgents, intelligence must be fresh and voluminous, which meant lavish expenditures for information; Furlong recommended that all field commanders have secret service funds available. In questioning suspects, Furlong continued, the goal of interrogation was complete personal data on every rebel, and no suspect should be allowed to sleep until thoroughly quizzed. To streamline the intelligence-security organization, a single officer should hold, concurrently, the posts of intelligence officer, provost marshal, and provost judge in each military district.

Furlong believed that food control was the most effective means to sever the people from the insurgents. This meant destroying the food supply in the countryside and rounding up the rural population, operations which would both starve and demoralize the rebels. Towns and reconcentration camps must then be securely guarded to prohibit traffic in food from urban areas. In assessing Spanish measures in Cuba, Furlong concluded that "the policy of reconcentration became absolutely necessary."

Furlong stated that active military operations against guerrillas should be handled by columns of two hundred men, armed and supplied for maximum speed. Pursuit must be relentless, and no surrenders should be accepted unless the guerrilla brought in his weapon.

Lieutenant Colonel Robert L. Bullard brought wider vision and as much study to his thinking on the problems of pacification. With Philippine service that ranged from field operations as a regimental commander to a provincial governorship, Bullard, an introspective West Pointer, stressed that political persuasion rather than military force was the heart of pacification.[27] Pacification, he wrote, "is no more than dealing with a people, handling and governing them according to their genius and character." This required a policy "composed of force and persuasion." Patience on the part of the military was absolutely necessary, but Bullard noted that there was a tendency to under-react when force was needed, which often caused greater destruction and bloodshed later. Reconcentration, however necessary in extreme cases of revolt, must be humane and well planned or its effects would be disastrous.

Bullard conceded that force alone could not win the final objective, the consent of the governed. Rather, he pointed out, the habits and thinking of the people must be gradually changed; he stressed religious education, the wide application of medical knowledge, and indoctrination of the young native political leaders and the children, and, in all matters, respect for the individual dignity of the people.

Furlong's and Bullard's writings on pacification are significant, for they represent the more thoughtful views of the officer corps. Furlong was detailed to the Military Information Division of the General Staff, and both officers held important posts in Cuba during the Second Intervention. There were other lessons, however, to be learned in the practical study of pacification not included in their writings. For all the study and all the techniques learned in the Philippines, the officers of the United States Army knew that colonial service was full of unforeseen hazards. As one general later phrased the dilemma:

Time and again since the nation assumed the role of World Power there have been thrust upon junior subalterns the determination of grave questions involving diplomacy, commerce, and the law, international, civil and criminal. A correct decision, with prompt and forceful action, may tide over a grave emergency, whilst an honest error may live to mar a record through a lifetime of loyal service.[28]

Yet the risks to reputation and career often only reinforced some officers' compulsions to "civilize" an occupied people, and this was equally true for Cuba as it was for the United States possessions.

1. R. Ernest Dupuy, *The Compact History of the United States Army* (New York, 1956), pp. 183–217.

2. The standard biography of Wood is Hermann Hagedorn, *Leonard Wood* (2 vols.; New York and London, 1931).

3. Theodore Roosevelt, *The Rough Riders* (*The Collected Works of Theodore Roosevelt*, Vol. XIII [24 vols.; New York, 1923–26]), p. 5.

4. Roosevelt to Charles W. Eliot, September 22, 1906, Theodore Roosevelt Papers, Library of Congress.

5. William Allen White, *Autobiography of William Allen White* (New York, 1946), p. 143. See also Funston's obituary, *Army and Navy Journal*, February 24, 1917; and the *New York Times*, February 20, 1917.

6. Reported in the *Army and Navy Journal*, April 13, 1907. For Funston's delightful account of his military career, see Frederick Funston, *Memories of Two Wars* (New York, 1911).

7. Samuel P. Huntington, *The Soldier and the State* (Cambridge, Massachusetts, 1957), pp. 222–69. For the American antimilitary tradition in the late nineteenth century, see Arthur A. Ekirch, Jr., *The Civilian and the Military* (New York, 1956), pp. 107–55.

8. William Harding Carter, *The American Army* (Indianapolis, 1915), pp. 1–27. General Carter was Secretary of War, Elihu Root's principal assistant in preparing the Army reforms of 1903.

9. Hugh L. Scott, *Some Memories of a Soldier* (New York, 1928), p. 218.

10. Philip C. Jessup, *Elihu Root* (New York, 1938), I, 215–407; Richard Leopold, *Elihu Root and the Conservative Tradition* (Boston,

1954), pp. 24–46. For the clearest exposition of the development of Root's thinking on colonial and military problems, see Robert Bacon and James Brown Scott (eds.), *The Military and Colonial Policy of the United States: Addresses and Reports by Elihu Root* (Cambridge, Mass. 1916); and U. S. War Department, *Five Years of the War Department Following the War with Spain, 1899–1903, as shown in the Annual Reports of the Secretary of War* (Washington, 1904).

11. The official account is best followed in the various reports in the U.S. War Department *Annual Reports*, from 1899 to 1905; the major printed source of documents for the war with Spain and the Philippine Insurrection is U.S. War Department, Adjutant General's Office, *Correspondence Relating to the War with Spain, April 15, 1898–July 30, 1902* (2 vols.; Washington, 1902). For a highly critical account of both governmental policy and the Army's conduct, see Moorfield Storey and Marcial Lichauco, *The Conquest of the Philippines by the United States, 1898–1925* (New York and London, 1926); and Leon Wolff, *Little Brown Brother* (Garden City, N.Y., 1961). More balanced accounts are by a member of the Philippine Commission, Dean C. Worcester, *The Philippines, Past and Present* (2 vols.; New York, 1914); and William T. Sexton, *Soldiers in the Sun* (Harrisburg, Pa., 1939), particularly pp. 237 ff.

For first hand accounts by American officers, see James Parker, *The Old Army: Some Memories, 1872–1918* (Philadelphia, 1929), pp. 222–367; Funston, *Memories of Two Wars*, pp. 188 ff.; William Raymond Bisbee, *Through Four American Wars: The Impressions and Experiences of Brigadier General William Henry Bisbee* (Boston, 1931), pp. 253–75; Scott, *Some Memories of a Soldier*, pp. 273–416.

12. "Annual Report of Maj. Gen. Arthur MacArthur . . . Commanding the Division of the Philippines," U. S. War Department, *Annual Reports, 1899–1900* (Washington, 1900), I, Part 5, 63.

13. Uldarcio S. Baclagon, *Philippine Campaigns* (Manila, 1952), p. 129.

14. Maj. Gen. Arthur MacArthur's testimony before the Senate Committee on the Philippines, U.S. Senate, *Affairs in the Philippines,* 57th Cong., 1st Sess., Sen. Doc. 331, I, 894–98. The record of the hearings cited above (3 volumes) is an excellent source for the conduct of pacification; another is the hearings held that year (1902) by the same committee, *Charges of Cruelty, Etc., to the Natives of the Philippines,* Sen. Doc. 205, I, 15.

American combat casualties showed the same disparity: 4,234 killed, 2,818 wounded.

15. Ganoe, *The History of the United States Army*, p. 411.

16. Both quotes from Mark Sullivan, *Our Times: The Turn of the Century* (New York and London, 1934), p. 342.

17. Mark Twain, "A Defense of General Funston," *North American Review,* CLXXIV (May, 1902), pp. 613–24.

18. Worcester, *The Philippines, Past and Present*, I, 289–93; "Report of the Secretary of War for 1902," *Five Years of the War Department,* pp. 256–57.

19. Testimony of Brig. Gen. R. P. Hughes before the Senate Committee on the Philippines, *Hearings,* Sen. Doc. 331, I, 569, as previously cited.

20. A good account of Taft's governorship in the Philippines is Henry F. Pringle, *The Life and Times of William Howard Taft* (New York, 1939), I, 163–225. See also Ralph Eldin Minger, "Taft, MacArthur, and the Establishment of Civil Government in the Philippines," *Ohio Historical Quarterly,* LXX (October, 1961), pp. 308–31.

21. Taft to Root, April 3, 1901, quoted by Pringle, *The Life and Times of William Howard Taft,* I, 205.

22. Bacon and Scott (eds.), *The Military and Colonial Policy of the United States,* p. 24; "Report of the Secretary of War for 1902," *Five Years in the War Department,* p. 259.

23. *Congressional Record,* 59th Cong., 1st Sess., XL, Part 4, 3838–40, 3895–96, 3980, 3986.

24. Taft to Wood, March 12, 1906, Leonard Wood Papers, Library of Congress.

25. This discussion is based on the author's research in the papers of Generals Leonard Wood, Robert L. Bullard, Tasker H. Bliss, Frank R. McCoy, Hugh L. Scott, James G. Harbord, Henry T. Allen, Frank Parker, Enoch L. Crowder, and John J. Pershing, in the *Journal of the Military Service Institution,* and in the following sources: Parker, *The Old Army: Some Memories,* 1872–1918; Carter, *The American Army;* Scott, *Some Memories of a Soldier;* Bisbee, *Through Four American Wars: The Impressions and Experiences of Brigadier General William Henry Bisbee;* Nelson A. Miles, *Personal Recollections and Observations of General Nelson A. Miles* (Chicago and New York, 1897); *Serving the Republic* (New York and London, 1911); William Harding Carter, *The Life of Lieutenant General Chaffee* (Chicago, 1917); and Richard C. Brown, "Social Attitudes of American Generals, 1898–1940," (unpublished Ph.D. dissertation, University of Wisconsin, 1951). Brown points out that General Order 100, the Army's rule governing treatment of civilians in war zones, was a mixture of "humanitarianism and military sternness."

26. Capt. J. W. Furlong, "Notes on Field Service in Cuba," November 2, 1907, File 4352, Army War College Document File, 1903–19, Records of the War Department General Staff, National Archives, Record Group 165. Hereafter cited as AWC Doc. File (with number), RG 165.

27. Lt. Col. R. L. Bullard was to become Lt. Gen. R. L. Bullard, commander of the First Division, III Corps, and Second Army of the American Expeditionary Force in World War I. His thoughts on pacification are from a manuscript, "Military Pacification," and the writings in his notebooks, particularly number 12, Bullard Papers, Library of Congress.

28. Carter, *The American Army,* p. 220.

# CHAPTER ONE

# CUBA, THE FRAGILE REPUBLIC

IT IS CLEAR in retrospect that the Cubans who planned and fought the thirty years' war against Spain chose an unpropitious time to launch their Republic. For Cuba, the coming of the twentieth century brought not only national independence but also the conditions that perpetuated colonial society, bound the country to the world market in raw materials, and bared it to the strategic and economic aspirations of the United States. Because of the heritage of Spanish rule, the social and economic transformations of three decades of civil war, and the impact of American economic expansionism and occupation, Cuba became a grotesque mutation of the Cuban patriots' utopian republic. Whatever the combination of causes, the patriots themselves personified the inability of Cuban society to develop political institutions and popular leaders through which differing values and aspirations could be accommodated without violence and exploitation. The roots of this pattern of political behavior lay deep in Cuba's past.[1]

## Cuba: Troubled Isle

Nature divided Cuba into distinct regions, which as late as 1900 were only loosely linked by railways, unpaved cart roads, and coastal steamers. The island itself was 730 miles long and varied from 22 to 160 miles in width. The rivers were short and seldom navigable inland. Cuba began and ended in mountains. At the western end of the island, the Cordillera

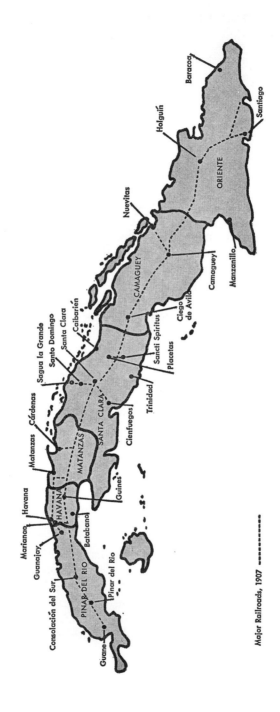

Map 1.—Major railroads, principal cities, and provinces, 1907

Major Railroads, 1907 ----------

de los Organos reached twenty-five hundred feet, but the land dropped off to the rolling plains and shallow valleys which characterized two-thirds of the island. As one traveled eastward, the land changed from the red clay highlands of tobacco-raising Pinar del Rio to the rich plains of Havana and Matazanas provinces. Then the island widened where the grasslands of Santa Clara and Camaguey supported sugar and cattle. Further eastward the hills blended into the rugged Sierra Maestre of Oriente, with peaks up to eight thousand feet. The mountains separated the jagged shoreline and plateaus from Cape Cruz to Cape Maisi from the fertile Cauto plain to the north.

Along Cuba's broken, island-bordered coast, tidal basins and sheer bluffs shared the shore with swamps choked by mangroves and lignum vitae. Inland the soil nourished over three thousand species of flora, ranging from royal palms and white pines to the flowering tangles of a rain forest. In 1907, after three hundred years of cultivation, 13 million acres of Cuba's 44,000 square miles were still primeval forest.

The climate was benign, but humid. The mean temperature was 77°. The seasons were determined by the rainfall, wet (May to October) and dry (November to April).

On this beautiful and productive land the Spanish planted a colony in 1512 and brought to it the institutions of Old Spain. By the nineteenth century Cuba had developed a national life that was typically Hispanic. Because of the continued domination by Spain, Cuba became even more colonial after the rest of Latin America won its freedom. The last half of the century, however, was an era of economic, social and political upheaval for Cuba, a period of change perhaps accelerated by the war for independence. Before the economic realities of the industrial revolution and the ideological spread of liberalism, the Hispanic institutions began to crack from political rigidity, and in the eyes of educated Cubans, Spanish rule was at best capricious and wasteful and lagged behind the realities of the nation's economic and intellectual growth.

In the late nineteenth century the mechanization of the sugar industry (a necessity for world competition) brought more land into the orbits of the sugar mills. The mills themselves changed from *ingenios* (the grinding equipment of a single plantation) to *centrales,* the depersonalized rural industrial complexes of mills, railroads, barracks, stores, and offices, fed sugar by satellite growers (*colonos*), either small owners or renters. Under the pressure to grow more and more sugar, the institution of Negro slavery became an anachronism, then disappeared altogether in the 1880's during the war for independence. At the same time, small farmers, tobacco planters, and cattlemen ceased to dominate the country's agricultural life.

The thirty years' war for independence, fought in the name of the most idealistic human goals, contributed to Cuba's institutional disintegration. It was a war not only for political freedom but also for racial emancipation, and also a civil war, waged between Cubans without quarter. Sustained by revolutionary ardor, it was never completely revolutionary in terms of institutional change.[2] As a war for independence, it was exploited by yet another foreign power, the United States. The war which won independence also mortgaged Cuba's future because it perpetuated the Spanish influence on Cuban affairs, accelerated American interest in Cuba's economic and political life, and created a class of insurgent leaders ill-prepared for the tasks of nation-building. This new political elite, sired by the insurrection, was a class unto itself, the *políticos.* The *políticos* embodied the socio-psychological heritage of the war: xenòphobia and *personalismo.* Under their leadership, Cuba was a state built on the social norms of guerrilla warfare.

In 1868 the independence movement had been the child of a politically dissatisfied Cuban planter elite. During the next ten years, death and exile gradually changed the leadership and character of the movement until it became an uneasy alliance of rural and urban workers, student radicals, Negro leaders, and exiled liberals, often intellectuals or professional men. The movement's component parts in 1895 were characterized by the democratic idealism of José Martí, the racial and economic reformism of Antonio Maceo, the non-revolutionary liberalism of Tomás Estrada Palma and Gonzalo de Quesada, and the military realism of Máximo Gómez. As a result of the war Cuban political behavior took a different shape; added to the traditional Spanish desires for power, prestige, and gold in government was an addiction to conspiracy and valorous patriotism. Cuba, with independence, remained the insurgent state, the political property of its *generales y doctores.*[3]

Postindependence Cuban society was in some respects static, in others dynamic. Judged by class attitudes and values, it remained traditional, divided into an upper class (those who hired labor) and lower class (those who worked with their hands).[4] Sixty per cent of the people were illiterate. In terms of raw population, Cuba had a net growth from 1899 to 1907 of 476,000 people or an increase of 39 per cent.[5] The birth rate, the single greatest growth factor, jumped from 9.6 per thousand (1901) to 19.8 (1905). Yet national, racial, and occupational divisions remained relatively fixed. With the end of the war, enough Spanish nationals flocked to Cuba to keep the island's aliens (80 per cent Spanish) at 11 per cent of the total population. In 1901 alone, 22,000 Spaniards, mostly unmarried men and boys bound for urban trades or commerce, entered Cuba. Much of the population which might have passed economically for a middle class was Spanish. Thus there remained a Spanish Cuba and a Cuban Cuba, the first largely urban, commercial-industrial, and economically important. The latter was both urban and rural and politically dominant. The antipathy of Cuban to Spaniard, exacerbated by war, continued into the new century.

In occupational terms about half of Cuba's work force (in 1907 some 770,000 in a population of two million) earned its living from the land. These *campesinos* (country-people) were not the typical Indio-Hispanic peasants of Latin America bound to a paternalistic hacienda or subsistence farm. They were, rather, predominately a Negro and white rural proletariat, earning wages as cane-cutters, tobaccomen, mill hands, and miners. Though some Cubans remained cattlemen and farmers, most of the workers were tied to sugar and tobacco. These two crops were rapidly converting Cuban agriculture to a cash-crop production and latifundia. The next largest group of Cubans were employed as domestic servants or in transportation. Matters of social position rather than income still influenced Cubans in selecting careers: in 1907 Cuba had more doctors than butchers, more lawyers than civil engineers.

The relatively stable distribution of people in occupations does not reflect, however, the changes in rural and urban life Cuba experienced from 1868 to 1898. The economic destructiveness of the guerrilla warfare, the abolition of slavery, and the transformation of the sugar business reduced the number of farm owners and produced a new urban class of chronically unemployed former slaves and small landholders living in the towns. This sector, often in competition with the Spanish for jobs, became a source of unrest, often demanding government jobs. The desire for official posts was national; one typical town of five hundred had a mayor, a secretary, a town doctor, and four policemen, drawing salaries from $35 to $75 a month for little work.

Racially, Cuba was a white country (70 per cent) with an easy attitude about admission to whiteness. The country, however Hispanic culturally, had its own racial tensions. Cuban history throughout the nineteenth century left a legacy of fear among the whites of race war and Africanization. In reality, by 1900 the white population, already the majority, was increasing more rapidly than the Negro. Slavery, however, left a tradition of social and economic inferiority that the Cuban Negro found difficult to reconcile with his important role as a soldier in the Army of Liberation. Among the upper class, such phrases as "they've a touch of the tar brush" or "his hair is not so nice" reflected a blurred but real color line. Even within the lower class, mulattos did not associate freely with Negroes. White and black Cubans lived "together, but not mixed."[6]

By 1900 the economic structure of Cuba had begun to take the form it retained for the next sixty years.[7] The major factor in the change was the influx of foreign capital to finance Cuba's postwar reconstruction and the expansion of the sugar industry. In terms of national wealth, sugar (dominated by alien entrepreneurs and foreign capital) was king. The cycle of the sugar business was tied to the season. The cane grew in the wet season, was harvested in the dry. The Cubans named these two periods for their impact on the nation's life. The growing season was *el tiempo muerto*, the time of unemployment and apathy. Harvest was *la zafra*, the vibrant months of work, of wages, of buying, of merry-making. The country lay at the feet of the sugar cycle: "We cannot live without *la zafra*; its power is total and its tyranny intolerable."[8] Since sugar was subject to violent price fluctuations in the world market, the tyranny was double.

Foreign capital and entrepreneurship also dominated the next largest crop, tobacco, at least in its marketing phase. Aliens also financed and developed the railways, steamship lines, manufacturing, banking, and commerce. The predominant stake was, in 1906, Spanish, with American and British investments close behind. American investment was variously estimated between $100 and $160 million. The striking thing about the alien business elite was its fear of competition and financial insecurity and its sense of desperate risk as it tried to capitalize on Cuba's wealth. The businessmen's special fears were as great as those of the Cubans.[9]

The institutions which might have eased the insecurity of Cuba's economic life had been weakened in the nineteenth century. The colonial government, for all its abuses, with the Catholic Church, had been the strongest national unifying force. Politically it was replaced by local and regional *jefes*. The legal system the Spanish left behind was as dehumanized and ambiguous in practice as ever. The rapacity of judges and advocates provoked a wry joke: "No one can afford either to win or to lose a lawsuit for the lawyers will take all you have in either case."[10] The Church had been loyal to the Crown during the insurrection; controlled by Spanish and Italian clerics, it was suspect and impotent after independence.

It depended on American sympathy to regain even a part of its limited financial wealth. Freemasonry and rationalism were in vogue.[11] The Church's philanthropic services lagged, and the people, particularly the Spanish, turned to their private clubs for succor. Other forms of association further divided the people, for whether university, secondary school, club, labor union, or intellectual circle, all were characteristically exclusive. The nation's press was generally irresponsible and biased by class, political, or national affiliation to the point of becoming a destructive rather than constructive force in politics.

One Spanish legacy, the tax system, was particularly burdensome, for import duties had been the colonial government's chief source of revenue. Heavy duties were levied on clothes, food, and other necessities of daily life. Land taxes, too, on developed property discouraged native investment. One observer estimated that in 1905 the per capita tax burden in Cuba was $12, in the United States, $3.55.[12]

Throughout the colonial period, the government of Cuba was intimately involved with the island's economy through land grants, subventions, taxation, and trade restrictions. For the individual Spaniard a colonial office provided a financial sinecure. To the Cubans, the government, which they did not share, was an economic institution for individual gain. Viewing the world's wealth in fixed terms rather than as a growing expression of human productivity, they equated holding office with individual economic activity. Political power was an accepted way of gaining wealth and status. Although the psychological need for public recognition made office-holding attractive, the economic motive was foremost in the drive for position. The concept of public service or public interest was alien. Appointment to office was preferable to election because in the first instance the officeholder had only to be loyal to the *patrón,* whereas in the second he was at the mercy of an electorate which could strip him of his livelihood. Conversely, each citizen, after independence and the adoption of virtually free suffrage, received one valuable vote to sell.

If, however, a Cuban became wealthy through business, he usually disassociated himself from partisan politics because, having achieved riches and security, he no longer needed political activity as an entree to material well-being. The withdrawal from partisan politics was a proclamation of economic success and high social status. Whatever protection he now wished from the government could be cultivated through individual contacts and largesse to bureaucrats, a return to the court politics of the colonial era. The wealthy Cuban did not demean himself by associating with co-operative organizations like political parties.

The exception to this behavior in Cuban society came from the former officers of the Army of Liberation. As a group they dominated Cuban politics for thirty years. Some were independently wealthy, others were not. By and large they saw themselves as the embodiment of Cuban sovereignty, characteristically feeling that a man who risks his life in battle for *la patria* should have the first option in deciding its future.[13] Many of these men grew up as guerrillas, and they loved rank, martial appearances, stirring declarations, and the adoration of their men. As a body the Cuban veterans, men schooled in the overthrow of government, were the most representative and popular political leaders in their society. Cuba's democratic form of government after independence enabled them to keep their battalions intact as voters.

Cuba, as many Americans saw it, was a bounteous land with an impossible people. First, there had been the Cuba of the glorious fighters for independence, who upon closer examination in 1898 turned out to be very human, often Negroid, and irresponsible and irrational.[14] The gallant heroes introduced to American readers by the revolutionary junta and the yellow press looked increasingly like those described by Edward F. Atkins, the most influential American sugar planter in Cuba: "The insurgents are . . . held together . . . by hopes of trouble between Spain and the United States, as well as by fear of being shot or hanged by their people. This is what is called 'esprit de corps'."[15]

Behind the American army in 1898 came a new generation of carpetbaggers to risk all in land development schemes, fruit farms, mines, and agricultural colonies. Though not numerous, these Americans saw themselves as the advance agents of civilization and prosperity. Yet they did little to help Cuban-American relations. As Havana resident Irene Wright observed:

> There is no person so perfectly calculated to "rub" a Latin "the wrong way" as the self-seeking, aggressive, unmannerly scouts we send to Cuba, among other frontiers, of whose faults, peculiarly enough, our national virtues and especially our strength are constituted.[16]

American relations with Cuba also had one myopic trait: Americans looked at Cuba and saw Havana. The nation's capital in government and vice, largest city, commercial and financial center, and port to the outside world, Havana had a hypnotic impact on foreign statesmen and capitalists. They gauged affairs in Cuba by events in Havana or at least the flow of news from the capital. Sometimes Havana was the only source of information, but the troubled rumors in Havana also distorted the outsider's understanding of the island's woes.

Who was the political Cuban? Lieutenant Colonel Robert L. Bullard thought he knew, and his description, whatever its flaws, has a timeless North American quality to it:

> The Cuban is intolerant of tyranny, but let him once obtain power and authority, and he is autocratic, dictatorial, inconsiderate, and without any quality of toleration or compromise. . . . Every Cuban understands these qualities have been the cause of official failure and downfall, yet when his term of power comes he seems unable to resist the temptation to become a despot.
>
> In all politics and public affairs he is a child. He is always able to satisfactorily excuse himself from all blame by shifting it to some one else. If not given his own way he will 'pick up his dolls' and refuse to play longer. The principle of the 'greatest good to the greatest number' means nothing to him and he views a majority vote against him with a deep sense of personal injustice . . .
>
> The Cuban puts dependence upon a strong central government. . . . He looks upon a strong central government to right all his wrongs, no matter how trivial. . . .

By reason of his inherited traditions from strong governments of Rome, Spain and the Catholic Church, the Cuban has a feeling of legal helplessness under superior orders however unjust, illegal and oppressive they may be and has a settled conviction that the only way to resist is to organize armed revolution.[17]

In light of its history and culture, independent Cuba was so socially, politically, and economically divided that it is debatable whether it was a nation in any but the territorial sense. It is little wonder that it appeared ungovernable to many Cubans and Americans. Yet the McKinley administration gave the United States Army a try from 1898 to 1902, and in its own way the Army attempted to create a Cuban nation.

## The Military Government of Cuba, 1898–1902

With the end of the war in Cuba and the termination of Spanish sovereignty on January 1, 1899, the United States assumed responsibility for the island's government. The announced American goal was to pacify Cuba and then turn over the government to the Cuban people, at some indefinite date. McKinley's appointee for the military governorship was Major General John R. Brooke, a cautious, apolitical, sixty-year-old cavalryman. A Civil War veteran with thirty-eight years of continuous service, Brooke's personal qualities proved his undoing. Tempered in the ways of the Old Army, he loyally sought direction from Washington in managing Cuban affairs. Unable to fathom the McKinley administration's desires for Cuba in 1899, he shied away from dictating reform on his own initiative. His chief subordinates felt no such compunction to await direction, and several of them already had civil programs underway in areas occupied by the Army in 1898.

A military government was formed to administer Cuba, placing command of the American army of occupation and supervision of the civil administration in the hands of a military governor and four major subordinates. Cuba was divided into four departments, the City of Havana (General William Ludlow), and three two-province departments. General Fitz-

hugh Lee, the former consul-general of Havana, commanded
Pinar del Rio—Havana; General James H. Wilson was in
charge in Mantazas—Santa Clara; and General Leonard
Wood in Santiago—Puerto Principe. At the national level
Brooke created four civil departments and various fiscal agen-
cies, the first staffed with Cuban secretaries, the latter with
Army officers. The provincial and municipal governments
were continued in the Spanish pattern, the offices filled by
Cubans appointed by the Military Governor and supervised
by the department commanders.[18]

More importantly, Brooke and his associates, backed by
the American army, were relatively free of internal political
pressure in Cuba. There was no organized resistance to their
rule, and many Cubans actively co-operated with them. Both
the form and style of the Military Government in 1899 were
near copies of the Spanish regime; the prewar pattern of
arbitrary rule, however concilatory and paternal, continued.

That there was no sharp break with the Spanish colonial
system can be explained in several ways. First, the major
task of the Military Government in its first year was to restore
public order, fight disease and starvation, and provide other
humanitarian services. These chores were accomplished primarily by the American army. In addition, Brooke received
no orders from Washington for governmental reform. President McKinley was still methodically plumbing American
opinion to help determine what to do about Cuba. His public
statements on Cuban policy in 1899 were models of ambivalence. At the War Department, the discredited Russell A.
Alger lingered on as Secretary, and the head of the newly
created Division of Customs and Insular Affairs did not fill
the leadership vacuum. Thus, the initiative for Cuban reform
lay with the Military Government and those Cubans who
could gain the sympathetic ear of an American general.

Faced with massive problems of national reconstruction,
Brooke found much in the Hispanic system of centralized
military-civil administration to recommend itself for his use.
He believed that Spanish law in most cases would adequately
protect both individual rights and property. Implicit in his

assumptions was the belief that law in Cuba was intrinsically a part of the country's social structure and reflected at least the tacit consent of the Cubans themselves. He realized, imperfectly, that Spanish law had some relation to the economic and social exploitation of the colonial government, but he believed that cultural-traditional factors worked against hasty reform.[19] Brooke had greater faith in government-by-law than did the Cubans, who were well aware of the inadequacies of Spanish rule and who had made civil disobedience a national way of life.

The immediate tasks of reconstruction, however, seemed to demand an authoritarian government, under whatever statutes. Reflecting on American rule in Cuba in 1899, one of Brooke's officers in Havana, Hugh L. Scott, believed conditions called for centralized power:

> A military government is the only kind fit to cope with such conditions [as existed in Cuba]. . . . as soon as a military intervention is proclaimed with force to back it, everything falls immediately into place. Foreigners and natives alike learn at once their status, and there is a legal basis of government. The will of the commanding general is supreme.

The Cubans themselves were no help in suggesting policy, Scott stated, for "they will usually tell you that they are *partida de la reforma*, blinking at you like an owl, but of what sort of reform they have not the vaguest conception."[20]

Throughout 1899, Brooke commanded a conservative, caretaker government designed primarily to maintain public order. He did little to institute domestic reform. He gave little attention to Cuba's ultimate well-being or its relationship to the United States, believing these questions beyond the scope of his duty. Brooke's values in government were efficiency and economy for their own sake; his major administrative accomplishments were to discharge flagrantly corrupt employees and to collect customs revenues honestly. Although these measures were improvements on Spanish rule, they were hardly calculated to produce long-term reforms. Yet they were legal, and Brooke valued legitimacy rather than innovation.

While Brooke wrestled with such sticky problems as paying off the Cuban insurgent army and discovering Washington's aims in Cuba, two of his subordinates were planning and working on a Cuban policy of their own. Generals Wilson and Wood were applying their considerable ability and political power to rehabilitate Cuba in such a way that the Cubans themselves would seek annexation to the United States. Though voluntary annexation was the goal of both men, their prescriptions for internal reform differed.

Major General James Harrison Wilson, commander of the department of Matanzas–Santa Clara, advocated a national program of economic reform sponsored by the Military Government.[21] Wilson, a West Point graduate and Civil War veteran, had left the service in 1870 for a career as a railroad executive. A successful businessman, he was also a former national committeeman of the Republican party. Like most of the industrialists of his day, Wilson was a firm believer in progress through economic growth. The efficiency and stability of any future Cuban government depended, Wilson stated, on the health of the island's economy, for wealth (or lack of it) dictated Cuban political behavior. Prosperity and social stability were possible in Cuba because the white race was in the majority, and their behavior, once they became affluent, would be conservative and responsible. In his experience, Wilson said, "the fortunate and prosperous are scarcely vicious."[22] Therefore he urged the Military Government to sponsor agricultural reconstruction through liberal loans and gifts of animals and tools. The United States should encourage Cuban prosperity, moreover, by opening its markets to sugar and joining the two nations in a customs and postal union. If the two countries were joined economically, the political merger, sought by the Cubans themselves, would soon follow.[23]

The beauty of Wilson's program was that it gave the Cubans the independence promised them in the Teller Amendment, the idealistic appendage to the war resolutions of 1898. One of its weaknesses was that it envisioned governmental activity beyond what Brooke and the War Department considered proper. It also assumed a Congressional willingness to lower trade barriers. Wilson's program was politically handicapped, because he and his most ardent champion, Senator Joseph B. Foraker of Ohio, were not on intimate terms with the McKinley administration. With Leonard Wood's succession to the military governorship, Wilson's views were given short shrift in Havana and Washington. Nevertheless, the form (the indirect control of Cuba through economic ties) if not the substance of the Wilson program became the foundation of the United States Cuban policy.

General Leonard Wood was Wilson's chief competitor for Brooke's job and Washington's ear. As military governor of the city of Santiago in 1898 and then of Cuba's two eastern-most provinces, Wood attacked the problems of reconstruction with energy and self-assurance.[24] In the course of his administration, a stunning success by humanitarian standards, he became Brooke's sharpest and most politically powerful critic. Unlike his superior, Wood firmly believed that drastic and far-reaching reforms were needed in Cuban society. As he wrote President McKinley in 1900:

> The great mass of public opinion is perfectly inert; especially is this true among the professional classes. The passive inactivity of one hundred and fifty years has settled over them and it is hard to get them out of old ruts and grooves. . . . We are dealing with a race that has been going down for a hundred years and into which we have got to infuse new life, new principles and new methods of doing things.[25]

Particularly frustrating for Wood was that "the better sort," the educated and wealthy people, were uninterested in public affairs. As Wood complained of the membership of the Cuban Constitutional Convention in 1901:

> The Convention represents at any rate the class to whom Cuba would be turned over in the case we withdraw, for the highly intelligent Cubans of the land-owning, industrial, and commercial classes are not in politics. The politicians are in a certain sense doctors without patients, lawyers without practice and demagogues living on the subscriptions of the people and their friends.[26]

Whatever the sorry condition of Cuban society, Wood believed Cuba should, after a long period of tutelage, be annexed to the United States, hopefully by choice of the Cubans themselves. In order to prepare the Cubans, Wood advocated their Americanization through the agency of the Military Government. More immediately he used his own power and prestige to impress the Cubans with the advantages of morality and high-mindedness in public office. By precept, exhortation, and force if need be, Wood was prepared to drive the Cubans from their old ways.[27]

In an article in the *North American Review*, Wood declared to his American audience that policy demanded a clean break with the past. Cuba needed "firm but liberal and just" government under American military commanders. The emphasis must be on developing citizenship and effective local government; this he was doing and "the people are beginning to realize that there is a certain satisfaction and independence to be gained by paying their own way."[28]

Wood was satisfied that the traditional principles of American citizenship were appropriate for Cuba, at least in the long run. While department commander he issued a paraphrase of the Bill of Rights to protect individual liberties. He waged a relentless campaign to eliminate crime, contamination, and corruption. To inculcate American values, he reformed the educational system under the supervision of an appointed board of three American officers and one Cuban. Instruction in English was to begin in kindergarten.[29]

In view of the righteousness of Wood's crusade, it is not surprising that he ran afoul of Brooke's central government. In sharp contrast to Wood's autocracy in Santiago, Brooke felt his way through the maze of Cuban politics, seeking advice from his Cuban secretaries, advocating caution, carefully avoiding conflict with the *políticos*. Where Brooke temporized, Wood brought dynamic leadership and militancy to the attack on Cuba's problems.

Just at the time the Military Government was established, Wood was embarking on an expensive, ambitious sanitation and road-building program in Santiago. Brooke soon demanded that all customs revenues (Wood's source of funds) be collected and distributed by his headquarters. Disgusted by this episode and others, Wood used his political contacts and a favorable press to discredit the Military Governor. Moreover, Wood thought that Brooke's inability to escape the evils of Spanish colonial administration threatened voluntary annexation by placing the American government in a bad light.[30]

Consistent with his view that clean government and new moral standards represented the best America could offer Cuba, Wood advocated that the Cuban economy be developed through private capital, especially American investment. Though he recognized that Cuban agriculture needed diversification and rehabilitation, he believed that this was not the business of the Military Government. Such paternalism would stifle individual responsibility, one of the new values he was inculcating. Rather than accept Wilson's loan program, Wood believed that private agricultural banks should make loans, "at good rates of interest," which could be as high as 10 per cent. In addition, as he pointed out in the section of his 1899 report entitled "Opportunities for Investment," foreign capital was desperately needed, and Cuba was rich with opportunities for enterprising Americans. Such views represented the economic phase of Americanization.

Before the end of 1899, events altered American policy toward domestic reform in Cuba. The first was the appointment of Elihu Root as Secretary of War. A distinguished lawyer and a philosophical skeptic, Root began a systematic analysis of America's colonial problems. In light of his subsequent influence on American policy, it is necessary to examine Root's views on Cuban society and the proper context for its reform. Root's assessment of the Cuban people did not differ from Wood's, but his concept of change varied. The Cubans, Root wrote President Charles W. Eliot of Harvard, "have no experience in anything except Spanish customs and Spanish methods which have grown up for centuries under

a system opposed to general education and self government."
Yet to produce lasting change, the Cubans must change themselves; "it cannot be done by having outsiders preach at
them."[31] Although there were many traditional barriers to
change, the United States could, by its example and a liberal
economic policy, support those Cubans who would provide
"conservative and thoughtful control of Cuba."[32] Essentially
Root believed in the efficacy of law and constitutionalism, but
not in forced change or the radical transplantation of cultural
values. He doubted that either the Cubans or Americans
wanted annexation or that the two cultures could ever be
compatible politically.

During the fall of 1899, as a result of his own study of the
Cuban problem, Root announced that the United States would
grant Cuba independence as quickly as a Cuban government
could be formed. This decision was implicit in Root's order
to complete rapidly the Cuban census. Root then made a
clear statement of American policy in his annual report,
published December 1:

> Our temporary occupation of the island of Cuba involves a very
> simple plan of operation, with some difficulties in its application which
> are apt to be overlooked by those who are impatient for immediate
> results. The control which we are exercising in trust for the people of
> Cuba should not be, and of course will not be, continued any longer
> than is necessary to enable the people to establish a suitable govern-
> ment. . . . Our present duty is limited to giving every assistance in
> our power to the establishment of such a government and to maintaining
> order and promoting the welfare of the people of Cuba during the
> period necessarily required for that process.[33]

With popular sentiment for Cuba's annexation dwindling
and the McKinley administration concerned with the Philippine Insurrection and the political potency of anti-imperialism
at home, Root had received a mandate to work for Cuban
independence. Ironically, Root chose as his foremost instrument of policy the champion of annexation, Leonard Wood.

On December 20, 1899, Wood replaced General Brooke
as military governor of Cuba.[34] He immediately began to

apply the operating principles and methods he had found so successful as a department commander. With independence in the offing, Wood, turning away from developing local self-government, concentrated on institutionalizing his public health program and educational reforms. He continued his drive for just, humane, efficient government. At the same time, Wood tried to delay independence as long as possible (though he was under severe pressure within Cuba and from Washington) in order to allow his reforms to take root.

Wood began his administration with his usual self-confidence, telling a correspondent of the St. Louis *Globe-Democrat* that "success in Cuba is so easy that it would be a crime to fail." He described his own task as doing "all we can for them [the Cubans] and to get out of the island as soon as we can."[35] This, and other statements, soothed critics in the United States and Cuba, for it was wide-spread knowledge that Wood favored a long period of tutelage and ultimate annexation.

With a deadline, however indefinite, hanging over the Military Government, Wood zealously attacked what he believed were Cuba's major problems. His purpose was to establish the standards of good government, by imposition if necessary. Major decisions on policy were his or Root's. Though 97 per cent of the government's employees were Cubans, none had a meaningful influence on matters of importance. Wood's Council of Notables, a group of distinguished Cubans, served more to check criticism than to give advice. In his first full year in office, Wood issued twice as many decrees as had Brooke, backed by an American army of occupation of eleven thousand men and the Rural Guard, a national constabulary of some one thousand Cuban veterans.

Wood, apparently with forethought, reigned with the noblesse of a Latin American *caudillo*. He was intensely military in appearance and bearing, made frequent tours about the island, became a skilled *jai-lai* player, and rode rough shod over the sensibilities of his critics.[36] In terms of material and humanitarian accomplishment, Wood's administration made significant advances in roadbuilding, harbor clearance, prison and judicial reform, the management of charities, sewerage system improvement, and in the repair and construction of public buildings. The outstanding achievement of the Military Government was, of course, the eradication of yellow fever, an epic of courage and perseverance. Within the government itself Wood weeded out grafters and incompetents. His most dramatic act was the removal of Estes G. Rathbone, Director-General of Posts and a crony of Senator Mark Hanna, for fraud.

Wood's Americanization program proceeded in his reform of the public school system. After an enthusiastic if disorganized beginning under Brooke, educational reform, administered by Lieutenant Matthew E. Hanna under laws patterned after those of his native Ohio, received top priority from the Military Government. Enrolments soared from twenty-one thousand in 1899 to over one hundred thousand children by the end of 1900. The curriculum, which included instruction in English and local government in the lowest grades, was taught from translated American textbooks. In addition, Wood persuaded Harvard to train Cuban teachers during summer vacations, and more than a thousand eventually journeyed to the United States for advanced training.

With all these successes, there were significant and disheartening failures. Efforts to use the jury system in criminal and civil proceedings, to introduce habeas corpus into the judicial system, and to create elected local school boards proved unworkable.

In all his enthusiasm for using the Military Government to engineer fundamental changes in Cuban life, Wood continued to hold his narrow view of the government's responsibility for Cuban prosperity. Though he recognized that the sugar planters were operating at a loss because of overproduction and high labor costs, he was unwilling to advocate more than tariff reduction by the United States.[37] In light of Congressional resistance to tariff revision, even this stand was bold. Wood recognized that a loan program was popular with Cuban farmers, but believed that the problem of agricultural credit could be solved by a "liberal degree of reciprocity." Working toward this goal, he urged Congress to reduce the sugar tariff 30 per cent and to abrogate the Foraker Amendment, thus opening Cuba to American investors under the sponsorship of the Military Government.

The most notable example of Wood's faith in private capital was his relationship with the Cuba Company. From 1900 to 1902 Wood assisted railroad entrepreneurs Sir William Van Horne, of the Canadian Pacific, and General Grenville M. Dodge, builder of the Union Pacific, to charter and construct a railway in eastern Cuba. In organizing the Cuba Company Van Horne and Dodge side-stepped the Foraker Amendment, which prohibited the Military Government from granting franchises, by accepting revokable permits. Wood and Root cleared the way for them, convinced that improved transportation to eastern Cuba would stimulate its economy. Without a doubt it did, but it also indicated Wood's willingness to use foreign investment to further the cause of annexation.

In a sense the entire story of the adoption of the Cuban Constitution of 1901 and of the genesis of the Platt Amendment may be read as a disavowal of the goals of Wood's reforms: Americanization and voluntary annexation. The Cuban Constitutional Convention, which began its deliberations in November, 1900, was never free from Wood's influence, but its work was largely its own.

The language of the Constitution of 1901 glowed with the idealism of nationalism, republicanism, and political liberalism. The Constitution provided for the personal freedoms denied Cubans during their war for independence. The form of government was unitary and presidential, but power was shared with a bicameral legislature and independent judiciary. The Constitution of 1901 worked no radical changes in the prevailing social and economic relationship of postwar Cuba. In the nation's political structure, specifically within the powers of the President, there were significant allowances for authoritarian rule. The President could suspend certain personal rights in times of emergency, remove provincial and municipal officials, grant pardons and amnesties, and carry over the annual budget if Congress failed to approve a new one. Lip-service was paid to the Military Government's educational and public health programs, but no specific responsibility was assumed to carry them through, much less continue them in the spirit in which they were begun.[38]

The Military Government wielded little influence in constitutionalizing Wood's reforms because its political energies were directed by Root to working out the future relationship of Cuba and the United States. The basic statement of American policy, later embodied as the Platt Amendment, is contained in a letter from Secretary Root to General Wood on February 1, 1901. Though Root's specific proposals were reworded and added to, the basic premise of his letter remained: that Cuba could best develop as an independent nation, but that her strategic position in the Caribbean, her history and her economy placed her in a unique relationship with the United States which necessitated some American control. Therefore, the two nations must bear the duties and obligations of this relationship. On Cuba's part this meant that its government must assume the responsibilities toward its people and other nations taken by the United States in the Treaty of Paris. The United States would meet its responsibility by guaranteeing Cuban independence and a stable, solvent, republican government.[39]

The final draft of Root's plan was written by the Senate committee of Orville H. Platt. An administration-sponsored measure, the Platt Amendment became law as part of the Army Appropriation Act of 1901. Debate was short, and the amendment passed by almost a straight party vote in both houses. Appended to the Cuban Constitution and later ratified as a treaty between the two nations, the Platt Amendment defined the relationship between the United States and Cuba for the next thirty-three years. As adopted it provided:

I. That the government of Cuba shall never enter into any treaty or other compact with any foreign power or powers which will impair or tend to impair the independence of Cuba, nor in any manner authorize or permit any foreign power or powers to obtain by colonization or for military or naval purposes or otherwise, lodgement in or control over any portion of said island.

II. That said government shall not assume or contract any public debt, to pay the interest upon which, and to make reasonable sinking fund provision for the ultimate discharge of which, the ordinary revenues of the island, after defraying the current expenses of government, shall be inadequate.

III. That the government of Cuba consents that the United States may exercise the right to intervene for the preservation of Cuban independence, the maintenance of a government adequate for the protection of life, property, and individual liberty, and for discharging the obligations with respect to Cuba imposed by the Treaty of Paris on the United States, now to be assumed and undertaken by the government of Cuba.

IV. That all acts of the United States in Cuba during its military occupancy thereof are ratified and validated, and all lawful rights acquired thereunder shall be maintained and protected.

V. The government of Cuba will execute, and as far as necessary extend, the plans already devised or other plans to be mutually agreed upon, for the sanitation of the cities of the island, to the end that a recurrence of epidemic and infectious diseases may be prevented, thereby assuring protection to the people and commerce of Cuba, as well as to the commerce of the southern ports of the United States and the people residing therein.

VI. That the Isle of Pines shall be omitted from the proposed constitutional boundaries of Cuba, the title thereto being left to future adjustment by treaty.

VII. That to enable the United States to maintain the independence of Cuba, and to protect the people thereof, as well as for its own defense, the government of Cuba will sell or lease to the United States lands necessary for coaling or naval stations at certain specified points, to be agreed upon with the President of the United States.

VIII. That by way of further assurances the government of Cuba will embody the foregoing provisions in a permanent treaty with the United States.[40]

The Platt Amendment, far-reaching in its implications, was "a work of extraordinary sagacity, from the American point of view."[41] The price of Cuban independence, it was accepted (with much unhappiness) as such by the Cuban Constitutional Convention. It was viewed as a prelude to annexation and was shortly denounced by seven of the sixteen delegates who voted for its acceptance. It also heartened the alien business community which had nearly despaired of American protection. The Platt Amendment also reflected a prevalent belief in Washington that further direct tutelage would be fruitless and might create violent resistance to the Military Government. It, too, articulated a national disillusionment with the burdens of colonial administration as well as the fulfilment of a promise to Cuba. In the future the United States would not attempt to change Cuban behavior; it would, instead, deal with Cuba, government-to-government, as national interest (in terms of security and economic gain) dictated. The Platt Amendment was designed to give the United States a maximum influence on the Cuban government with a minimum of responsibility for the character of Cuban life.

In Cuba there was some protest against those articles (II, IV, and V) drafted to protect the work of the Military Government, but the greatest outcry was against the amendment as a whole and Article III specifically. To allay Cuban fears, Elihu Root, during discussion with a Cuban delegation in Washington, stated that Article III did not sanction intervention in Cuban domestic affairs. It was simply an extension of the Monroe Doctrine by treaty. There would be no "intermeddling or intervention in any manner" in internal affairs. Root, however, added the proviso, which he repeated for Domingo Méndez Capote, that the United States might intervene "when there may exist a true state of anarchy within the Republic."[42]

Senator Joseph B. Foraker's analysis of the effects of the Platt Amendment was more far-sighted. During the Senate debate, he predicted that Article III might bring about the intervention it was supposed to deter. America's pledge to guarantee Cuban peace would work to the advantage of the political "outs," for they might nullify any election by rising in rebellion and force the United States to intervene.[43] A similar view was held by the noted British political commentator and statesman, James Bryce. He believed that any interpretation of Article III less strict than Root's could lead to intervention in the event of insurrection. "There may be," Bryce wrote, "civil strife, or disorders, which, though scarcely amounting to war, the Executive cannot suppress." Intervention then would be necessary to maintain the guarantees of the Platt Amendment, and intervention would resurrect the question of annexation, a latent hope of many living in Cuba.[44]

The formal withdrawal of the Military Government on May 20, 1902, marked the end of Wood's reform program. The principle of leadership by example and government by morality disappeared with the United States Army. Wood was hailed as a great colonial governor by such knowledgeable judges as Lord Cromer and General H. H. Kitchener, who credited him with the regeneration of Cuba, "an accomplishment unequaled by any race in any age."[45]

Wood's rationale for change was based on an absolute moral code, free enterprise economics, the theory of the public interest, and a just social order through law, all alien concepts to the Cuban people. He realized that radical change was necessary in Cuba, but, however ambitious his Americanization program, his reforms were half-measures. He missed the crux of General Wilson's argument: the economic conditions in Cuba so prejudiced political stability that a radical and rapid change in the island's economic structure was mandatory. Private enterprise, particularly foreign investment, would simply deepen the woes of an already exploitative colonial economy. To keep the Cubans from turning to the government as a source of personal income, the government itself would have to act to provide other economic alternatives.

It is true that Wood, much to his disappointment, did not win enough time to institutionalize his Puritan revolution. He was never able to find enough educated Cubans who were willing to compromise their personal prestige and their sense of nationality to serve in an American government. In the case of the conservative commercial and planter elite, Wood found it practically impossible to interest them in holding office. They were unwilling to surrender their social exclusiveness and international business connections, both of which rested on their avoidance of Cuban politics. Ironically, the administration, which Wood hoped would show the Cubans the best of the American political tradition, was best remembered for the efficiency of its highly personalist rule. Wood gave Cuba the "effective tyranny" that Spain had failed to provide.

The Military Government left Cuba several legacies. In its three years of operation it gave many Cubans the vision of what American occupation meant: an end to violence, better health, justice, and economic growth, all at the price of Cuban political independence and Hispanic culture. It is no wonder that Cubans viewed the United States with a mixture of hope and fear. On the other hand, despite Wood's reforms, the American government no longer accepted responsibility for institutional changes within Cuba. To this degree Cuba was independent. The United States, however, placed restrictions upon the Cuban government that further weakened its limited ability and will to deal with Cuba's problems. All these factors contributed to the political developments that led to the Second Intervention.

## The Politics of Faction, 1900–1906

While the Army administered Cuba, the leading figures of the independence movement formed political organizations to contend in the promised elections. These organizations were based on personal and regional loyalties.[46] At the time of the municipal elections in June, 1900, three major factions appeared. The two largest groups, the Nationalists and Federal Republicans, were dominated by Cuban veterans. The Nationalists were identified by their co-operation with the Military Government at the national level. They were men from Havana or the western provinces, supported by Máximo Gómez. They claimed to favor a strong central government. The Federal Republicans represented the interests of Santa Clara and its civil governor, a former insurgent general, José

Miguel Gómez, but it had strength in Matanzas and Oriente also. Both factions favored immediate independence. The Unión Democrática, the third political group, was led by Havana conservatives, many of whom favored continued American tutelage. In the election itself, regional loyalties prevailed; the Federal Republicans elected all their candidates in Santa Clara and Matanzas, the Nationalists theirs in Havana. The Unión Democrática, labeled the American party, collapsed from lack of support.

In the elections for delegates to the Constitutional Convention in the fall of 1900, the same alignments held, despite Wood's restriction of the suffrage to literates, property owners, and veterans. Elected by province on the basis of population, the delegates, whether Nationalist or Federal Republican, were (with one exception) leaders of the independence movement and unfriendly to American control. Among the thirty-one men were "generals of the wars of independence, distinguished conspirators, patriots ennobled by emigration and banishment, noted specialists in Public Law."[47] Among the more prominent members were Gonzalo de Quesada, member of the revolutionary junta and soon to be minister to the United States; General Juan Ríus Rivera, former Secretary of Agriculture, Industry, and Commerce and civil governor of Havana; General Emilio Núñez, governor of Havana; General Alejandro Rodríguez, former mayor of Havana and commander of the Rural Guard; Havana lawyer Alfredo Zayas; General Pedro Betancourt and Domingo Méndez Capote, political bosses from Matanzas; Salvador Cisneros Betancourt, planter from Camaguey, ex-president of the insurgent government and former Marquis of Santa Lucia; Juan Gualberto Gómez, Negro orator and editor from Oriente. The Santa Clara delegation included General José Miguel Gómez, General José de Jesus Monteagudo, General José B. Alemán, mulatto lawyer Martín Morúa Delgado, General José Luis Robau and Colonel Enrique Villuendas, all in the ruling clique of the Federal Republicans. In all, the delegates were Cuba's political elite.

For the elections of 1901, the political factions realigned themselves over the issue of the presidential nomination. The Nationalists wanted to run Máximo Gómez, still a national hero despite his difference with the veterans over bonuses. He rejected the proposal, saying, "Men of war, for war, and those of peace, for peace."[48]

The Nationalists then turned to Tomás Estrada Palma, former head of the revolutionary junta. Estrada Palma had been a major figure in the independence movement for thirty years. Born in Oriente in 1835, educated in Spain, he was chosen president of the revolutionary government in 1877. Captured and exiled the same year, he did not return to Cuba until his election as president. After the Peace of Zanjon (1878) he went to Honduras where he married the daughter of the President, served as postmaster-general, and saw his father-in-law assassinated. Emigrating to the United States, he founded a school for Cuban children at Central Valley, New York. A firm patriot and friend of José Martí, Estrada Palma became the central figure in the revolutionary junta when the insurrection began again in 1895. He raised funds, arms, munitions, and men for the Army of Liberation and served as the insurgent government's delegate in Washington. Undeniably, he played an important role in the movement, but, outside of the insurgent leadership, he was virtually unknown to Cubans. He was so closely identified with the United States that he seemed the American candidate. He was openly sympathetic to American democracy and to commercial ties with the United States, and apparently never completely dismissed the possibility of union with the United States. His critics later interpreted his statements that political independence would not automatically serve the welfare of the Cuban people to mean that he was an agent of American expansionism.

Estrada Palma's personal life was exemplary; he was honest, kindly, and modest. A slight, elderly man with a drooping white mustache and carefully combed hair, he looked the perfect grandfather. Age, however, had made him rigid in his judgments on people and matters of loyalty, honor, duty, and patriotism. He was extremely sensitive to personal criticism.

Although Estrada Palma valued democracy, he was a political and economic conservative. He was an advocate of balanced budgets, governmental austerity, and obedience to authority. He believed Cuba's future was democratic, but it would have to evolve from education and practice. As president he commented on Cuba's insufficient preparation in self-government, stating that

. . . the efficacy of the democratic system resides precisely in this, in being open in everything, in criticizing and discussing everything. But from there (the ideal) to the highly personalized, angry attacks of present day politics, there is a great abyss.

All defamatory statements deserve censure, but I have granted even the most misguided of those who try me, benevolency and inexhaustible leniency.

Many confuse, unfortunately, liberty with license. I, on the other hand, have never used a single one of the thousand recourses power offers me in order officially to quiet the defamers. This is the reason that up to the gates of Havana, and even within the capital itself, the most extreme and rabid opponents enjoy true immunity.

From such a chance I am demonstrating, religiously, respect for liberty: acquiescent, tolerating the exaggerated, and at times hurt, feeling that the concept of liberty itself is attacked when my character is questioned.

There are inevitable evils, and this is one of them. The great Washington was bitterly attacked, with notorious injustice, and he was Washington.

In Cuba we have a Republic, but there are no citizens. They will be shaped as they become imbued with true democracy, which is sane and disciplined. . . . Until now, our status as colonials has not allowed us to educate ourselves politically. We must give ourselves a full trial.[49]

A major factor in Estrada Palma's nomination was that his long exile had freed him to a large degree from the bitter factionalism within the revolutionary leadership in Cuba. On the other hand, he was well known to the American government and was highly regarded by the McKinley administration. The United States government knew he was a firm Cuban patriot, and a friend to private enterprise and the rights of foreign citizens. It also approved of his belief that the Cubans should be led by a responsible, educated elite until the people learned orderliness and restraint in public affairs. In light of Estrada Palma's values and comparing his service to Cuba with that of Generals Máximo Gómez and García, his elevation to the presidency was comparable to having Benjamin Franklin instead of George Washington as the United States first president.

Estrada Palma's candidacy was supported by most of the prominent men associated with the Constitutional Convention, Nationalists and Federal Republicans alike. He was endorsed by such diverse types as Máximo Gómez, Méndez Capote, Emilio Núñez, José Miguel Gómez, Morúa Delgado, and Gonzalo de Quesada. His campaign was based on promises of prosperity and national unity. General Bartolomé Masó decided to run against him as an anti–Platt Amendment candidate, but withdrew from the race when Leonard Wood refused to place Masó partisans on the board supervising the elections. Duly elected under the supervision of the Military Government, Estrada Palma returned to his native land in May, 1902, to become president after twenty-five years in exile.

Estrada Palma's first term was full of difficulty, but his administration had some major successes, primarily in its relations with the United States.[50] Between 1902 and 1905, the Cuban government negotiated a Treaty of Reciprocity which widened Cuba's share of the American sugar market, reduced America's demand for naval bases to two sites, and firmly defended Cuba's claim to the Isle of Pines. Domestically, Estrada Palma, supported by a "non-partisan" cabinet of men known for their conservatism and administrative ability, worked to continue the programs in sanitation, education, and public works begun by the Military Government. Estrada Palma built the nation's credit by reducing the public debt and by cautious administration. In his budgets, receipts exceeded expenditures, and the Treasury developed a surplus estimated by the government's critics at $25 million by 1906.

The Estrada Palma government, despite the American minister's complaints about its skilful defense of Cuba's interests, lived up to the expectations of the Roosevelt administration.

Within Cuba, however, the political and economic situation was less than promising. The spirit of annexationism still lived in the aliens and in Cuban conservatives, and their hold on the island's wealth forced Estrada Palma to hear their views. As the adrenalin of independence drained away from the bureaucracy, inefficiency and corruption spread. To quiet the veterans and stimulate the economy, Estrada Palma negotiated a $35 million loan with Speyer and Company, a New York banking house. With this loan, he paid part of a bonus voted the veterans by the Cuban congress. Although the sugar industry began to recover, its patterns of employment and the distribution of its profits still created unrest in the growing season, the *tiempo muerto*. In 1903 and 1904, there were strikes in the cities and banditry in the countryside. Spanish immigration, encouraged as a means of building a white yeoman class, instead increased the competition for urban jobs. Although Estrada Palma tried to offset unemployment with public-works spending, he could not get the congress to vote the funds. His own fiscal policies kept the cost of living high.[51]

Politically, Estrada Palma did not take a party label or try to exert party leadership. In the congress the Nationalists and Federal Republicans proved unwilling to implement the Constitution. They turned their energies, instead, to voting themselves immunity, passing veteran bonuses (one of which Estrada Palma vetoed), bickering over patronage. Personal ambitions and regional rivalries determined a politician's position on a given issue. The congress was most unified on one point, opposition to the United States and those whose interests its legation supported: sugar growers, the Catholic Church, investors, the alien business community, and annexationists. The Estrada Palma government became the object of criticism from the politicians because it was blamed for the economy's failure to meet expectations, for spending too much money for public works in Havana, for being too polite to Americans, for being too careful with its funds, and for being insensitive to the patriots in congress.[52]

Although there were many issues, the congressional elections of 1904 were determined again by personality and region. The parties reformed accordingly. The Federal Republicans became the Conservative Republicans, an alliance between the followers of Ricardo Dolz (a conservative) of Havana and the Miguelistas (followers of José Miguel Gómez, regarded as radicals) of Santa Clara. The Nationalists became the National Liberals, and ran with the blessing of Máximo Gómez and against the Platt Amendment. The elections were controlled by whichever faction held local power; fraud was common.

The factions underwent even more radical shifts in 1905, a presidential election year.[53] The Conservative Republicans split in an argument on party organization, but the issue was the candidacy. The Havana wing, under Dolz and Méndez Capote, favored provincial representation. The Miguelistas wanted the party controlled on the basis of the number of representatives the party elected to congress, which would have favored José Miguel's candidacy. Unable to reconcile their differences with the *habaneros*, the Miguelistas joined the National Liberals on the promise that Gómez would be nominated. The new alliance, called the Liberal party, named Gómez and Alfredo Zayas, the party president, as their slate. One National Liberal, General Emilio Núñez, governor of Havana, was unhappy with this move, as he too had presidential ambitions. Taking the label Nationalist, Núñez hoped to win the election on the strength of his friendship with Máximo Gómez and his own Havana following. The old general's death in June, 1905, however, dimmed Núñez' chances. He then joined the new Moderate party, formerly the Conservative Republicans.

Hoping to continue his administration and to block the Gómez-Zayas faction, which he considered unscrupulous and radical, Estrada Palma reluctantly decided to run for re-election at the head of the Moderate ticket. He also believed the Moderate leaders were more sympathetic to his legislative goals and economic policy than the Liberals. He was paired with Méndez Capote, the party president. Estrada Palma's decision, motivated by a sincere desire to continue the programs he believed best for Cuba's development, immediately cast the two political alliances as a government party and an opposition.

Estrada Palma's first move which bound him to the Moderates was to reorganize his cabinet. The new secretaries, called the "Fighting Cabinet" for their war records and, said the Liberals, for their intention to use force to win the elections, were led by Generals Fernando Freyre de Andrade and Rafael Montalvo. The former, as Secretary of Government, commanded the Rural Guard and the election machinery. He immediately went to work to insure a Moderate victory by removing unfriendly provincial and municipal officials. Theoretically the Constitution protected these officials, but the congress had failed to pass a law providing for their election. In the absence of such a law the President had the power (under the Spanish codes) to remove appointees. The same situation held true for the judiciary. Since the Constitutional provisions for bipartisan election boards had not been implemented either, the election could be controlled simply by changing the local officials. This was what Freyre de Andrade did, and he did so with enthusiasm. In the Liberal strongholds in Pinar del Rio, Havana and Santa Clara, the purge was widespread. The outraged Liberals replied with riots, counter-intimidation and arson, but much of the local protest was not party-inspired.[54]

The government also increased its following by the liberal granting of pardons and by filling the bureaucracy with partisans. Policemen, teachers, and public health officers were among those replaced with Moderates. The degree of Estrada Palma's complicity in these acts is uncertain, but it is unlikely that he was simply the ignorant tool of his Moderate secretaries. It is more likely that he believed his own re-election was crucial to Cuba's existence and he was willing to condone most, if not all, the measures necessary to insure his victory.

Unrest increased during the *tiempo muerto* of 1905 as the fall elections approached. The Liberals charged that Estrada Palma was using political violence to bring on American intervention and annexation.[55] One of his accusers, the popular Miguelista and secretary of the Constitutional Convention, Enrique Villuendas, was killed in a gun battle with police in Cienfuegos the day before the provincial-municipal elections. The Liberals added assassination to their charges. The following-day, September 23, 1905, the Moderates swept the elections, although the Liberals, through equally effective coercion, held on to some posts in Santa Clara and Pinar del Rio. Violence was used by both parties. After the election a Moderate newspaper admitted that 432,000 names were on the registers, although Cuba probably had no more than 300,000 eligible voters.[56] In the national elections which followed on December 1, the Moderates and Estrada Palma won their soiled mandate as the Liberals boycotted the polls.

That the Liberals shortly began to plan a revolt seems certain, but the coming of *la zafra* deprived them of many potential rebels. There was, nonetheless, scattered violence. The most inauspicious incident was the attack on the Rural Guard post at Guanabacoa near Havana on February 24, 1906. There a group of some thirty insurgents killed two Guards, wounded others, and captured guns and horses. On the diplomatic front, José Miguel Gómez went to New York in October to lecture the newspapers there on Moderate injustice. In one interview he blandly suggested that it was the United States duty to right the election wrongs in the name of constitutionalism and democracy.[57] By the time of Estrada Palma's second inauguration (May 20, 1906), the Liberals had despaired of any peaceful settlement, and a revolt in 1906 was only a matter of timing and organization.

As the *tiempo muerto* of 1906 again brought Cuba to an economic standstill, the rumors of revolt grew along with the scanty crops of sugar and tobacco.[58] The Republic stood on the threshold of a new experience, its first civil war as a sovereign nation. Behind it lay the long years of struggle against Spain. Yet little had changed. Life for the *guajiro* was still *el tiempo muerto* and *la zafra*. The American soldiers had come and gone. With Estrada Palma there had been peace for awhile, and life was a little easier; but now the men talked war and unearthed rifles and cartridges. What had become of the military heroes, the patriot statesmen of the war with Spain?

The answer was that they were the same men they had always been, the products of a system of government that exploited the political ignorance of the people. They were the children of a society and an economy that had unevenly distributed its rewards for three hundred years and showed little evidence of changing. Without any experience in the peaceful accommodation of conflicting interests, seldom without any motive other than self-satisfaction, Cuba's popular politicians moved their country toward civil war. Under the circumstances, it was unreasonable to hope that the United States would stand aloof. Just as surely as revolt was the product of Cuba's failure to develop responsible party government, so too was American intervention a predictable product of general insurrection. The great imponderable was the character such intervention would take.

1. The picture of Cuba circa 1808–1800 is drawn from the following works: Wyatt MacGaffey and Clifford R. Barnett, *Cuba* (New Haven, Conn., 1962); Lowry Nelson, *Rural Cuba* (Minneapolis, 1950); Robert Freeman Smith (ed.), *Background to Revolution: The Development of Modern Cuba* (New York, 1966); Gonzalo de Quesada, *Cuba* (Washington, 1905); José R. Álvarez Díaz *et al.*, *Un estudio sobre Cuba: colonia—república—experimento socialista* (Miami, Fla., 1963); Raymond Leslie Buell *et al.*, *Problems of the New Cuba*, A Report by the Commission on Cuban Affairs (New York, 1935).

Of particular value among works by Americans in this era are Irene Wright, *Cuba* (New York, 1910) and Edward F. Atkins, *Sixty Years in Cuba* (Cambridge, Mass., 1926). Miss Wright, as a reporter for *Diario del la Marina* (Havana) and agricultural agent, was a ten year resident in Cuba and a serious student of its culture. Atkins was an influential sugar planter, owner of several large estates in Santa Clara province.

2. The best-documented, incisive history of Cuba for the war of liberation is Hermino Portell Vilá, *Historia de Cuba en sus relaciones con los Estados Unidos y España* (4 vols.; Havana, 1938–1941). *Cf.* Philip Foner, *A History of Cuba and Its Relations with the United States* (2 vols.; New York, 1962, 1964). On the role of the Negro in the revolutionary movement see also Lawrence F. Nichols, "The Bronze Titan: the Mulatto Hero of Cuban Independence, Antonio Maceo" (unpublished Ph.D dissertation, Duke University, 1954).

3. Portell Vilá claims that the tragedy of the United States intervention in 1898 and the occupation that followed was that it polarized Cuban politics around the question of economic and political ties to the United States. The reactionaries and the demagogues that the United States had to deal with in 1906 were creatures of its own making. Portell Vilá, *Historia de Cuba,* IV, 499.

For a moving fictional account of Cuban life from 1868 to 1920, see Carlos Loveira, *Generales y doctores,* ed. Shasta M. Bryant and J. Riis Owre (New York, 1965).

4. Lowry Nelson, *Rural Cuba,* pp. 139–61.

5. The statistics are from Office of the Director, Census of Cuba, U.S. War Department, *Report on the Census of Cuba, 1899* (Washington, 1900); and Henry Gannett and Victor H. Olmstead (eds.), *Cuba: Population, History, and Resources, 1907* (Washington, 1909). The latter work is based on the 1907 census conducted by the Provisional Government. For a summary, see Henry Gannett, "Conditions in Cuba Revealed by the Census," *National Geographic Magazine,* XX (February, 1909), 200–202. See also Álvarez Díaz, *Estudio sobre Cuba,* pp. 373–96.

6. Wright, *Cuba,* p. 88.

7. MacGaffey and Barnett, *Cuba,* chap. iii; Nelson, *Rural Cuba,* pp. 79–138; Wright, *Cuba,* pp. 134–35, 164, 235, Álvarez Díaz, *Estudio sobre Cuba,* pp. 471–88. For the relation of poverty to rural violence, see Alberto Arredondo, *Cuba: tierra indefensa* (Havana, 1945), pp. 173–205. For a description of the sugar industry, see Willis Fletcher Johnson, *The History of Cuba* (New York, 1920), V, 15, 160–82.

8. Manuel Márquez Sterling, *Alrededor de nuestra psicologia* (Havana, 1906), p. 14. *Alrededor* is a vivid description of the social and psychological upheaval which independence and industrialized agriculture brought to Cuba; the author was a noted Cuban patriot, journalist, author, and diplomat. Another striking account of the impact of sugar and tobacco on Cuban life is Fernando Ortiz, *Cuban Counterpoint,* trans. by Harriet de Onís (New York, 1947).

9. Atkins, *Sixty Years in Cuba, passim,* and Walter Vaughan, *The Life and Work of Sir William Van Horne* (New York, 1920), pp. 267–317. Van Horne, builder of the Canadian Pacific Railroad, was the moving spirit behind the construction of the Cuban Railroad, which linked Oriente Province with western Cuba.

10. Scott, *Some Memories of a Soldier,* p. 239.

11. J. Lloyd Mecham, *Church and State in Latin America* (Chapel Hill, N.C., 1934), pp. 354–59.

12. Wright, *Cuba,* p. 198.

13. Márquez Sterling, *Alrededor de nuestra psicologia,* p. 214. The best source of documentary evidence on the subject is Manuel Secades y Japón and Horacio Díaz Pardo (eds.) *La justicia en Cuba: los veteranos y los indultos* (Havana, 1908) and *La justicia en Cuba: Patriotas y traidores* (2 vols., Havana, 1912, 1914). For an example of the hagiography of the War of Independence, see Emerterio S. Santovenia, *Huellas de gloria: frases historicas cubanas* (Havana, 1944).

14. Charles Johnson Post, *The Little War of Private Post* (New York, 1961), p. 81; Freidel, *The Splendid Little War,* p. 93–95; Theodore Roosevelt, *The Rough Riders,* pp. 54, 57, as previously cited.

15. Atkins, *Sixty Years in Cuba,* p. 278.

16. Wright, *Cuba* p. 98. For a critical account, see Enrique Collazo, *Los Americanos en Cuba* (2 vols., Havana, 1905).

17. "Cubans," manuscript by Lt. Col. Robert L. Bullard, Bullard Papers.

18. The most recent scholarly printed account of the military occupation and the evolution of American policy for Cuba is David F. Healy, *The United States in Cuba, 1898–1902: Generals, Politicians, and the Search for Policy* (Madison, Wisc., 1963). Professor Healy's study emphasizes the political pressures in Cuba and the United States that produced the Platt Amendment and the Reciprocity Treaty of 1903. Older but valuable accounts may be found in Charles E. Chapman, *A History of the Cuban Republic* (New York, 1927); Russell H. Fitzgibbon, *Cuba and the United States, 1900–1935* (Menasha, Wisc., 1935); John Kendrick Bangs, *Uncle Sam Trustee* (New York, 1902); and Albert G. Robinson, *Cuba and the Intervention* (New York, 1905). See also James Harold Hitchman, "Leonard Wood and the Cuban Question, 1898–1902" (unpublished Ph.D. dissertation, University of California, Berkeley, 1965).

19. "Civil Report of Major General John R. Brooke, Military Governor of Cuba," U.S. War Department, *Annual Reports, 1899* (Washington, 1900), I, Part VI, 5–476. Brooke's views on the relation of law to government-inspired reform may be found on page 164 of his report, hereafter cited as *Civil Report, 1899.*

20. Scott, *Some Memories of a Soldier,* pp. 234, 248–49.

21. James H. Wilson, *Under the Old Flag* (New York and London, 1912), I, 472–516.

22. *Civil Report, 1899,* p. 337. The gist of Wilson's argument is contained in pp. 330–41 of Brooke's report.

23. Healy, *The United States in Cuba,* pp. 92–95.

24. For two contemporary accounts of Wood's work, see Theodore Roosevelt, "General Leonard Wood: A Model American Military Administrator," *Outlook,* LXI (January 7, 1899), 19–23; and Ray Stannard Baker, "General Leonard Wood," *McClure's Magazine,* XIV (Feb-

ruary, 1900), 368–79. For a detailed account of Wood's work in Santiago and Habana, see Hagedorn, *Leonard Wood*, I, 184–392.

25. Wood to McKinley, April 12, 1900. Quoted in Hagedorn, *Leonard Wood*, I, 285.

26. *Ibid.*, p. 323.

27. For an eye-witness report, see Robert P. Porter, *Industrial Cuba* (New York, 1899), pp. 63–65. Porter was McKinley's special commissioner in Cuba; he lauded Wood, but advised against forced annexation.

28. Leonard Wood, "The Existing Conditions and Needs in Cuba, *North American Review*, CLXVIII (May, 1899), 593–601. Wood repeatedly told Cubans that "one cannot advance liberty by the same methods and same laws that served tyranny." Rafael Martínez Ortiz, *Cuba: los primeros años de independencia* (2d ed.; Paris, 1924), I, 388.

29. Wood's report on the Department of Santiago—Puerto Principe is part of Brooke's *Civil Report, 1899*, pp. 834–57. For the text of the Provisional Constitution of Santiago de Cuba, see Ramón Infiesta, *Historia constitucional de Cuba* (Havana, 1951), pp. 354–55.

30. Wood to Roosevelt, July 12, 1899, and August 18, 1899. Quoted in Hagedorn, *Leonard Wood*, I, 251–52.

31. Root to Eliot, May 4, 1900. Quoted in Philip C. Jessup, *Elihu Root* (New York, 1938), I, 288.

32. *Ibid.*, pp. 304–5.

33. "Annual Report of the Secretary of War," U.S. War Department, *Annual Reports, 1899* (Washington, 1900), I, 31–32.

34. The primary printed source for Wood's proconsulship is his multi-volumed reports: *Civil Report of Brigadier General Leonard Wood, Military Governor of Cuba, for the period from December 20, 1899, to December 31, 1900* (12 vols.; Washington, 1901); *Civil Report of Brigadier General Leonard Wood, Military Governor of Cuba, for the period January 1, 1901, to December 31, 1901* (15 vols., Washington, 1902); *Civil Report of Brigadier General Leonard Wood, Military Governor of Cuba, for the period January 1, to May 20, 1902* (6 vols., Washington, 1902).

For his own analysis of his administration, see Leonard Wood, "The Military Government of Cuba," *Annals of the American Academy of Political and Social Science*, XXI (March, 1903), 153–82.

35. Hagedorn, *Leonard Wood*, I, 260–61.

36. Scott, *Some Memories of a Soldier*, p. 237. The conservatives revered Wood and hoped his authoritarian regime would continue indefinitely. Wright, *Cuba*, p. 190.

37. Wood's economic views may be found in the following sections of his *Civil Reports:* 1900—I, 89–92; 1901—I, 33; 1902—I, 12–13. For a contrasting view, see the report of Perfecto Lacoste, Secretary of Agriculture, Commerce, and Industries in *Civil Report, 1900*, VII, 10–15.

38. For a complete copy of the Constitution of 1901, see *Civil Report, 1902*, I, 243–64. For analysis, see Infiesta, *Historia constitucional de Cuba*, pp. 283–323.

39. Root to Wood, February 9, 1901. Reprinted in *Five Years of the War Department*, pp. 187–90.

40. U.S., *Statutes at Large*, XXXI, 897.

41. Enrique José Varona, *Mirando en torno* (Havana, 1906), p. 47. The literature on the Platt Amendment is voluminous. See Healy, *The United States in Cuba*, pp. 150–78; Chapman, *A History of the Cuban Republic*, pp. 126–51; Fitzgibbon, *Cuba and the United States*, pp. 73–85; Hagedorn, *Leonard Wood*, I, 421–23; and Jessup, *Elihu Root*, I, 310–31. Accounts from the Cuban standpoint are Manuel Márquez Sterling, *Proceso historico de la Enmienda Platt, 1897–1934* (2 vols.; Havana, 1941); Rafael Martínez Ortiz, *Cuba: los primeros años de independencia* (2 vols.; 2d ed., Paris, 1924); Portell Vilá, *Historia de Cuba*, IV, 7–290; Emilio Roig de Leuchsenring, *Historia de la Enmienda Platt* (2 vols.; Havana, 1935); Jorge Mañach, "Revolution in Cuba," *Foreign Affairs*, XII (October, 1933), 46–56.

42. República de Cuba, Sentado, *Memoria, 1902–1904*, "Report of the Committee Appointed to Confer with the Government of the United States, Giving an Account of the Results of Its Labors." No. 7, Document M. Copy in subject file "Cuba," Root Papers, Library of Congress.

43. *Congressional Record*, 56th Cong., 2d Sess. XXXIV, 3151.

44. James Bryce, "Some Reflections on the State of Cuba," *North American Review*, CLXXIV (March, 1902), 449–56.

45. Scott, *Some Memories of a Soldier*, p. 270; Hagedorn, *Leonard Wood*, I, 400, 412.

46. Chapman, *A History of the Cuban Republic*, pp. 130–32; Johnson, *The History of Cuba*, IV, 260–64; Martínez Ortiz, *Cuba: los primeros años de independencia*, II, 330–33, 407.

47. Infiesta, *Historia constitucional de Cuba*, pp. 286–87 n.

48. Quoted by Chapman, *A History of the Cuban Republic*, p. 143.

49. Quoted in Carlos de Velasco, *Estrada Palma: contribución historico* (Havana, 1911), pp. 33–34. The biographical sketch of Estrada Palma is based on Pánfilo D. Camacho, *Estrada Palma, el Gobernante Honrado* (Havana, 1938); Carlos Márquez Sterling, *Don Tomas: Biografia de una epoca* (Havana, 1953); Martínez Ortiz, *Cuba: los primeros años de independencia*, I, 330–33; Portell Vilá, *Historia de Cuba*, IV, 263–90; Roig de Leuchsenring, *Historia de Enmienda Platt*, I, 15–23; Chapman, *A History of the Cuban Republic*, pp. 152–54; Scott, *Some Memories of a Soldier*, p. 263.

50. Major accounts of the Estrada Palma administration may be found in Portell Vilá, *Historia de Cuba*, IV, 420–520; Chapman, *A History of the Cuban Republic*, pp. 152–94; Fitzgibbon, *Cuba and the United States*, pp. 94–111.

51. Report of Sr. Despaigne, Administración de Aduana, to Capt. Frank R. McCoy, November 8, 1906, Tasker H. Bliss Papers, Library of Congress; J. M. Cortes to Gen. T. H. Bliss, August 25; September 9, 15, 22, 29; October 6; November 18, all 1906, Bliss Papers.

52. H. G. Squiers, Minister to Cuba, to Secretary of State John Hay, September 19 and October 17, 1903, U.S. Department of State, *Foreign*

*Relations of the United States, 1903* (Washington, 1904), pp. 374–75; Márquez Sterling, *Don Tomás,* pp. 397 ff.

53. Report of William H. Taft and Robert Bacon, "Cuban Pacification" in "Report of the Secretary of War," U.S. War Department, *Annual Reports, 1906* (Washington, 1906), I, 451–53. This report (Appendix E in the Secretary's report) is, with appendixes, the basic source of published material on the Second Intervention. Hereafter cited as Taft-Bacon *Report.*

54. Martínez Ortiz, *Cuba: los primeros años de independencia,* II, 515–18.

55. *Ibid.,* pp. 539, 543–55; Portell Vilá, *Historia de Cuba,* IV, 433.

56. Editorial, *La Discusión* (Havana), November 11, 1905. For a catalogue of Liberal charges, see the statement of the Executive Committee of the Liberal party, September 27, 1905. Both reprinted in Taft-Bacon *Report,* pp. 495–500.

57. *Diario de la Marina* (Havana), October 4, 1905; Portell Vilá, *Historia de Cuba,* IV, 441–42. Portell Vilá believes Gómez was encouraged to revolt by New York businessmen interested in annexation. One, at least, did not; James H. Wilson told Gómez that revolt was worse than unfair elections. Wilson to A. Figueroa, December 6, 1905, James H. Wilson Papers, Library of Congress.

58. Frank Steinhart, U.S. Consul General, Havana, to Gen. Leonard Wood, July 13, 1906, Wood Papers.

# CHAPTER TWO

# THE AUGUST REVOLUTION

DESPITE isolated outbreaks of violence and a host of conflicting rumors, in July, 1906, the the Estrada Palma government seemed firmly entrenched. The Liberal leaders, however, had not given up their plans for open revolt. Rather, they had decided to stage a *golpe de estado* by seizing the Havana police stations and capturing the President and his cabinet.[1] They then planned, presuming that United States would have no cause to intervene, to have a rump Cuban congress (less the 1905 electees) establish a provisional government and hold new elections.[2] The junta itself included the top leadership of the Liberal party: José Miguel Gómez, Alfredo Zayas, José de Jesus Monteagudo, Demetrio Castillo Duany, Justo and Carlos García Vélez, Juan Gualberto Gómez, and Manuel Lazo.[3] The junta's plans were café-talk in Havana by August 1, and the government, unable to ignore the conspiracy, may have been about to act when the actual rebellion began.

On August 16 in the westernmost province of Pinar del Rio, a former guerrilla colonel and Liberal congressman, Faustino (Pino) Guerra, called several hundred men to his colors (a Cuban flag trimmed with black crepe), and the revolt was underway.[4] Guerra, apparently fearing that the government would smash the plot, took the field without orders from Manuel Lazo, the most influential Liberal in the province. Guerra himself was an engaging person, but hardly a Liberal strongman. He was best known as a gambler, horseman, accordian player, and bon vivant. Slim, ruggedly handsome, dark, mustachioed, and hook-nosed, Pino Guerra was a finished guerrilla chieftain, having served with Antonio Maceo.

Guerra's call-to-arms shocked the government into action. Its first moves may have been its most disastrous, for Estrada Palma arrested the leading members of the revolutionary junta. Within a week he had José Miguel Gómez, Castillo Duany, Monteagudo, García Vélez, Juan Gualberto Gómez, and most of their fellow plotters safely behind bars.[5] The remaining conspirators went into hiding, and in most cases did not get to the rebel armies during the next five weeks. The most important fugitive was Alfredo Zayas, president of the Liberal party. The arrests, however, had two important effects. The first was to put the revolt in the hands of a second rank of local military chieftains; the other was to make the rebels' recruiting easier and their antigovernment propaganda more credible.[6]

Hard on the heels of the arrests, more rebel bands formed in Havana Province (under Enrique Loynaz del Castillo and Ernesto Asbert) and in Santa Clara, so that after one week the rebels had two thousand men on the loose. Mounted and armed with rifles and revolvers of varying serviceability, the scattered columns were commanded by self-appointed generals and colonels, who called their forces the Constitutional Army. The privates of the officer-heavy Constitutional Army were, largely, unemployed rural workers, "illiterates without land, wanting adventure and novelty . . . to them all causes were good if they offered an opportunity to do the August." [7] "Doing the August," or "going to the woods" to improve one's lot, was an old Cuban custom, and as long as the insurgent officers kept up the picnic atmosphere there would be plenty of recruits. The revolt gave the Cuban *campesino* an incomparable opportunity for "saving the country and at the same time eating meat." [8]

The political goals of the Constitutional Army generals were no different from those of the Liberal party. As Pino Guerra led his swelling column of horsemen around Pinar del Rio, knocking aside or avoiding scattered detachments of the

Rural Guard, he took several opportunities to make his aims clear. To reporters (who found him most co-operative), Guerra explained that "our plans are to establish a reign of Law according to that prescribed in the Constitution, annulling past elections, the product of assassination, fraud and violence; we want to bring to power legislators elected by the popular will."[9] He complained about Moderate corruption and extravagance, but he continued to insist that election frauds were the cause of the revolt, and that the rebels simply wanted a return to the Constitution.[10]

In Havana Province, Ernesto Asbert called for new elections, even if it meant American intervention: "We prefer a new American intervention that will guarantee future legal elections."[11] If the American government does not intervene, he continued, "we will overthrow the Palma Administration or make everything in the island American. We would much rather trust Roosevelt than Palma."[12] In New York City, Colonel Charles Aquirre opened an insurgent press office, and shortly news releases stressing the rebels' restraint and pure motives were common in the city's newspaper offices.

The insurgent columns marched about their home provinces throughout the rest of August, avoiding pitched battles, collecting men, horses, and supplies, and generally behaving themselves. Though the rebel generals collected "contributions" from fearful planters, there was little destruction and even less violence. Essentially the rebel strategy was to create an atmosphere of impending violence and thus intimidate the government. As Guerra told reporters, "we are holding back to give the government an opportunity to recognize its errors and restore peace to the people of Cuba without the necessity of bloodshed."[13]

The rebels' principal tactic was to disrupt communications while at the same time threatening to burn out landholders. Trains and coastal steamers were robbed of official mail, and a couple of railway culverts destroyed. For every culvert dynamited or cane field endangered, reports of ten times as much destruction reached Havana. With the telegraph lines down, the government could not verify the reports. In reality the rebels were taking horses, arms, and food by promissory note and respecting private property.[14] In Santa Clara, where a rebel column of a thousand was parading under General Eduardo Guzmán, the planters found Guzmán's demands firm, but polite:

> The exegiencies [sic] of the war, every day more exacting, and the necessity of preparing for active military operations obliges me to exact a small obligatory war loan, which amount I divide amongst the rich landowners of this district.
>
> My interest is not to receive money, but ammunition, and to that effect I solicit from you the remittance of ten thousand rounds of cartridges either of Mausser [sic] or Remington style to my Headquarters in the non-prorogable time of eight days. The security of your properties will be complete because I maintain the most absolute order with my forces and I will give you a receipt for the amount disbursed by you in the purchase of war materials, obliging myself to obtain this Division the payment of same in any case.[15]

The insurgents, however, did not entirely avoid combat, for there were several clashes with the Rural Guard. Near Santiago a Guard lieutenant died in ambush; on August 22, Guerra's column captured the detachment at San Luis (Pinar del Rio) and the next day "occupied" the town of San Juan y Martinez. In Havana Province a Guard patrol shot up an insurgent column, killing its leader, Quentin Banderas. On August 25, Guerra with two thousand horsemen rode into the city of Guines and routed the Guards there, killing three and wounding six. In Santa Clara, the Guard dispersed one rebel band only to find that the officials of Las Cruces (alcalde, councilors, police, and Guards) declaring for the revolution. Riding about with impunity the rebels, by the end of August, numbered four thousand under Guerra, four thousand in Havana with Asbert and Loynaz del Castillo, and another six thousand scattered throughout the island.[16]

Estrada Palma and the Moderates were surprised and confounded by the rapidity with which the insurrection grew, and their acts to crush the revolt were marked by confusion, hesitancy, and a notable lack of success. First, Estrada Palma increased the Rural Guard by two thousand men, but, failing to find recruits, he then offered volunteers $2.50 a day to form a government militia. In addition, he created a Foreign Legion of Artillery of alien volunteers, commanded by an exotic group of Englishmen, Americans, and Germans, to handle the government's Colt machine guns. As the mobilization went on, the Cuban Secretary of State, Dr. Juan O'Farrill, assured the American chargé, Jacob Sleeper, that the government would soon raise twenty thousand men and crush the revolt in two months' time.[17] Despite the government's optimism, economic conditions in Cuba deteriorated rapidly as credit dried up, planters despaired of protection, and the rebels harassed communications.[18]

## Roosevelt Considers Intervention

In the United States, the outbreak of the August Revolution found the Roosevelt administration and the American people with their minds far from Cuba. The summer of 1906 had already been exciting. On June 25, Harry K. Thaw had murdered architect Stanford White over his attentions to Harry's wife, Evelyn. Then in August, the President had dismissed two companies of Negro infantrymen for shooting up Brownsville, Texas. On August 29, William Jennings Bryan returned from an eight month tour of "decadent" Europe and at a rally at Madison Square Garden stunned Tammany with a proposal to nationalize the railroads. The New York newspapers were locked in mortal combat over William Randolph Hearst's candidacy for the state's governorship; Hearstism was synonomous with demagoguery—in Republican circles. The popular songs were "Waltz Me around Again, Willy" and "Why Did I Pick a Lemon in the Garden of Love." Serious readers were engrossed in H. G. Wells' *The Future of America,* Jack London's *White Fang,* and Upton Sinclair's *The Jungle.*

The government had scattered from Washington to escape the discomforts of August along the Potomac. The Congress was home campaigning, and the leaders of the executive branch had fled to their summer homes. Theodore Roosevelt was strenuously relaxing at Oyster Bay; Secretary of War William Howard Taft was fishing in Quebec; Assistant Secretary of State Robert Bacon was vacationing in Maine; and Secretary of the Navy Charles J. Bonaparte was taking the breezes at Lenox, Massachusetts. Only Elihu Root, the Secretary of State, was hard at work, speech-making and banqueting his way home from the Third Pan American Conference at Rio de Janiero. In Washington Alvey A. Adee was watching the cables at the State Department, and Generals Fred C. Ainsworth and J. Franklin Bell were moving the papers at the War Department. The legation in Havana was just as relaxed (until the revolt), for the minister, Edward V. Morgan, an able career diplomat, was vacationing in Europe.

At the time of the Cuban insurrection, Roosevelt's Caribbean policy was in the delicate process of readjustment. After five years of tension and conflict, years that saw the Canal Zone seized, a customs receivership established in the Dominican Republic, Venezuela protected, and American diplomats and vessels involved in minor conflicts throughout Central America, Roosevelt and Root in 1906 embarked on a general reinterpretation of the American presence in the Caribbean. Their principal aim was to reassure the Latin Americans that the Monroe Doctrine and Roosevelt's Corollary did not make their countries protectorates of the United States.[19] At the opening session of the Rio Conference on July 31, Root had stirred the audience with a firm statement of the United States friendship and respect for the Latin American republics:

We wish for no victories but those of peace; for no territory except our own; for no sovereignty except sovereignty over ourselves. We deem the independence and equal rights of the smallest and weakest member of the family of nations entitled to as much respect as those of the greatest empire; and we deem the observance of that respect the chief guaranty of the weak against oppression of the strong. We neither claim nor desire any rights or privileges or powers that we do not freely concede to every American republic. We wish to increase our prosperity, to expand our trade, to grow in wealth, in wisdom and in spirit; but our conception of the true way to accomplish this is not to pull down others and profit by their ruin, but to help all friends to a common prosperity and a common growth, that we may all become greater and stronger together.[20]

Although Root's speeches quieted some anti-American criticism, they did not signify any change in the United States power relationship with the Caribbean republics. The United States was intimately concerned with the affairs of these countries, Theodore Roosevelt wrote Henry Cabot Lodge, since their well-being affected the United States security (i.e., the Panama Canal) and foreign trade. Despite what Root said, the United States had not foresworn intervention itself, only awkward, antagonizing intervention. In the future, Roosevelt confided, interference by the United States would be " . . . to secure the well-being of the dependencies, or quasi-dependencies, themselves; that there should be the minimum of such interference which will accomplish the result; and that it should where possible be veiled as to avoid hurting the feelings of those in whose behalf we are interfering."[21]

The revolt in Cuba was a week underway before Roosevelt or Taft took interest in it, and their first concern was to assist the Estrada Palma government and survey the military aspects of possible intervention. Neither acted to change the United States diplomatic attitude toward the revolt: that the Cuban government must protect American lives and property and pay for damages.[22] Roosevelt's first act in dealing with the Cuban crisis was to clear the way for Estrada Palma to purchase five million cartridges through the co-operation of the War Department on August 25.[23] Taft on the same day ordered General Bell to report the General Staff's estimate on the troops available for Cuban service.

General Bell's views on the revolt, sent directly to the President, were hardly encouraging.[24] Although the General Staff had planned a force of fifteen thousand men in three expeditions, which Bell believed adequate, the Chief of Staff further outlined the probable character of operations against the insurgents. If the Army were to campaign for the Cuban government, it was quite likely to run into the same problems it faced in the Philippines:

> It is one of the most difficult operations in the world, as military history abundantly shows, to completely disarm a hostile population as skillful in the arts of concealment and deception as is the Latin Race. . . . In dealing with such people, Mr. President, it is not a question of military strength and fighting quality. The heart breaking feature of it all is that you organize an army and it goes forth with military ardor, with all the pomp and panoply of war, enthusiastically to meet and conquer the enemy, only to discover it can find nothing to fight.

Instead, Bell continued, the guerrillas and terrorists hid among the sympathetic people who provided arms, food, recruits, and information, and a pacification program became essential. If the President was considering supporting Estrada Palma, Bell wrote, the Army should immediately send officers to Cuba to collect military intelligence: the insurgents' names, arms, suppliers, residence, and occupation. A widespread network of spies would have to get the names of "every individual secretly connected with their supply, information and communication service" if the rebellion was to be broken.

Though Bell's experience with insurgents was limited to the Philippines, his analysis of the Cuban rebels' potential for guerrilla warfare coincided with Brigadier General Frederick Funston's views. On August 28, Funston wrote Bell to give the Chief of Staff the essence of his two years of experience in the Army of Liberation.[25] In 1898, Funston said, the United States Army had an erroneous impression of the Cuban insurgents because it saw the worst troops in the Army of Liberation. The Cuban insurgents were formidable guerrillas because of their mobility, scouting skills, and intelligence services. Although they were not good marksmen, they were experts in the ambush and were never ambushed themselves. Their cavalry was excellent. Funston believed that the Cubans had never lost the military initiative in 1895–98.

The Spanish were defeated, Funston continued, because they could not match the speed of the rebel forces or the insurgents' sources of information. If American soldiers were to be committed against the Constitutional Army, Funston suggested that the bulk of the troops be cavalry and mounted infantry organized in self-sustaining columns of five hundred to a thousand men. Because the Cubans' greatest weakness was their difficulty in feeding columns of more than four thousand, the Army could count on having to pursue the guerrilla bands as they foraged. Funston thought that the Americans could break up the Cuban columns initially against adverse odds of five-to-one, but that a guerrilla war would call for a larger troop commitment.

Roosevelt, after studying Bell's letter and the General Staff's preliminary study, wrote the Chief of Staff that he agreed with his analysis and approved the dispatch of two Army officers to report on military conditions in Cuba, for Bell was not satisfied that the newspapers, his only source of information, were reliable.[26] The officers, Major Eugene F. Ladd and Captain Dwight E. Aultman, were both veterans of Wood's Military Government and experts in Cuban affairs. Ladd had been the island's auditor and treasurer, and Aultman, until 1904, adviser to Cuba's Corps of Artillery.

Upon learning of Bell's letter and Roosevelt's decision to send military observers to Cuba, Taft wrote the President and clearly stated the central consideration in the United States subsequent reaction to the deepening crisis in Cuba: "What Bell says is entirely true, that if we sent our men there to suppress disorder we would have a fight on our hands very much like we had in the Philippines. . . . "[27]

At this point, Roosevelt was not yet ready to commit the United States to open support of Estrada Palma, but clearly he was willing to supply the Cuban government with munitions and to investigate the possibility of action against the rebels. His military advisers had been frank and realistic, but they had not urged armed intervention. The President, who did not even mention the Cuban crisis in a September 4 letter to Elihu Root, was waiting for a clearer picture of the insurrection.[28]

In Cuba the political and military initiative lay with the insurgents, and they did not surrender it. Part of the rebels' calculations was that the United States could be forced to intervene to their advantage if there was clear danger to foreign property and irrefutable proof of the government's corruption and weakness. As General Eduardo Guzmán put it:

We desire . . . peace because we desire the welfare of our country and because we are all patriots . . . if the Government do [sic] not come around to concede what we ask, which is strictly just, I can assure you that the forces of Santa Clara . . . will commence their offensive work against the public forces and against the properties of foreigners, with the sole end that the Americans shall come as quickly as possible, as we prefer to live under the shelter of the justice of a foreign power than submit ourselves to tyranny under the flag which has cost us so much to acquire.[29]

Already the pleas of American planters and British railway managers were flooding the legation. Certainly the Constitutional Army had the ability to destroy foreign property, but its generals showed more interest in threats than arson. Still they made their point; as one American plantation manager wrote Jacob Sleeper:

The Cuban professor, who teaches school here, made a visit to the headquarters of the rebels and the man in charge told him that if the Cuban Government succeeded in whipping them that they would destroy all the foreign property that they could find. Owing to the fact that the element that has enlisted with the rebels is the worst element on the Island, we do not feel safe in our present locality as there is not a rural guard or policeman in thirty miles of us and all kinds of trouble could be made as we *have no protection whatever*. There are about forty Americans in this locality and we hope that you will take this matter up with the Cuban Government at once and see that we have some protection.[30]

Win or lose, the insurgents threatened to begin burning property on September 15, and kept up their cry for mass resignations in the government, peace, amnesty, and new elections, all under the United States supervision if need be.[31]

From the viewpoint of the Estrada Palma government, the situation was growing increasingly desperate. From the outset, Estrada Palma and his closest advisers had counted on

American support, under the terms of Article III of the Platt Amendment, in the case of open rebellion against their regime.[32] The government's reasoning probably followed that of an article written by Enrique José Varona on August 31. Cuba's foremost author and political philosopher believed the Platt Amendment promised support only to a *de jure* government, " . . . to aid, consequently, the present government. To proceed in another way would be to reopen the thorny Cuban problem; and that does not suit the administration in Washington, and enters now neither in the preoccupations, nor in the interests of the people of the United States."[33] Yet the United States appeared reluctant to offer aid, and the American chargé, Jacob Sleeper, did little more than carp about the lack of protection for foreign property.

The Cuban people themselves found the government's embarrassment amusing. In the countryside the *campesinos* were reveling in the anti-authoritarian spirit of the moment. The government's militiamen were enjoying their good wages and were reluctant to risk not being able to spend their dollars. They suspected the Foreign Legion of Artillery with its machine guns was much too eager for combat. As for the *habanero*, he too feared a fight. A reporter asked one businessman why there was no cheering when the government forces shuffled unwillingly out of Havana. "Why should I cheer," the merchant replied. "They are getting two dollars a day, American, besides fifty cents for food. And when it is all over we pay, you and I. For my part, I don't see why there must be all this fighting. There will be more elections some day. And if they fight very long, business will be ruined."[34] Yet the government recognized that an American intervention would be distasteful to many Cubans and politically perilous for those who invited it, and if it could avoid at least the stigma of intervention that would be a major victory.[35]

On September 1, the Cuban situation was tangled, but some important generalizations should be made at this point. First, the insurgents were out in large enough numbers to cause the havoc promised, but as yet they had destroyed only a few bridges and culverts of the Western Railway, a British-owned line which had been carrying government troops to Pinar del Rio. There had been several inconsequential clashes with the Rural Guard with few casualties. The government's response, thus far, had been to raise several thousand useless militiamen and to offer a general amnesty to the rebels. Roosevelt had supported Estrada Palma with munitions, but, weighing the consequences of expanding that assistance to include troops, he had concluded that the political risks were too great. Until armed intervention became more clearly justifiable, the United States would insist only that foreign property be respected by both sides. Nonetheless, Cuba was faced with economic collapse if the insurrection could not be ended before *la zafra*, if the sugar and tobacco crops went up in flame, and if credit and the government's revenues continued their downward spiral.

### The Veterans, Steinhart, and the Failure of Compromise

On September 1, a third party entered the Cuban civil war in an effort to end the crisis without the United States intervention.[36] A committee of noted veterans of the Army of Liberation, led by Generals Agustin Cebreco and Mario García Menocal, offered to mediate the differences between the government and the Liberals. The committee included veterans of all political affiliations.[37] Menocal became the group's spokesman. He was forty, an engineering graduate of Cornell University, an able soldier, and, in 1906, manager of the Cuban-American Sugar Company's Chaparra estate, the world's largest sugar property. By September 8, the Veterans believed that both the rebels and the government were ready for a truce and compromise settlement to void the 1905 elections, to hold new elections on the basis of a reformed electoral law, to provide for municipal autonomy and an independent judiciary and civil service, and to have a general amnesty.[38]

Estrada Palma was still hoping to entice the United States into the conflict on his side, but his government thus far had been unable to get Sleeper even to recommend dispatching American troops to guard foreign property. Sleeper reported that the revolt was growing and that American interests were endangered, but he had not asked for American forces.[39] Militarily, the government hoped that one solid victory over Guerra would either dishearten the rebels or encourage Roosevelt to give further assistance. This was not to be.

In Pinar del Rio, a government force of eight hundred under Colonel Avalos Acosta had been chasing Guerra for two weeks. To reinforce Avalos, an armored train guarded by two hundred militiamen and the Foreign Legion of Artillery's machine guns was sent from Havana. Twice ambushed and once reinforced, the armored train was besieged by the rebels near Consolación del Sur on September 8. "It was a lovely battle—unlimited ammunition to burn and nobody hurt," William Inglis, an American reporter, said. After a fierce exchange of fire for many hours, giving the encounter "all the elements of battle except casualties," both sides politely exchanged and refused demands for surrender.[40] Before either force suffered the embarrassment of running out of ammunition, Colonel Avalos' column hit Guerra's flank, held by six hundred men under the brothers Paez, at a cluster of farmhouses called Hato Nuevo. Exchanging a few harmless volleys, the government forces launched one of history's least damaging bayonet charges, driving the rebels off and losing only one man killed and twelve wounded. The Rural Guard claimed it buried eleven insurgents. Avalos' attack, nonetheless, got the train fight off dead center, and Guerra's force withdrew. Guerra marched unmolested to San Diego, a mountain resort, where he took the waters, enjoyed first-class cuisine, and listened to the happy serenades of his warriors. The armored train, pocked with a few bullet holes, returned to Havana, and the rebels were as well armed and unchastened as ever.[41]

At this crucial moment in the civil war, the Cuban government turned for aid to Frank M. Steinhart, the United States consul-general in Havana. For several years before 1906 and for many years afterward, Steinhart was one of Cuba's most influential alien residents. Born in Bavaria and raised in Pennsylvania, he joined the United States Army as a young man. Through luck and pluck, he rose rapidly to sergeant in General Philip Sheridan's headquarters. At the same time he earned a law degree. As Leonard Wood's chief civilian clerk after 1899, he turned his acute, encyclopedic mind to handling the delicate political details Wood gave him.[42] He stayed on in Havana after 1902 as an official of the Havana Electric Railway Company and an agent for Antonio San Miguel, a wealthy Spanish entrepreneur. In 1903, on the recommendation of his former generals and the Cuban business community, he was appointed consul-general on the basis of his "thorough knowledge of Cuban affairs, the People and language."[43]

Without question, Estrada Palma was correct in believing that Steinhart would be unequivocal in urging American support for the Cuban government, and that Steinhart was committed to Wood's belief in a conservative, elitist control of Cuban affairs.[44] In a letter dated September 5 to William Loeb, Roosevelt's private secretary, Steinhart asked for the President's views on intervention.[45] He portrayed Estrada Palma as despondent and fearful, the armed forces as unable to halt the insurgents, Sleeper as "an ass," and Cuba's economic condition as collapsing. Steinhart believed that the President might have a month to consider intervention, but if help should be requested, troops should be rapidly dispatched to prevent chaos. Three days later (September 8) Steinhart sent the simple cablegram that began to draw Roosevelt into the intervention he was so anxious to avoid:

*Absolutely Confidential.* Secretary of State, Cuba, has requested me, in name of President Palma, to ask President Roosevelt send immediately two vessels—one to Habana, other to Cienfuegos. They must come at once. Government forces are unable to quell rebellion. The Government is unable to protect life and property. President Palma will convene Congress next Friday, and Congress will ask for our forcible intervention. It must be kept secret and confidential that Palma asked for vessels. No one here except President, Secretary of State and myself knows it. Very anxiously awaiting reply. Send answer to

STEINHART
Consul General[46]

Roosevelt's reaction to Steinhart's plea was immediate; he ordered Secretary of the Navy Charles J. Bonaparte to dispatch warships to Havana and Cienfuegos. There were, however, no detailed presidential instructions indicating the vessels' mission.[47] Despite his dispatch of the two warships, Roosevelt still did not want to intercede on either side of the Cuban civil war and was even less enthusiastic about reopening the question of Cuban-American relations.[48] Instead he cautioned Acting Secretary of State Bacon to warn Steinhart that, as distasteful as the rebels were, "immediate intervention" was out of the question and that Estrada Palma must use "all the resources at his command to quell the revolt. . . . "[49] On September 10, Bacon cabled Steinhart that two ships were on the way, but Estrada Palma must either compromise with the Liberals or beat them in the field, and that "until such efforts are made we are not prepared to consider the question of intervention at all."[50] Steinhart acknowledged the dispatch of the ships, which, he said, coupled with the "victory" at Consolación del Sur, heartened the Cuban government. On the same day, the British minister in Havana wired his government that only American intervention, whether in support of Estrada Palma or not, could save Cuba from economic ruin.[51] On September 11, Bacon again cabled Steinhart that the President believed "actual, immediate intervention to be out of the question," that Estrada Palma must exhaust his own resources before Roosevelt would consider intervention.[52]

If Roosevelt wanted Estrada Palma to work toward a compromise, the news that the United States Navy was on the way and that the United States expected the Cuban government to save itself had just the opposite effect. On September 10 and 11, the government suspended constitutional rights in three provinces, arrested more Liberals, rescinded its amnesty order, renewed military operations, put Havana under a curfew, and rejected the veterans' peace plan.[53] A representative of the veterans in the field, Colonel Gerardo Machado, reported to Menocal that the Rural Guard and militia had just killed some prisoners; Machado and other veterans then joined the Constitutional Army.[54] Menocal, who had believed that Estrada Palma had overcome the Moderates' objections to compromise, now found the President unwilling to negotiate " . . . though we were ignorant of the causes that could have brought about such a radical and unexpected change in the President's attitude." The veterans recognized that Estrada Palma's new militancy was an insurmountable obstacle to settlement and broke off negotiations.[55]

The results of Estrada Palma's new interest in prosecuting the war were increased insurgent attacks, dynamitings of British railroad properties and rumors of sugar property burnings.[56] Steinhart's cables showed how rapidly the situation deteriorated. In his first wire on September 12, he believed diplomatic pressure might end the rebellion; by that afternoon he was forwarding a request from Estrada Palma for two or three thousand troops to prevent a massacre in Havana.[57] It was into this tense and unpredictable situation that Roosevelt's two warships sailed, without restrictive instructions, and it was at this moment that the President's hope for peace through persuasion was dashed completely through events in Cuba.

## The United States Navy Intervenes

On the afternoon of September 12, the cruiser "Denver" steamed into Havana harbor and anchored off O'Reilly and Obispo streets with its guns cleared for action. The Americans in the watching crowd cheered, the Cubans were silent and scowling.[58] The city itself, its low white buildings with red tile roofs stretching off in the smoke and haze of the Cuban afternoon, was peaceful. In the harbor the smells of tar, fish, tobacco, and rotting fruit mixed with the cries of the bumboat merchants. Along the Malecón, strollers looked out curiously at the United States Navy.

The day before the gunboat "Marietta," Commander William F. Fullam in command, arrived in Cienfuegos. The "Marietta" was fresh from Commodore W. H. H. Southerland's squadron in Dominican waters where it had been carrying government troops and showing the flag in threatened ports. By coincidence, Commander Fullam was a leading advocate of using sailors as ships' landing parties and of abolishing the Marine Corps; there was a touch of eagerness in his reports to prove his sailors' fighting qualities. Immediately upon anchoring, Fullam was besieged by American planters begging protection. If the sailors did not come ashore, the planters told Fullam, the insurgents would put their *centrales* to the torch. Under the instructions wired him by Secretary Bonaparte on September 12, he could use his own discretion about landing sailors to protect American property.[59] Assuming in the absence of further instructions that he could act in "case of necessity," Fullam decided on September 14 to land men to protect Hormiguero, Constancia, and Soledad *centrales*.[60] He then put a force of four officers, seventy men, and two machine guns ashore and called for reinforcements, with the ecstatic approval of the sugar planters. He personally doubted that the rebels would resist since they seemed to welcome intervention.[61]

Fullam might have been chagrined if he had known of events in Havana. The day before his men went ashore at Cienfuegos, another landing party had disembarked at Havana and then, under direct orders from Roosevelt, gone back to the "Denver." Shortly after his ship's arrival on September 12, Commander J. C. Colwell, "Denver's" captain, visited Estrada Palma. The President, Colwell discovered, was delighted by "Denver's" appearance, which he said strengthened his government.[62] The city, Colwell learned, was rife with rumors of treason, massacre, race war, looting, and arson. As a result of a conference with Estrada Palma, Sleeper, and Steinhart, Colwell ordered a battalion of sailors (some 120 men) and three field pieces ashore to prevent an uprising in Havana. The landing party took up positions in the Plaza de Armas which controlled the main thoroughfares and, not incidentally, protected the President's palace. No sooner were the sailors ashore than two things happened: a delegation of the Liberal's Central Revolutionary Committee, led by Zayas, approached Colwell and offered to surrender their forces to him, and Sleeper learned that Roosevelt did not want any Americans to land without his orders.[63] The new order read: "Vessels sent to Cuban waters are under orders of the President, who will determine when and how they shall be used for protection of American life and property. Ships may be used for asylum." Sleeper tried to get the sailors back aboard "Denver" that night, but Colwell put him off until the next morning because he believed his men's presence had stopped mob rule in Havana and because he thought he could negotiate the rebels' surrender.[64] Colwell admitted, however, that the government had used the time the Americans were ashore to regroup its troops, distribute more arms and to continue fortifying the city. During the night a force of Rural Guards under General Alejandro Rodríguez sallied out to meet the rebels, but were scattered in a skirmish near Wajay. The fight was most notable because General Rodríguez had his monogrammed raincoat captured by the rebels and Loynaz del Castillo was brained with a machete by one of his own men.

On September 14, also, Estrada Palma convened a special session of congress, but his message to them was not a call for peace or compromise. Rather, he asked for support and approval of his war decrees.[65] By that afternoon, however, "Denver's" landing party was gone from the Plaza de Armas. Estrada Palma was most disturbed. He had asked for open intervention on September 13. Americans had come ashore (albeit to protect lives and property), but Roosevelt had withdrawn them. His reaction was to increase the pressure on Roosevelt. Steinhart broke the news to the President: Estrada Palma, Méndez Capote, and the cabinet were determined now to resign and have the congress adjourn. "The consequences will be absence of legal power, and therefore the prevailing state of anarchy will continue unless the United States Government will adopt the measures necessary to avoid this danger."[66]

## Roosevelt Acquiesces in Intervention

The landings from "Denver" and "Marietta" may have saved lives and property, but their greatest importance to the Cuban civil war was their impact on the strategy of both the government and the rebel leadership. Both sides apparently saw the landings as the first step of an American military intervention, and both renewed their efforts to insure that intervention would serve their purposes. Fearing continued fighting and an insurgent victory, Estrada Palma was determined to throw the government into the United States hands if Roosevelt would not support him militarily. He was convinced that Cuba's future peace and economic stability were at stake, that under the Platt Amendment Roosevelt must act to prevent the Republic's collapse.[67]

The Liberal leaders were equally interested in American intervention because they thought if free elections were held they would win and, in any event, their government would need the United States approval to survive. Despite threats, their treatment of American property was hardly destructive. Rather, they held the sugar plantations hostage, while, for Roosevelt's benefit, they demonstrated Estrada Palma's military weakness. The Liberals gambled that Roosevelt would avoid a guerrilla war if possible, that he could not bear, politically, the expenses of a permanent or violent occupation. They interpreted the landings to save lives and property as the first step in American mediation and from that point did little more than encourage the rumors of chaos and destruction, which they knew Roosevelt could not ignore.[68]

At Oyster Bay, Theodore Roosevelt struggled to find a way out of the Cuban impasse, which to a degree he had created for himself. By dispatching "Denver" and "Marietta" without orders, by urging Estrada Palma to fight on, by acting to protect American lives and property, he had encouraged the contestants in the civil war to increase their pressure for American intervention. In the face of what appeared to be an explosive situation around Havana, where Guerra, Asbert, and Loynaz del Castillo had joined their columns, Roosevelt hurriedly sent more ships and Marines to Cuban waters. Even before "Denver" and "Marietta" put parties ashore, he wired Bacon:

> We should have a large force of marines in Havana at the earliest possible moment on any ships able to carry them. Cable Steinhart . . . that we will send ships and marines as soon as possible for the protection of American life and property.[69]

Roosevelt, on September 13, was still anxious to avoid intervention, and he recognized that Estrada Palma's unpopularity and military weakness made it unwise to intervene on his behalf. The Cubans were "not suffering from any real grievance whatsoever," yet they had plunged themselves into a civil war that endangered their very existence as a nation. To find a solution to "what is happening in Cuba . . . I expect to do some tall thinking in the effort to bring about a condition which shall, if possible, put an end to anarchy without necessitating a reoccupation of the island by our troops."[70]

The next day Roosevelt acquiesced to American involvement in the Cuban insurrection when he increased his military commitment to "protect American interests by fulfilling American obligations to Cuba."[71] After a conference with Secretary Bonaparte, Roosevelt had the Navy dispatch three battleships, a cruiser, and the transport "Dixie," carrying a Marine battalion, into Cuban waters. The Marine Corps also formed two more battalions at Norfolk and the League Island Navy Yard; these embarked on September 16 and 17.[72]

In an effort to halt the fighting (which was largely halted anyway) and perhaps encourage new negotiations among the Cubans, Roosevelt resorted to personal diplomacy. In a long letter to Gonzalo de Quesada, the Cuban minister in Washington, a letter concurrently delivered to Estrada Palma and the Cuban press, the President made his last attempt to avoid a military intervention.[73] He first reviewed for the Cubans his own sincere interest in their welfare and the last seven years "of profound peace and of steadily growing prosperity." Now "the evil of anarchy" menaced Cuba's "peace, prosperity and independence. . . . " Whoever was responsible for the revolt, all Cubans must now recognize the danger to their sovereignty. But if Cuba continued to show that she had "fallen into the insurrectionary habit," then the United States had no other choice but to intervene. All Cuban patriots were therefore adjured to find a peaceful solution to their differences.

Roosevelt emphasized, however, that he could not ignore the obligations imposed on both nations by Article III of the Platt Amendment, and, since he had information that American lives and property were endangered, he was constrained to act. In his judgment, it was imperative that hostilities cease immediately and that "some arrangement" for "the permanent pacification" of the island be established. To achieve these ends, he was sending Secretary of War Taft and Assistant Secretary of State Bacon to Havana to reconcile the warring factions.

Although the negotiations of the Taft-Bacon Peace Mission were far more publicized, praised, and criticized than Roosevelt's acts up to September 14, the character of the American intervention was shaped by the events leading up to the dispatch of the Peace Mission. By the time it arrived in Havana, occupation was virtually inevitable. The most important factor was that both the Estrada Palma government and the Liberal insurgents calculated on forcing American intervention in their support. Roosevelt's reactions to the Cuban civil war left both parties in doubt as to his final position. Estrada Palma first received quick presidential attention on his request for ammunition and an equally prompt response to his request for warships. The insurgents' public statements, on the other hand, showed deeper political and military wisdom. They judged that Roosevelt would not risk an unpopular war on the side of a weak and "unjust" government.

Roosevelt's grasp of the Cuban crisis was complicated by the Steinhart-Sleeper competition at the Havana end of the diplomatic channel, but both men accurately passed on the news they received and neither controlled Cuban affairs. As sympathetic as Steinhart was to the Estrada Palma government, he did not have to encourage the Cuban president to ask for help. More serious was Steinhart's judgment on Sleeper's competency, but his own prejudices and interests were known to Roosevelt and Bacon. While they communicated to Estrada Palma through Steinhart, they also weighed Sleeper's cablegrams which continued to come to them. However misleading or excited Steinhart and Sleeper might have been, it was Roosevelt who failed to realize how inaccurate one of his basic assumptions was: that the Cubans would compromise their differences rather than turn the island over to the United States to govern again. Perhaps if Roosevelt had had Elihu Root's counsel, he would have seen some other diplomatic alternative, but even Root could not have changed the military implications of a Cuban intervention.

The crucial decision not to support Estrada Palma, for this is what the Gonzalo de Quesada letter was, rested primarily on military considerations. Roosevelt, Taft, Bell, and Funston were in essential agreement that a guerrilla war in Cuba was a real possibility and that such a war would be costly in lives, American property, and the administration's popularity at home. Throughout their deliberations, they were aware that they risked another war on the Philippine model if they aided Estrada Palma. Furthermore, though the Army and Navy were better prepared than in 1898, troops and ships could not be moved rapidly enough to save the Cuban economy if the insurgents decided to live up to their September 15 deadline to destroy foreign property. The naval intervention, by itself, was of little assistance to the planters in the back country.

The hurried dispatch of "Denver" and "Marietta," accompanied by Roosevelt's belated restriction of their instructions, increased the hope of Estrada Palma and the insurgents that the United States would intervene in their favor. The landings to protect lives and property had a significant impact on the course of the rebellion, for afterward neither side showed any inclination to compromise. Instead both parties polarized around the men working to increase the American involvement. Estrada Palma's decision to resign, which must be linked with the re-embarkation of "Denver's" sailors, was never modified, for he considered the United States failure to support him foolish, dishonorable, and unfaithful to the Platt Amendment. Face to face with "Marietta's" parties around Cienfuegos, the insurgents, on the other hand, were quick to impress the Americans with how co-operative they could be with the occupying forces.[74]

Whether Roosevelt realized the impact of the landings or simply did not care after September 14 is uncertain. With the approval of both the State Department and the Secretary of the Navy, the landings continued after the dispatch of the Taft-Bacon Peace Mission.[75] The transport "Dixie" put her Marine battalion ashore to replace Fullam's sailors around the *centrales*. At the same time the Mission was working to avoid an occupation, the Marines extended American protection to foreign properties in Santa Clara.

Roosevelt's letter to Gonzalo de Quesada, which followed the news of the landings, did not encourage an all-Cuban compromise as the President had hoped, however slightly. To the Cubans, his message was as enigmatic as his earlier statements and acts.[76] Was or was not the United States intervening, and on whose behalf? Though Roosevelt's plea to stop fighting did have some effect, his announcement of Taft and Bacon's departure for Cuba reinforced rather than discouraged the efforts of the Cuban government and the insurgents to make the United States responsible for ending the revolt. If Roosevelt believed Taft could argue the United States out of its involvement in the Cuban insurrection, he badly misjudged the skill, the subtlety, and ambitions of the *políticos*. Roosevelt's unwillingness to accept the risk of a Cuban war committed the United States to intervention on the insurgents' terms. It also established the policy of the military occupation that followed intervention and influenced the course of Cuba's political development.

1. Portell Vilá, *Historia de Cuba*, IV, pp. 455–56.

2. "Manifesto of the Revolution," July 28, 1906, reprinted in the Taft-Bacon *Report*, p. 505. The "Manifesto" was first made public in the first week of September. *World* (New York), September 5, 1906.

3. For a reliable Cuban account, see Martínez Ortiz, *Cuba: los primeros años de independencia*, II, pp. 614–70; Capt. F. R. McCoy to Maj. Gen. Leonard Wood, October 18, 1906, Wood Papers.

4. Jacob Sleeper, chargé d'affaires, American legation, Havana, to Secretary of State, August 21, 1906, as printed in U.S. Department of State, *Foreign Relations of the United States, 1906* (Washington, 1909), I, 454. Hereafter cited as *Foreign Relations, 1906*.

The author has examined the original diplomatic correspondence in Case 244, *Numerical File, 1906–1910*, Vols. XXXVI–XXXVIII, General Records of the Department of State, National Archives, Record Group 59, but for convenience has cited *Foreign Relations, 1906* or the Taft-Bacon *Report* except when a particular passage or entire document does not appear in either. In that case the original is cited. Further references to the *Numerical File* are cited as (case), *Num. File, 1906–1910* (Vol.), RG 59.

For the beginning of the revolt, see also Wright, *Cuba*, p. 173.

5. For the status of the Liberal *políticos* and the officers of the Constitutional Army, the author has used an extensive biographical study compiled by the Military Information Division (MID), Army of Cuban Pacification (ACP), in December, 1906, Serial 4352-E-11, AWC Doc. File, RG 165.

6. As Sir William Van Horne put it: "The disturbance in Cuba, which was at first confined between the Rural Guard and a disorderly element in the extreme west, was raised to the dignity of an insurrection by the arrest of a lot of political leaders, including the late candidate for the presidency against Mr. Palma."—Quoted in Vaughan, *The Life and Letters of Sir William Van Horne*, p. 315.

7. Martínez Ortiz, *Cuba: los primeros años de independencia*, II, 450.

8. Lt. Col. R. L. Bullard's manuscript autobiography, Bullard Papers.

9. Martínez Ortiz, *Cuba: los primeros años de independencia*, II, 621.

10. Faustino Guerra, "Causes of the Cuban Insurrection," *North American Review*, CLXXXIII (September 21, 1906), Part I, 538–40.

11. *La Discusión* (Havana), August 29, 1906. Eduardo Guzmán called the revolt a "demonstration" and promised not to destroy foreign property. *World* (New York), September 13, 1906.

12. *Times* (London), September 7, 1906.

13. *Havana Daily Telegraph,* August 25, 1906, appended to Report 160, Sleeper to Secretary of State, August 25, 1906, Case 244, *Num. File, 1906–1910,* Vol. XXXVI, RG 59.

14. Wright, *Cuba,* p. 179; *Havana Daily Telegraph,* August 27, 1906. On August 28, *La Discusión* reported fifty incidents, all of horse requisitioning, and many *falsos rumores.*

15. General Eduardo Guzmán to the manager, Central Parque Alto, appended to the report of Cmdr. W. F. Fullam, USN, to Bureau of Navigation, September 18, 1906, Area 8 (Caribbean) File for September, 1906, in the Naval Records Collection of the Office of Naval Records and Library, National Archives, Record Group 45. Hereafter cited as Area 8 File, (month), RG 45.

16. Taft-Bacon *Report,* p. 457; *New York Times,* August 21–26, 1906; Sleeper to Secretary of State, August 28–September 1, 1906, *Foreign Relations, 1906,* pp. 457–65.

17. Sleeper to Secretary of State, August 25 and 28, 1906, *Foreign Relations, 1906,* pp. 456–59.

18. Sleeper to Secretary of State, August 25 and September 1, 1906, *Foreign Relations, 1906,* pp. 456, 464–65; Taft-Bacon *Report,* pp. 456–57; *Washington Post,* September 2, 1906.

19. This was the central theme of Root's addresses in Brazil, Uruguay, Chile, Argentina, Peru, Colombia, and Panama. See U.S. Department of State, *Speeches Incident to the Visit of Secretary Root to South America: July 4 to September 30, 1906* (Washington, 1906), *passim.*

20. Quoted in James Brown Scott, "Elihu Root," in Samuel Flagg Bemis (ed.), *The American Secretaries of State and Their Diplomacy* (New York, 1927——), IX, 217.

21. Roosevelt to Henry Cabot Lodge, April 30, 1906, Roosevelt Papers.

22. Acting Secretary of State Alvey A. Adee to Sleeper, August 31, 1906, *Foreign Relations, 1906,* pp. 463–64.

23. Roosevelt to Taft, August 27, 1906, Roosevelt Papers; Maj. Gen. F. C. Ainsworth to William Loeb, Roosevelt's secretary, August 27, 1906; Ainsworth to Loeb, August 29, 1906; Loeb to Ainsworth, August 29, 1906, Roosevelt Papers and File 1158957, Document File, 1890–1917, Records of the Adjutant General's Office, National Archives, Record Group 94. Hereafter cited as Doc. File (number), RG 94.

24. Brig. Gen. J. F. Bell to Roosevelt, August 30, 1906, Roosevelt Papers.

Portell Vilá (*Historia de Cuba,* IV, 450) says Taft ordered Bell to send troops from the Philippines to Cuba on August 26. Two Army transports, "Meade" and "Ingalls," did leave Manila on September 1 via Suez for the East Coast, but the troops were not included in the contingency plans. The vessels were to relieve the shortage of shipping on the Atlantic coast where only the "Sumner" was stationed. Portell Vilá is mistaken when he says Roosevelt began to move troops to Cuba before Estrada Palma requested them. See Parts II and III, Army

War College Serial 11, "Cuba," September 3, 1906, AWC Doc. File, RG 165.

25. Brig. Gen. Frederick Funston to Brig. Gen. J. F. Bell, August 28, 1906, Appendix 1 to Army War College Serial 11, "Cuba," as previously cited.

26. Roosevelt to Bell, September 1, 1906, Roosevelt Papers; Bell to Leonard Wood, May 1, 1911, Wood Papers. In the letter to Wood, Bell complained that in 1906 he could not get information on conditions in Cuba from the State Department: "I had to base all our preparations on mere suspicion." Bell added that the presence of the Secretary of War in Washington might have unblocked the cable clog at State.

27. Taft to Roosevelt, September 2, 1906, Roosevelt Papers.

28. Roosevelt to Root, September 4, 1906; Roosevelt to Taft, September 4, 1906, Roosevelt Papers.

29. Interview with General Eduardo Guzmán, reported in *La Correspondencia* (Cienfuegos), September 6, 1906, translated copy in Cuba Subject File, Admiral William F. Fullam Papers, Library of Congress.

30. W. A. Page, manager of Buenaventura and Redención plantations, Bahía Honda, to American legation, September 2, 1906, Case 244/91, *Num. File, 1906–1910*, Vol. XXXVII RG 59.

For reports of other complaints, see Sleeper to Secretary of State, September 4, 6, 8, 1906, with enclosures, *Foreign Relations, 1906*, pp. 467–73; *New York Times*, September 10, 1906.

31. Sleeper to Secretary of State, September 7 and 8, 1906, *Foreign Relations, 1906*, p. 470–72; *La Lucha* (Havana) and *La Discusión*, August 29, 1906; *New York Times*, September 10, 1906. See also "Manifesto of the Central Revolutionary Committee," September 1, 1906, reprinted in Secades and Díaz Pardo (eds.), *La justicia en Cuba: patriotas y traidores*, II, 24–25.

32. Estrada Palma to Claudio G. Mendoza, October 10, 1906, James H. Wilson Papers; also reprinted in Taft-Bacon *Report*, pp. 12–15; Camacho, *Estrada Palma*, pp. 227–28; Taft-Bacon *Report*, p. 455; Márquez Sterling, *Proceso historico de la Enmienda Platt*, I, 312–13; Johnson, *The History of Cuba*, IV, 282; Portell Vilá, *Historia de Cuba*, IV, 458; *Times* (London), August 25, 1906.

33. Enrique José Varona, *Mirando en torno* (Havana, 1910), p. 7.

34. William Inglis, "The Armed Struggle for Control of Cuba," *Harper's Weekly*, L (September 22, 1906), pp. 1344–47.

Inglis was present through most of the revolt and subsequent American intervention in 1906. For the role of the newspaper reporters, see Wright, *Cuba*, p. 175.

35. The Moderate paper *La Discusión* attempted to turn popular feeling against the Liberals with editorials like the one printed August 31. If war continued, *La Discusión* said, the Americans would intervene: "Beside us would pass with jingling spurs and beery lear the American officer, master of all, and drawing all to himself, even the smiles and glances of our adorable virgins.

"And is it for that Cubans are fighting against Cubans?"

"The survivors of our heroic and holy struggles for independence are rending one another and opening the way for the entrance of Fins [*sic*], Germans, Americans, and Spaniards, who shall come to enjoy the fecundity and richness of our soil, the freshness of our air, the murmur of our rivers, the sweetness of our pale moonlit nights, the caresses of our seas, and even the love of our women.

"Can the Negroes wish themselves to bring the knife to cut their throats?

"The whites, are they not like frogs, asking for a master, a hard master, who will stay forever.

"This republic, so rich, so youthful, so beautiful, so envied, by all, is it to be cast out and delivered to the Yankee, merely because elections were carried out well or ill?

"Are there not to be, after all, more elections, and are there not means to make these elections be as they should rather than place our neck under the heel of Uncle Sam?"

36. Sleeper to Secretary of State, September 1, 1906, *Foreign Relations, 1906*, pp. 464–65.

37. Thirty-eight signatories of Compromise Proposal printed in the *Havana Daily Telegraph*, September 10, 1906.

Prominent Liberals among the Veterans were Tomás Recio, Enrique Collazo, and Manuel Lazo.

38. Menocal's "Bases," September 7, 1906, reprinted in Secades and Díaz Pardo (eds.), *La justicia en Cuba: patriotas y traidores*, II 64. For Menocal's account and related Veteran correspondence see *Ibid.*, pp. 29–30, 32–33, 61–64, or Taft-Bacon *Report*, pp. 500–502.

39. Sleeper to Secretary of State, September 6 and 7, 1906, *Foreign Relations, 1906*, pp. 469-72.

40. William Inglis, "How Cubans Fight Cubans," *Harper's Weekly*, L (October 6, 1906), 1416–18, 1434–35. See also *Havana Daily Telegraph*, September 8, 1906, and the *New York Times*, September 10, 1906.

41. William Inglis, "With the Rebel Leader in the Cuban Hills," *Harper's Weekly*, L (September 29, 1906), 1380–83.

42. Hagedorn, *Leonard Wood*, I, 265, 312–13; "Record of Frank Steinhart's Military and Civil Services Under the War Department," n.d. (1902?), Cuba Subject File, Wood Papers.

43. Steinhart File, 4E3, 28–7–1, Box 236, Foreign Service Records, RG 59.

Steinhart had planned to resign as consul-general on January 1, 1907, to become the Havana representative of the New York investment house of Speyer and Company. At Taft's insistence, he remained in his post until July, 1907, when he resigned to negotiate a loan for the Cuban government.

44. Portell Vilá, *Historia de Cuba*, IV, 458.

45. Steinhart to Loeb, September 5, 1906, Case 244/310, *Num. File, 1906–1910*, Vol. XXXVII, RG 59.

46. Steinhart to Secretary of State, September 8, 1906, Taft-Bacon *Report*, pp. 444–45.

Steinhart's assumption of the role of the United States diplomatic spokesman in Cuba coincided, interestingly, with the publication in the New York *World* of a cable attributed to Sleeper: "Revolution spreading. All quiet." This cable is supposed to have enraged Roosevelt, who then turned to Steinhart. (Chapman, *A History of the Cuban Republic*, p. 199.) Sleeper denied to *La Lucha* and the State Department that he ever sent such a message, and the author's examination of volumes 36, 37, and 38 of the *Numerical File* failed to uncover such a cable. Sleeper's fall from grace (Roosevelt to Bacon, September 10, 1906, Roosevelt Papers) seems to have begun with Steinhart's letter to Loeb.

47. Two telegrams, Roosevelt to Charles J. Bonaparte, September 8, 1906, Area 8 File (September, 1906), RG 45. The first telegram directed the Secretary of the Navy to report the availability of vessels, the second dispatched them to Cuban waters to protect American lives and property.

48. Roosevelt to George Otto Trevelyan, September 9, 1906, Roosevelt Papers.

49. Roosevelt to Bacon, September 10, 1906, Roosevelt Papers.

50. Bacon to Steinhart, September 10, 1906, *Foreign Relations, 1906*, p. 474.

51. Steinhart to Secretary of State, September 10, 1906, *Foreign Relations, 1906*, p. 474; G. W. E. Griffith, British minister to Cuba, to Sir Edward Grey, Foreign Secretary, September 10, 1906, Foreign Office File 371–56, Public Record Office, London. Hereafter cited as FO (file number), PRO.

52. Bacon to Steinhart, September 11, 1906, *Foreign Relations, 1906*, p. 475.

53. República de Cuba, Decree 380, *Gaceta oficial* (September-October, 1906), p. 2004; *Washington Post*, September 11 and 12, 1906; *The World* (New York), September 11, 1906.

The Moderates' counter peace proposal "La Obra de la Paz," September 11, 1906, promised the reforms suggested by the Liberals and Veterans except for nullification of the 1905 elections. Secades and Díaz Pardo, *La justicia en Cuba: patriotas y traidores*, II, 43–44.

54. Machado to Menocal, September 12, 1906, reprinted in Secades and Díaz Pardo, *La Justicia en Cuba: patriotas y traidores*, II, 46–47.

55. *Ibid.*, pp. 61–64. *cf.* Horacio Ferrer, *Con el rifle al hombro* (Havana, 1950), p. 182.

56. Steinhart and Sleeper to the Secretary of State, September 12 and 13, 1906, *Foreign Relations, 1906*, pp. 476-77.

57. Steinhart to Secretary of State, September 12, 1906, *Foreign Relations, 1906*, p. 476.

58. Wright, *Cuba*, p. 78. For the subsequent account of "Denver's" stay in Havana, the author has used the report of her captain, Cmdr. J. C. Colwell, USN, to the Secretary of the Navy, October 4, 1906, Area 8 File (October, 1906), RG 45.

59. Secretary of the Navy to Commanding Officers, "Denver," "Marietta," "Dixie," September 12, 1906, Case 244/106½, *Num. File, 1906–1910,* Vol. XXXVIII, RG 59.

60. Two cables, Cmdr. W. F. Fullam, USN, to Secretary of the Navy, September 14, 1906, Area 8 File (September, 1906), RG 45, and Fullam Papers.

61. Fullam to the Secretary of the Navy, September 15, 1906, Area 8 File (September, 1906), RG 45. Copy also in Case 244/130, *Num. File, 1906–1910,* Vol. 37, RG 59.

*La Discusión* on September 15 reported that American sailors had landed to support government troops and were emplacing guns around Cienfuegos to drive off the rebels.

When Fullam learned from Sleeper on September 16 that he should not have landed, he was disgusted: "The U.S. Charge de Affairs [*sic*] at Havana told consul *not* to land until he heard from Washington. I cannot understand his action, and I am glad that I did not wait, because I feel that we *did right*. We were sent here to protect American Interests, and when Mr. Childs and Mr. Hughes *asked* for help we gave it to them to the best of our ability."—Fullam to Lt. J. V. Klemann, USN, September 16, 1906. See also Fullam to Secretary of the Navy, September 18, 1906, Area 8 File (September, 1906), RG 45.

62. Colwell's report, October 4, 1906, previously cited. "Denver's Sailors Guard Palace" were the headlines in the *Washington Post,* September 14, 1906.

63. *Ibid.;* Roosevelt to Bacon, September 13, 1906, Roosevelt Papers; Cablegram, Bacon to Sleeper, September 13, 1906, Case 244/149, *Num. File, 1906–1910,* Vol. XXXVII, RG 59.

64. Colwell to Bureau of Navigation, September 14, 1906, Case 244/131, *Num. File, 1906–1910,* Vol. XXXVII, RG 59.

65. "Message of President Tomas Estrada Palma to the Cuban Congress," September 14, 1906, reprinted in *Foreign Relations, 1906* pp. 483-85.

The next day Estrada Palma increased the Rural Guard by another 5,000 men and appropriated more funds for the war. *La Discusión* (September 15, 1906.)

66. Steinhart to Secretary of State, September 14, 1906, *Foreign Relations, 1906,* p. 479.

For the background of Estrada Palma's decision, see Sleeper to Secretary of State, September 15, 1906, *Foreign Relations, 1906,* pp. 482–83.

67. Estrada Palma letter, October 10, 1906, reprinted in *Republic of Cuba: Report of the Provisional Administration from October 13th, 1906 to December 1st, 1907, by Charles E. Magoon, Provisional Governor* (Havana, 1908), pp. 12–15. Hereafter cited as Magoon, *Report, 1906–1907.*

68. Sleeper to Secretary of State, September 14, 1906, and Roosevelt to Bacon, September 14, 1906, *Foreign Relations, 1906,* pp. 479-80.

69. Roosevelt to Bacon, September 12, 1906, Case 244/117, September 12, 1906, *Num. File, 1906–1910,* Vol. XXXVII, RG 59.

70. Roosevelt to Charles W. Eliot, September 13, 1906, Roosevelt Papers.

71. Roosevelt to Bacon, September 14, 1906, *Foreign Relations, 1906,* p. 480.

72. Bonaparte to Bureau of Navigation, September 14, 1906, Area 8 File (September, 1906), RG 45. "Annual Report of the Colonel Commandant of the United States Marine Corps . . . 1906," in *Annual Report of the Colonel Commandant of the United States Marine Corps to the Secretary of the Navy, 1893–1906* (Washington, 1906), pp. 21-22.

Two more Marine battalions, formed in thirty-six hours, embarked on September 25 and by the first week in October there were twenty-eight hundred Marines ashore or afloat near Cuba.

73. Roosevelt to Gonzalo de Quesada, September 14, 1906, *Foreign Relations, 1906,* pp. 480–81. The Cuban minister was in fact vacationing in Europe and did not see the letter until after the Peace Mission departed from Washington.

74. Lt. J. V. Klemann, USN, to Fullam, September 25, 1906, and Fullam to Secretary of the Navy, October 29, 1906, both in the Fullam Papers.

75. Bonaparte to Roosevelt, September 18 and 19, 1906, Bonaparte Papers, Library of Congress, and Secretary of the Navy to Commanding Officer, "Marietta," September 19, 1906, Fullam Papers. Bonaparte informed the President that the State Department wrote "practically all orders" for the vessels in Cuban waters.

76. Márquez Sterling, *Proceso historico de la Enmienda Platt,* I, 346–47.

# CHAPTER THREE

# THE SECOND INTERVENTION

F ROM the oubreak of revolt in Cuba to the dispatch of the Taft-Bacon Peace Mission, Roosevelt's major concern was to avoid involving the United States in a guerrilla war in Cuba. Such a war would quite likely strip the continental United States of troops, become expensive in lives and money, and be enormously unpopular with the American voter. Yet the complex, muddy insurrection in Cuba simmered on, and Roosevelt could not escape the conclusion that, whatever happened to the Taft-Bacon negotiations, American forces might be needed in Cuba. Therefore, as Taft left for Cuba and even as he later met with the *políticos* in Havana, the military phase of Roosevelt's Cuban diplomacy gathered strength. It was to become increasingly important in the President's deliberations and in its effect upon the course of the negotiations of the Taft-Bacon Mission.

On his way to Havana, Taft detrained in Washington to assemble his party and to meet with Generals Bell and Ainsworth to review the plans for the deployment of troops to Cuba. On September 15 Taft reported to Roosevelt that the force was organized on paper, orders were ready, and that the three expeditions (each of approximately six thousand men) could be supported logistically.[1] A copy of the General Staff's plan reached Roosevelt two days later, and after examining it, he returned it to the War Department for revision.[2] Roosevelt's major criticism of the General Staff's plan was that it did not reflect General Funston's recommendation that the Army, if it had to fight the insurgents, should use primarily cavalry and mounted infantry.[3] General Bell replied that he was more or less in agreement with Funston's assessment of possible operations and that the back-up (or second) expedition would be composed solely of cavalry.[4]

While the plan emphasized matters of organization, supply, and transportation, the analysis of the problems of campaigning in Cuba and the type of warfare that might be expected could not have increased Roosevelt's willingness to commit troops in support of Estrada Palma. The General Staff pointed out the limitations imposed by Cuba's lack of roads, the problems of supply and security, and the terrain advantages a guerrilla force would have in waging a prolonged war.[5] The Army's operations against the insurgents would entail a long occupation and large numbers of soldiers "for occupying railways, bases of supply and strategic points to enable mounted troops [to] operate safely in [the] interior."[6] The British military attaché in Washington, after a conversation with Captain Dwight E. Aultman who had recently returned from his fact-finding mission to Cuba, believed that as many as forty thousand soldiers might be needed in Cuba. If so, Roosevelt would have to raise another thirty-five thousand men to keep the Army properly prepared, and such men would be raw recruits not available for immediate service. A war in Cuba would strip the Army posts in the United States of all experienced troops capable of national defense or expeditionary duty elsewhere.[7]

Even as Taft and Bacon bargained with the *políticos* in Havana and occasionally threatened to land troops, Army officers in Washington told the press how unappealing they found the prospects of pacifying Cuba. Members of the General Staff saw war in Cuba as "a campaign of chasing and reconcentration," needing perhaps one hundred thousand men.[8] The *New York Times* reported:

Officers who have had experience in the Philippines especially have no desire to take part in settling the Cuban mess by force. They say that there is only one way of ending a guerilla campaign down there

. . . and that is by reconcentration, which would be certain to raise a storm of protest in this country.[9]

The *Washington Post*'s headlines on September 22 read "Reconcentrado is the Hint Given Cuba . . . May Adopt Weyler's Policy." In another article on September 23, the *New York Times* again drew a parallel between Cuba and the Philippines. In discussing General Bell's campaign in Batangas, "a form of concentration which resulted in establishing peace," it reported that this experience prepared the Army for "the sort of work that would have to be done in Cuba."[10] As for an Army consensus on a Cuban war, the *New York Times* found the officers it interviewed in agreement that a counterguerrilla campaign would be "long and extremely arduous, with no opportunity for distinguishing one's self, and the result . . . will be the annexation of Cuba."[11]

The political dilemma which might grow from a fighting intervention in Cuba did not escape the British press. The *Times* thought the whole business enormously amusing if the United States Army and an American general had "to resort to the devices of the much-abused General Weyler—reconcentrado camps, *trochas*, and the rest."[12] The *Graphic* approved of Roosevelt's "judicious threats" to dampen the *políticos*' pleas for intervention and recognized that to support Estrada Palma would be foolish: "With the conquest of the Philippines still uncompleted, a guerrilla war in Cuba, such as the veterans of the Spanish war could have sustained, would have been exceedingly disagreeable."[13]

The naval intervention, ordered by Roosevelt on September 8 and 14, continued during Taft's negotiations in Havana. By the night of September 21, there were three battleships ("Louisiana," "New Jersey," "Virginia") and two cruisers ("Denver" and "Des Moines") in Havana harbor. The next day two more cruisers arrived with eight hundred Marines. By October 1, three more battleships and two more cruisers had arrived and the number of available Marines increased by two thousand.[14] At Cienfuegos on September 23, Commander Fullam placed the Cuban Central Railway under the

United States protection and put sailors and Marines aboard its trains.[15] In all, Estrada Palma, by surveying the naval buildup, could gamble that the United States would not let the revolt go on, even to the point of taking temporary political control in Cuba and occupying the island to the end of the disorder.

The military situation in Cuba, as the Taft-Bacon Mission soon found, was growing tense, for the officers of both the insurgents and the government militia were on the verge of losing control of their unruly followers.[16] Although the insurgents had, in the first month of operations, limited themselves to requisitioning horses and arms, the rebel army had grown so large that its soldiers had to forage widely to eat. With each day the risk of general disorder and destruction increased.[17] By September 27, Sir William Van Horne was writing that if the United States did not end the revolt quickly "it may require an army of 150,000 men and prolonged guerrilla warfare to secure the United States in the peaceable occupation of the country."[18]

It was against this background of increasing combustibility that Secretary of War William Howard Taft attempted to negotiate a peaceful compromise that would keep the United States from occupying and governing Cuba.

## Taft in Havana, Roosevelt at Oyster Bay

Leaving Roosevelt at Oyster Bay on September 14, William Howard Taft and Robert Bacon headed for Havana bearing the President's confidence, his faint hope for peace without intervention, and the burden of his previous military commitments.[19] Taft was painfully aware that the Peace Mission was a frail hope. To Elihu Root he wrote that he found his position "quite embarrassing" because he knew so little of Cuba. He thought only that the Cuban government was "a house of cards" and that the United States must act to salvage the Cuban nation.[20] To Roosevelt, Taft expressed doubt about his qualifications for fulfilling the President's expectations: " . . . This trip is a little like purchasing a pig in a poke, I know so little of the actual situation."[21] The mission's second member was no happier about his job. Robert Bacon, the taciturn, cosmopolitan lawyer from the House of Morgan and Assistant Secretary of State, thought the United States should have supported Estrada Palma from the first, a position he never modified.[22]

Taft's biggest worry in Washington, after seeing that the General Staff's plans were prepared, was whether intervention was constitutional. He was assured that, in the opinion of Judge Advocate General George B. Davis, it was. Roosevelt was duly notified of the good news.[23] The President's reaction was predictable: although he appreciated the opinion, he would not "dream" of waiting for a Congressional mandate to act, and his decision to intervene, if "necessary," would be a useful precedent for future Presidents.[24] Both Roosevelt and Taft recognized, however, that constitutional sanctions were handy tools to silence domestic critics.

Taft then organized his Mission and entrained for Tampa on the afternoon of September 16. Besides Bacon and some clerks, he took along Captain Frank R. McCoy, Leonard Wood's aide then detailed to the Army War College, and Frank S. Cairns, a former Cuban customs officer and secret service operative for Wood. Both men spoke Spanish and had a wide knowledge of Cuban politics. On the ride south, Taft and Bacon were briefed on Cuban affairs by Albert G. Robinson, author, reporter for the New York Sun, and long time friend of Cuban nationalism. Robinson made two major points: that Estrada Palma would be difficult to deal with because he believed if he failed no other Cuban government could succeed, and that unless peace and credit were quickly re-established Cuba faced economic collapse.[25]

Aboard the cruiser "Des Moines" the next day (September 18), Taft and Bacon discussed the Cuban situation with McCoy and Cairns. McCoy cautioned Taft about Robinson; he was a radical and unduly friendly with the insurgents and

some unscrupulous Americans in Havana. It was true that
Estrada Palma was stubborn, perhaps through age, but it
was also a fact that Méndez Capote and the Moderates would
undercut the President if they felt the need. McCoy and
Cairns agreed that José Miguel Gómez was popular, but
Alfredo Zayas was a "scoundrel and shyster . . . the cheapest
demagogue on the island." Steinhart, on the other hand, was
knowledgeable and absolutely trustworthy.[26]

The atmosphere in Havana, as the city awaited the Peace
Mission, was best described by an American reporter: "If the
Queen should lead Alice straight from Wonderland into the
heart of this amazing Cuban war, they would both feel perfectly at home."[27] Early on the morning of September 19,
the "Des Moines" anchored in Havana harbor and the Peace
Mission set to work. Amid cheers of "Viva Taft y Bacon . . .
Viva Mis'tah Roo-velt," Taft stepped ashore in top hat and
morning clothes with Bacon taking advantage of his shadow.

The first conferences were with Dr. Juan O'Farrill, the
Secretary of State, and President Estrada Palma. The latter
gave Taft and Bacon a long lecture on the virtues of his
administration and the treachery of the rebels. If anything
was clear after Estrada Palma finished, it was that compromise was going to be difficult.[28] The commissioners' first concern, however, was to get the insurgents and government
forces to observe the truce declared by Estrada Palma after
the publication of the Gonzalo de Quesada letter. By threatening to land sailors and Marines, Taft, through McCoy,
Ladd, and Cairns, was able to get General Montalvo (the
new Secretary of Government), General Rodríguez, and
Colonel Avalos to hold their positions and the insurgents
(Guerra, Asbert, and Loynaz del Castillo) to do likewise.[29]
At the same time, the American officers made a quick tour
of the rebel camps, where they found the insurgents numerous
(around twelve thousand), poorly armed, and quite popular
with the rural people. Clearly, the rebels were capable of
great destruction (estimated at $100 million worth or the size
of American investments), and their foraging was becoming
uncontrolled. The government troops were too few and inef-

fective. In Taft's words, "we cannot maintain the Palma government except by forcible intervention against the whole weight of public opinion in the island."[30]

Establishing themselves at Minister E. V. Morgan's home in the suburb of Marianao, which was between the lines, Taft and Bacon began to piece together the Cuban political puzzle, hoping that a compromise might be found. They learned that Freyre de Andrade, now a congressman, and Montalvo admitted rigging the 1905 elections and that some Moderates were belligerent to the point where they "were willing to do anything to force intervention."[31] The Moderate party, represented by Méndez Capote, would, however, abide by the peace commissioners' decisions, and at least some Moderates consented to have the 1905 elections voided if the rebellion would end.[32]

The initial difficulty in dealing with the insurgent-Liberal leadership was to insure that whoever negotiated for the Liberals spoke also for the rebel generals. Agreement was quickly reached in a conference among Alfredo Zayas (who "played the game well from first to last," according to McCoy), the imprisoned members of the revolutionary junta, and the rebel generals: Zayas would speak for the Liberals and the Constitutional Army.[33]

Taft decided that the Peace Mission would negotiate from the compromise proposed by Menocal and the veterans, which he thought was a fair solution. Taft believed that if the congressional elections of 1905 were nullified and new elections held, Estrada Palma would still be acceptable to the Liberals. Estrada Palma had his faults, but his honesty and "disinterested" patriotism were unquestioned and having him in office would give the next government "constitutional continuity" and the confidence of businessmen. Taft also realized the presidency was the most powerful force in the Cuban government, and Estrada Palma was more to his philosophical liking than the other candidates he had met.[34]

On the basis of their earlier statements, both parties seemed agreed that new laws for elections, the judicial system, the civil service, and provincial and municipal organization were needed. The main points of contention were the restoration of the officials removed in 1905 and 1906 and the validity of the elections of 1905. Taft concluded that the congressional elections must be voided, while Estrada Palma's office could be negotiated. The problem was the rebel generals' popularity and their potential for mischief. As for American goals, Taft wrote Roosevelt:

> Of course what you and I want is peace, and to get these insurgents to lay down their arms and go back into the country, and I am willing to sacrifice a good deal to do this, because it is possible the next government will have sense enough to lay the foundation of an army that will suppress future resorts to violence in remedying political wrongs.[35]

Thus far in the negotiations Roosevelt concurred with Taft's views, though he doubted that Estrada Palma could be saved. He believed the compromise plan would work because the Moderates "must accede" or fall from power. But if the insurgents did not accept the terms, Taft should ask them for counter-proposals rather than threaten intervention.[36] Only as a last resort should Taft land troops "to save life and property in Havana," and in any case the use of the word "intervention" must be avoided.[37]

On September 24, Taft formally approached the Revolutionary Committee (Zayas and his fellow Liberals) with the compromise. The essence of Taft's plan was:

1. Estrada Palma would continue as President for a full term.
2. Senators and representatives elected in 1905 would resign.
3. An electoral law would be drafted by a mixed commission and new elections would be held, perhaps as early as January.
4. New laws would be enacted to protect municipal autonomy, establish judicial independence, and create a non-partisan civil service.
5. All the provincial and municipal officials elected in 1905 would have to stand for re-election.
6. The rebels would disarm and disband under a general amnesty.

Though the Liberals wanted Estrada Palma's powers of appointment curtailed and their partisans restored immediately to provincial and municipal office, "they indicated the probability of their acquiescence."[38] The Moderates and Estrada Palma, however, held to the position they had presented to Menocal when they learned the "Denver" was on the way: the elections of 1905 must stand; the Liberal party must limit "its requirements to the settlement of a future right."[39] Otherwise, Estrada Palma said, he would not continue in office. He added that the compromise was "useless," that the commissioners were "prejudiced," and that it was "inconsistent with his dignity and honor" to accept such a solution.[40] Taft's reaction was just what Estrada Palma must have expected, for the Secretary, despairing of a compromise and fearing war, asked Roosevelt for more ships and men.[41] The next day, when Estrada Palma again notified Taft he would resign and take the whole government down, Taft asked the President's permission to land troops and assume control of the Cuban government "until a more permanent policy may be determined."[42]

Roosevelt, however, was not yet ready to accept the inevitability of an American occupation of Cuba. While Taft was assaulting the Cuban civil war frontally in Havana, the President was guarding the administration's flanks and rear, and he was fearful that they were not yet secure. On September 22, he had warned Taft that "it is important from the standpoint of public sentiment here that we shall make it plain that we are exhausting every effort to come to an agreement before we intervene."[43]

Roosevelt saw the Cuban problem reopening all the old issues of annexation, imperialism and Army authoritarianism in the insular possessions. One of his major worries was that American business interests had financed the revolt, but an investigation by Frank Cairns indicated that voluntary American contributions to the Liberals' war chest had been few.[44] Still there was the problem of Roosevelt's influential Congressional critics. Ben Tillman, John Sharp Williams, and Joseph W. Bailey, he wrote Charles W. Eliot, were always ready to jump him on the imperialism issue.[45] From within his own party, he heard from Joseph B. Foraker and Albert G. Beveridge. The first warned him that it was unconstitutional to intervene without Congressional assent; the second suggested he "take the Island—advice about as rational as requests I used to get at the time of the anthracite coal strike, to 'take the coal barons by the throat.'"[46] Yet, as the *Times* of London observed, neither the Republicans nor the Democrats could gain much from a Cuban intervention, for the former had been lauding the restraint in the new Roosevelt-Root Latin American policy statements and the latter had been hailing Cuba as a noble example of what the United States might expect if the Philippines were granted independence.[47]

Diplomatically, Roosevelt was under no real pressure because Great Britain, France, and Germany believed the United States would protect their nationals without active intercession; only Spain wanted to organize a common voice to urge the United States to intervene. The Great Powers, however, feared damaging their good relations with the Roosevelt administration.[48] From a conversation with the American minister to Spain, Lord Acton, the British minister, gathered that the United States did not want to annex Cuba and that it was agreeably surprised by the mild reaction of the European press to the Cuban crisis.[49] The lack of foreign interest was awkward for both the Cuban government and Roosevelt. At one stage, Estrada Palma's ministers supposedly considered having their troops destroy German and British property to increase the pressure on the United States.[50] Roosevelt, on the other hand, upon learning that the European diplomats in Havana favored intervention, observed:

I should not be at all sorry to have the foreign consuls act as to intervention of their governments . . . because it would make our course clearer and give us an even more complete justification.[51]

When Taft reported that the compromise plan had failed on September 25, Roosevelt equivocated on intervention. First, he made a personal appeal to Estrada Palma to rise above honor to save his country, which Estrada Palma was already convinced he was doing by resigning and forcing the Americans to take control. Roosevelt was confused as to how conditions could have "changed so completely," and urged Taft to keep trying, to work closely with the Liberals to find a compromise: "I do not believe we should, simply because Palma has proven obstinate, put ourselves in the place of his unpopular government and face all the likelihood of a long drawn-out and very destructive guerrilla warfare."[52] Still, Taft could land troops if necessary.

In Havana, Taft worked to patch together another compromise before Estrada Palma resigned. With the Liberal goals almost achieved, Alfredo Zayas co-operated with him in order to head off an actual occupation. The Moderate position remained unchanged. Taft began to feel the chances for nonintervention slipping away: " . . . our suggestion as a basis of compromise seems to be thought a great victory for the Liberals . . . Palma and the Moderates will now take away their dolls and not play." Although he did not like "temporizing and compromising" with rebels because it "is a bad precedent," " . . . we did not make and were not responsible for the situation which we found."[53]

Roosevelt agreed with Taft that dealing with rebels was an evil thing, but that the Secretary had probably saved Havana from rioting and arson. The President urged Taft not to give up, but to avoid using the word "intervention." The whole affair was regrettable, but not "in the slightest degree due to any act of ours."[54] In another cable the same day (September 26) Roosevelt had more afterthoughts about the compromises offered the rebels, and concluded that the concessions, considering Estrada Palma's military weakness, were "the least of two very serious evils." The President feared the revolt had set a bad precedent, that of remedying political disputes by force, but that however likely another revolt, the Cubans should have one more chance at self-government.[55]

Although Taft expected hostilities to begin again between the ill-disciplined militia and the insurgents and doubted that Estrada Palma would change his mind, he still hoped a provisional Cuban government could be formed. Estrada

Palma had called another special session of congress to accept his resignation on September 28; the Peace Mission had but two days to find a replacement. Zayas was working with some Moderates, Taft reported, and he himself had warned them that any intervention would be temporary. This warning, he hoped, would dishearten the annexationists in the Moderate party.[56] When Taft worried about the constitutionality of a new government, Roosevelt told him the problem was meaningless. The American goal was still any settlement which avoided war and intervention:

> Remember that we have to do not only what is best for the island but what we can get public sentiment in this country to support, and there will be very grave dissatisfaction here with our intervention unless we can show clearly that we have exhausted every method by which it is possible to obtain peace and the perpetuation of the government with some show of order prior to our taking control ourselves.[57]

The provisional government scheme, however, did not gain much support, and Taft, upon learning that the Moderates were planning a counterinsurrection, again asked for Roosevelt's approval for immediate intervention. The President's reply re-emphasized the need to justify intervention to the American public:

> . . . I do not see that two revolutions would be . . . more objectionable than one, and as far as our attitude before the people of the United States is concerned it would make our position even better, for if we have to intervene I shall not object to any additional proof that the intervention was inevitable. . . . If we have to put down the insurrection it will, of course, take many months and a large force, and the people of this country will need to be convinced that there was no later alternative. . . .[58]

On September 28, Taft, Zayas, and other Cuban *políticos* went on with the charade of forming another government before the congress met that afternoon. By now Taft realized that both the Liberals and Moderates favored an American occupation, the former to have their new elections, the latter because they hoped it would bring annexation:

But neither party is willing to take the responsibility of saying so out loud. Accordingly they are going to take the cowardly fashion of breaking a quorum and running away and leaving old Palma, (who after all is a good deal of a hero, really the only hero I know of in the Cuban revolution), hanging by his gills between Heaven and Earth.[59]

The Moderates were even prepared to scatter the congress by force if it attempted to choose a Liberal as provisional president.[60] During the day, Taft cleared the wording of an intervention proclamation with Roosevelt (who was observing naval gunnery practice at Buzzard's Bay) and reviewed the course of the negotiations. He reassured the President that the insurgents would not fight the Americans and that last minute Moderate delaying tactics should not deter the United States from intervening. Roosevelt finally gave Taft the go-ahead to land Marines and to take control when the Cuban government no longer existed.[61]

At nine o'clock that evening a fraction of the Cuban congress met for the second time that day in an atmosphere charged with emotion. There were the predictable impassioned speeches by the island's most accomplished orators, and then, rather than accept the President's resignation, a delegation of senators went to see him. Estrada Palma listened to their pleas to remain in office, and admitted that his personal desire was to do so. As William Inglis reported the President's last moments in office:

[Estrada Palma said] "But here, we have a question of the dignity of the government. We are deprived of authority by an armed element which has risen against us. I must go."
Not another word was spoken. The President of the Senate seized the right hand of Don Tomás and drew his left arm around the aged man in a close embrace. Tears were in the eyes of both. As Dolz turned away, he was sobbing. Duque Estrada, Mario Garcia Kohly, Fortun, all the rest, embraced the President and turned away weeping. But the old man neither wept or spoke. He seemed dazed. The Cuban Republic, savagely torn by her own greedy sons, was dying before him. And a little while later he heard passing his palace the measured tramp of American marines on their way to guard the millions in the state Treasury—the real cause of the revolution.[62]

The citizens of Havana waited expectantly for the political drama to play itself out. As Lieutenant of Artillery Horacio Ferrer watched the Cuban flag over Morro Castle lowered at sunset, he sadly reflected that it would never be run up the staff again.[63] Around midnight Estrada Palma formally submitted his resignation to the peace commissioners.

In the early hours of September 29, William Howard Taft worked to make the occupation as popular as possible. Upon receiving Estrada Palma's resignation, the Secretary of War called the Marines ashore and issued a proclamation stating that in the absence of a Cuban government, the United States, "to restore order," had temporarily assumed political control of the island. He established a provisional government, naming himself governor. The Cuban flag would continue to fly and the laws of the Republic would remain in effect. The Provisional Governor called upon "all citizens and residents of Cuba to assist in the work of restoring order, tranquillity, and public confidence."[64] The second American occupation of Cuba had formally begun.

## Occupation and Disarmament: October, 1906

With intervention and occupation a fact, Roosevelt accepted it as an inevitable and temporary alternative to "a destructive and wearisome civil war," occasioned by Estrada Palma's military weakness.[65] He was satisfied that Taft had done all he could to get a compromise, that annexation was still unwise, and that the Republican party would not be politically penalized for the intervention.[66] Back in Washington, the President talked with Sir Mortimer Durand, the British ambassador; Roosevelt "seemed very confident about restoration of order. He said he had no wish to annex either Cuba or San Domingo."[67] In another conversation Elihu Root told Durand that the intervention would be terminated as quickly as possible, and, in a letter persuading Gonzalo de Quesada to stay at his post, the Secretary of State stressed the need now to work again for Cuba's independence:

To secure the successful accomplishment of this purpose as speedily as possible, all friends of Cuba ought to unite their earnest efforts. With hopeful courage and determination on the part of Cuba's real friends all this wretched business will soon be over, and we shall look back upon it as merely a hard lesson in the course of Cuba's development in the art of self-government.[68]

At the Havana end of the "wretched business," William Howard Taft also did all that pleasant speeches could do to disarm the Cubans and to insure that they did not misunderstand the United States intentions. In an address at the opening day exercises of the National University, the Provisional Governor spoke with Hispanic courtesy and delicacy. He praised the accomplishments of Spanish culture and the progress of the nation: "The island of Cuba, established as a Republic four years ago, made such rapid progress in four years as almost to intoxicate those of us who believed in popular government." Now, however, Cuban democracy had faltered, and it was necessary for the United States to catch Cuba in "its stumble in the progress toward self-government." Sadly but willingly, the United States, proudly showing its readiness "to expend its blood and treasure" for the "progress of popular government," would help Cuba move forward again. Taft's major suggestion was to be less class conscious, less committed to utopian ideals, and much more interested in business:

Therefore I urge upon the young men who are going out into life to-day . . . that they devote their attention, if they have estates in the island, to the betterment of those estates; and that others who have not estates, if they can get into commercial houses and into commercial pursuits, do so that when twenty-five years hence, a sympathetic stranger comes here again he may not find the governing or political class, the commercial class, the class representing the sciences and the professions, all different and divided, so that you do not have the benefit of a mixture of all those classes to form that without which a successful republic is absolutely impossible—a safe, conservative, patriotic, self-sacrificing public opinion.

Exhorting the Cubans to "be not discouraged," Taft concluded his speech with the lesson that disappointment often leads to new successes and then finished with a rousing " ¡ Viva la República de Cuba!"[69]

In the meantime Marines of the hastily formed Provisional Marine Brigade landed and fanned out across the countryside to guard sugar properties and railway facilities and to garrison the troubled towns where insurgents and the militia still glowered at each other along rifle barrels. Led by the legendary Colonel L. W. T. Waller, pacifier of Samar, the two-thousand-man brigade, broken into company detachments, kept the peace until the Army arrived.[70] The Marines met only threatening gestures from the disgruntled militia. The insurgents were singularly co-operative. One Marine officer, First Lieutenant William P. Upshur, described the whole business to his parents as a welcome change from shipboard life. His first letter began with a classic phrase for Marines: "No doubt you have been wondering what under the sun has become of me." He quickly assured his parents that the landings had been safe and the journey of his company to Pinar del Rio uneventful:

> The whole thing is exactly like Richard Harding Davises [sic] description of a revolution. We have the dirty rabble of Negroes armed with every tipe [sic] of antiquated weapon (a general to about 8 men) the palms and other tropical vegetation, the queer houses and of course the palace. . . . the people are harmless . . . our detachment could clear the island of them in a jiffy.[71]

Duty in Pinar del Rio was excellent, the shopping good, the people friendly, and when the Marines left in late October the town band and color guard, carrying the Cuban and American flags, marched with Upshur's company to the station. Earlier there had been banquets and speeches; at the station a cheering crowd bid the Marines farewell.[72]

Throughout the island the business of disarmament and demobilization went on during October. The work was directed by Brigadier General Frederick Funston, who had arrived in Havana late in September to assist Taft and command the American forces in Cuba.

On September 29, the Revolutionary Committee had agreed that the Constitutional Army would disband, surrender its arms and horses, and return home. Taft appointed a Disarmament Commission of Cuban veterans and American officers to co-operate with the Liberal generals to this end.[73] The Commission members joined the rebel columns and began the trying task of sending the celebrating insurgents home.[74] Aided by the pull of work in the sugar and tobacco fields, the commissioners were able to disperse the insurgents. Guerra's troops were bought off with ham sandwiches and were allowed to carry their weapons home with them before they were confiscated. In Ernesto Asbert's camp, disarming was slowed by many violent arguments and posing for photographs; there Funston found only 693 rusty rifles from seven thousand men, no ammunition, no pistols, and no machetes.[75] Major Ladd had much the same experience with Loynaz del Castillo's men; he estimated that about 12 per cent of the arms were surrendered. Loynaz del Castillo, in fact, told his men that "the Constitutional Army is not dissolved but in an apparent way" and that they should hold their weapons, for "we know that the American government is willing to grant almost anything before having to fire a gun in Cuba."[76] In an interview Pino Guerra analyzed the rebel position in a more positive fashion: "The revolution is ended and we have won, so we are supremely content."[77]

Working to get the insurgents back to their homes in time for the harvest, the Disarmament Commission did not quibble over the number of arms it received. As Major Ladd reported, it was concerned that it collected only 3,153 weapons from twenty-five thousand men, but more arms could easily be obtained anyway, and the prime consideration was to disband the Constitutional Army. By October 8, the insurgents had returned to their homes and the militia was mustered out of the service. In the latter's case, the government's rifles were largely recovered. The number of arms that remained in the peoples' hands, however, was a continuing source of concern to the Provisional Government.[78]

One incident marred the process of disarmament, as far as Taft was concerned, and that was the disposition of the insurgents' horses. During the revolt the insurgents had gathered mounts wherever they found them, and no record of ownership was attempted. Horse-trading had been common during the revolt and the alteration of a mount's physical characteristics was easy. Yet the insurgent generals had promised to restore "property which was taken by them for military purposes," and Taft wanted their horses returned. At the time, Taft was not in the best of humor: "I have to put up with the strutting about of insurgent generals in their uniforms, and their complaints by the other side of them, although in my heart . . . profane expressions of disgust press for utterance."[79] Taft was in no mood to give the rebels any more than they had already won. Funston and Ladd did their best to round up the horses; certificates were drafted in Spanish vesting temporary custody of each horse with the insurgent possessing it, with "ownership to be determined later," but between the drafting and printing this phrase was lost. Before the Disarmament Commission could correct the error, the rebel officers hurriedly issued the original certificates.[80] Both Funston and Ladd believed the incident (if regrettable) was minor, and that rebel possession of the horses was instrumental in getting them to go home.[81] Taft thought questions of private property were most serious, and, greatly disturbed, he asked Roosevelt if the Provisional Government could indemnify the owners, and Roosevelt agreed.[82]

The most significant repercussion of the horse incident was that Taft relieved Funston and sent him back to his post in California, replacing him with the Chief of Staff, Brigadier General Bell. Although Taft said Funston was no longer needed in Cuba because there would be no military operations, he relieved the general for not being respectful of private property (about eight thousand horses) in violation of the truce agreements. Taft was through with the unorthodox and mercurial Funston: "He has two o'clock courage and ability to meet an emergency that such courage gives

him, but when it comes to organization and execution of
plans I think he is lacking."[83] In military circles, Funston's relief was laid to friction with some of his former Cuban comrades, but the Army did not miss the point that pacification
still caused sticky problems with their civil superiors.[84]

Even as Taft gloomily considered the problems of intervention and occupation, the Cubans themselves celebrated
the end of the revolt and the coming of *la zafra*. William
Inglis saw Guerra's insurgents return to Pinar del Rio, and
he was infected by the passion of the hand-waving, scream-
ing crowd at the station. As the train pulled in, it was met with
thunderous *vivas* from the mob packed along the platform:

Mob: "Viva los Liberales!"
Rebels: "Viva Cuba!"
Mob: "Viva nos liberadores!"
Rebels "Viva la Constitución!'
Everybody: "Viva los Americanos. Viva la Paz! Viva Taft y Bacon!
Viva-a-a-a Mit'ter Roo-velt!" [85]

In Havana, the Liberals began to collect contributions to
erect a statue of Roosevelt, and Commander Colwell of the
"Denver" got a gold watch and a banquet in his honor from
the grateful revolutionary junta.[86] With Taft's announcement
of a general amnesty on October 10 and with the insurgent
army dispersed, the August Revolution, to the insurgents'
way of thinking, drew to a happy and successful close.[87]

Uncomfortably settled in the palace, "as cheerful as Spring
Grove cemetery," Provisional Governor William Howard Taft,
in his scant moments of reflection, thought that the Cuban
intervention had been "wretched from the beginning." In letters to Elihu Root and his brother Charles, Taft reviewed
the events of September, and the dominant tone of his account was futility.[88] The cause of the revolt, he believed,
was the coercion in the Porfirio Díaz style used to thwart the
popular will in the elections of 1905. "The theory is all right,
but the practice failed because there was no Díaz and there
was no force to suppress the revolution which followed."

When he arrived in Havana, he learned two inescapable facts: the insurgents had arms and men enough to wreak havoc, and the Moderates wanted annexation. He and Roosevelt had agreed to steer a course between war and annexation, and their goal was "to get the people dispersed and down to work in the tobacco and sugar fields." Affairs in Havana had been a "nightmare"; if the United States had supported the Cuban government, there would have been war and the destruction of American-owned property. If it had not intervened at all, the result would have been the same.[89] Now the United States, Taft wrote the President, as it acted the role of receiver or trustee for Cuba, must make the best of a bad situation. It must show the "South Americans that we are here against our will and only for the purpose of aiding Cuba. . . ."[90]

As appraised by the sophisticated Captain Frank McCoy, who understood the Cuban people and their problems, "some kind of intervention was absolutely necessary" for Cuba had truly been in turmoil.[91] The revolt "was a fight between the 'Ins' and 'Outs' with no principle at stake," sparked by the Moderates when they adopted "the Porfirio Díaz scheme of running a Latin-American Republic, without the force necessary to solve the problem . . . " Instead the government had "relied on the Platt Amendment, with its backing of the United States." In the Peace Mission's negotiations, the Liberals "outplayed" the Moderates, who worried about "their sacred honor and dignity" and "sulked in their tents." Taft, McCoy wrote Wood, "soon found he was up against a different lot of people" from the Filipinos, but on the whole (since Wood couldn't be there) the Secretary "handled the thing ably and with wonderful tact for a new comer to Cuba."

Both Taft's and McCoy's accounts reveal the commissioners' feeling that their mission had successfully stopped the war on the insurgents' terms and that the chance of any other settlement had been closed before they arrived in Cuba.

In the meantime, Roosevelt made sure that the Cubans would bear the historical responsibility for this situation by publishing the diplomatic correspondence leading to the

Peace Mission before the occupation was a week old.[92] The Taft-Roosevelt correspondence and the full report of the Peace Mission were made public two months later. The documents printed in the Taft-Bacon *Report* and *Foreign Affairs, 1906* have in fact perpetuated the Roosevelt administration's interpretation of the Peace Mission's conduct, and American historians (critics and apologists alike) have largely accepted Roosevelt's evidence.[93] Conceding Roosevelt's thesis that he did not want intervention for both the United States and Cuban interest, one must still conclude the Taft-Bacon Mission was sent as much to protect Roosevelt's political leadership at home as it was to stop the war in Cuba. To a large degree, Taft's job was to negotiate the United States out of the impasse Roosevelt helped create when he sent ammunition and ships to Havana. In the eyes of Cubans of varying political persuasions, the United States, until the Taft-Bacon Mission arrived, was stiffening the otherwise impotent Cuban government.[94]

The contemporary Cuban reaction was a mixture of relief, political self-justification, and despair with the nation's political weakness, but few dismissed the revolt lightly. Representative of the Liberal-nationalist viewpoint, Enrique Collazo described the revolt as the necessary destruction of a non-Cuban government built upon the moral and economic prejudices of Leonard Wood and Estrada Palma.[95] Outraged by the political nihilism of 1906, Roque E. Garrigó emotionally deplored the Cubans' inability to reach the social harmony of their ideal:

> In the Nation, in the provinces and in the Cuban municipalities, there are, nor can there be, more than two points of view: that of the privileged ones, vile adulterers of the [political] system now marvelously full of their bastard ambitions, their stupidities and their frauds; and that of those who suffer in placid tranquillity, lacking the spirit of true citizenship, in unqualified fear of the abusers.[96]

For Enrique José Varona, who had watched the events of September take place with characteristic sang-froid, the American commissioners had destroyed the Cuban government because they feared the loss of the foreign property held hostage by the rebels. Varona could see no other reason why the United States government had abandoned the rule of law, which was one of its guiding principles. He believed that the influence of foreign capital was the "major social force" in Cuba, that with its vast resources foreign capital had moved in its own self-defense to end the war and halt the politics of violence and destruction:

> Thus far it has limited itself to crushing the Government of Sr. Estrada; and it will substitute another when it becomes advantageous. Without bias it will take tomorrow the necessary steps as they appear to it in order to avoid the disagreeable need of repeating the operation.
> Thus our first revolt will be liquidated. Those who worry about the future of the Cubans in their own country will help in liquidation with sadness, shame and fear.[97]

Among Cuban historians the machinations of pro-annexation property owners and the deleterious effect of the Platt Amendment on Cuban domestic politics have vied as the major causes of the intervention. Few have denied the event's importance. Martínez Ortiz believed the August Revolution was a greater disruption of the nation's life and a greater source of disillusionment and insecurity than the war for independence; he thought that if the war had continued the nation would have dissolved in social revolution. Roig de Leuchsenring cast the Platt Amendment as the chief villain because it encouraged the *políticos* to plead and threaten to gain American support and then evade their responsibilities when the United States became involved. Portell Vilá stated that the instability of Cuban post-colonial society made revolt inevitable, for which intervention was a poor solution and annexation a constant threat. The Platt Amendment gave the American and Spanish property owners all the promise they needed to agitate for intervention.[98]

There is little doubt that Roosevelt and Taft believed that nothing could be worse for any society than to be sundered by rebellion and to have law and order collapse. As far as Cuba was concerned, Roosevelt and Taft were friendly with the Estrada Palma government and the conservative values under which it governed. Why then did they, in effect, allow it to collapse? To a large degree they realized that sanctioning rebellion would be an unhealthy thing for Cuba internally and that the destruction of foreign property would be the island's economic (and perhaps political) ruin. Yet the single most important factor in the matrix of social, economic, and geopolitical considerations that they weighed was their fear of the American public reaction to a military pacification of Cuba. In this fear, the President and Secretary of War were reinforced by the advice of their military advisers and diplomatic representatives in Cuba.

Roosevelt and Taft, however, rode the historical analogy of the Philippine Insurrection much harder than did Generals Funston and Bell. Doubtless for reasons of institutional self-protection and their concept of national security, these senior officers and the General Staff were not anxious to intervene in support of Estrada Palma. Their plans and correspondence indicate, though, that they believed they could suppress the rebellion (if not save the sugar mills) with eighteen thousand troops if they could be relatively free in conducting the pacification on their own terms. It was the particulars of these terms that concerned the President.

Faced with the possibility of active military intervention in Cuba, Roosevelt armed himself with a large supply of justifications. Which ones were for his conscience and which for public consumption is hard to say. Clearly, the constitutional-legal sanctions that encouraged him to act served both. His concern for Cuba's peace and well-being was real enough, but so was his desire to escape the interventionist-imperialist label. Incongruously the two justifications he used to start the naval intervention of September 8 (that he was acting "to protect American lives and property" and to pre-empt European intervention) were designed to satisfy American public opinion and yet the act of naval intervention served to prolong the Cuban rebellion and end the possibility of compromise. The arrival of "Denver" and "Marietta" were the key events which directly influenced the style and timing of the subsequent occupation, determining that it would be peaceful and result in a political victory for the Liberals. Believing that a failure to protect foreign lives and property would cause a storm of protest in the United States, Roosevelt felt compelled to send ships to Cuba. By doing so, he narrowed his chances of avoiding an occupation.

The Cuban government and the rebels calculated on winning American influence to their side, and Roosevelt did nothing to discourage their hope for American intervention. The Cubans were correct in assuming that Roosevelt could not let the war go on; they were willing to gamble that intervention would work to their advantage. The rebels made the most astute assessment of American reaction by guessing that Roosevelt would not fight to support a weak regime established by rigged elections. The Moderates, on the other hand, committed a basic mistake when they equated Roosevelt's bellicose righteousness with a personal freedom to order troops to fight in defense of law, order, constitutional government, and the sanctity of property. Insensitive themselves to the popular restraints upon democratic government, they thought Roosevelt would risk an unpopular war simply to uphold political abstractions.

1. Taft to Roosevelt, September 15, 1906, Roosevelt Papers.

2. Roosevelt to Taft, September 17, 1906, Roosevelt Papers.

3. Roosevelt to Brig. Gen. J. F. Bell, September 20, 1906, Roosevelt Papers.

4. Bell to Roosevelt, September 22, 1906, Roosevelt Papers.

The revision was incorporated in the Army War College's "Memorandum to the Assistant Secretary of War," September 22, 1906, Appendix 3 to Serial 11, "Cuba," AWC Doc. File, RG 165.

5. Part I, Serial 11, "Cuba," September 3, 1906, AWC Doc. File, RG 165.

6. Brig. Gen. F. C. Ainsworth to Maj. E. F. Ladd, September 27, 1906, Doc. File 1168399, RG 94.

7. Memo, Lt. Col. Count Edward Gleichen to Sir H. M. Durand, British ambassador to the United States, attached to letter, Durand to Sir Edward Grey, October 5, 1906, FO 371-56, PRO.

8. *New York Times,* September 22, 1906; *Washington Post,* September 27, 1906. The *Post* reported the General Staff was ready to deploy 45,000 men, all the Regulars in the United States.

0. *Now York Timoo,* Soptombor 21, 1006.

10. *Ibid.,* September 23, 1906.

11. *Ibid.,* September 22, 1906.

12. *Times* (London), September 21, 1906.

13. *Graphic* (London), September 22, 1906.

14. Report of Capt. A. R. Couden, USN, to Secretary of the Navy, October 11, 1906, Area 8 File (October, 1906), RG 45.

15. Fullam to Bureau of Navigation, September 23, 1906, Area 8 File (September, 1906), RG 45.

16. Ladd to Ainsworth, September 15, 22, and 25, 1906, Doc. File 1164984, RG 94.

17. Taft-Bacon *Report,* 450; Cmdr. J. T. Newton, USN, to Bureau of Navigation, September 27, 1906, Case 244/235, *Num. File, 1906–1910,* Vol. XXXVII, RG 59; Harry Gannett, administrator of the Trinidad Sugar Company, to Sir Edward Grey, September 18, 1906, FO 371–56, PRO.

18. Sir William Van Horne to G. M. Dodge, September 27, 1906, Case 244/276, *Num. File, 1906–1910,* Vol. XXXVII, RG 59.

19. The basic printed source on the Taft-Bacon Mission is the Commissioners' *Report,* previously cited, in which is reprinted the Taft-Roosevelt correspondence (edited) and various related papers, including peace proposals, letters to the Cuban government, reports of the Disarmament Commission, and other miscellaneous documents. The original copies are scattered throughout the Taft and Roosevelt Papers in the Library of Congress and in the archives of the State Department. Unedited copies of the Taft-Roosevelt correspondence are included in the Records of the Provisional Government of Cuba, National Archives, Record Group 199. For ease of reference the author has used the Taft-Bacon *Report* for citations except where documents do not appear there ui have been edited.

Reliablo aooounto of Taft'o Cuban oxporionoo baoed on tho Taft Papers are Ralph Eldin Minger, "William Howard Taft and the United States Intervention in Cuba in 1906," *Hispanic American Historical Review,* XLI (February, 1961), 75–89, and Henry F. Pringle, *The Life and Times of William Howard Taft* (New York and Toronto, 1939), I, 305–10.

20. Taft to Root, September 15, 1906, Root Papers.

21. Taft to Roosevelt, September 16, 1906, Roosevelt Papers.

22. James Brown Scott, *Robert Bacon: Life and Letters* (New York, 1923), pp. 117–18.

23. Memo from tho Judgo Advocato Goncral to tho Socrctary of War, September 15, 1906, Taft-Bacon *Report,* pp. 493–95. The essence of Davis' brief was that intervention was legal under the Platt Amend-

ment and the responsibility of the President, who could use all of his powers to suppress rebellion.

24. Roosevelt to Taft, September 17, 1906, Roosevelt Papers.

25. Transcript of interview with Albert G. Robinson, New York *Sun,* September 17, 1906, Taft Papers.

26. "Memorandum of a Conference Between Hon. William Howard Taft, Secretary of War, Hon. Robert Bacon, Acting Secretary of State, Captain F. R. McCoy, U.S.A. and Mr. F. S. Cairns, held on the U.S.S. Des Moines, Tuesday, September 18, 1906," Taft Papers.

27. William Inglis, "The Disappointed Rebels in Wait about Havana," *Harper's Weekly,* L (October 13, 1906), 1454.

28. Taft to Roosevelt, September 20, 1906, Taft-Bacon *Report,* pp. 502–4. At one point, Taft is supposed to have said that the times called for self-sacrifice and patriotism, to which Estrada Palma replied, "Mr. Secretary, I do not intend to take any lessons in patriotism from you." William Inglis, "The Collapse of the Cuban House of Cards," *Harper's Weekly,* L (October 20, 1906), 1490.

29. "Truce Correspondence," Exhibit 7, Taft-Bacon *Report,* pp. 502–4.

30. Taft to Roosevelt, September 20 and 21, 1906, Taft-Bacon *Report,* pp. 469–71.

31. McCoy to Wood, October 18, 1906, Wood Papers; "List of Callers on Secretary Taft during his mission to Havana as Special Envoy from his arrival, September 19," with personal data on callers, File 002, Confidential Correspondence, Provisional Governor of Cuba, Records of the Provisional Government of Cuba, 1906–1909, National Archives, Record Group 199. The Confidential Correspondence is hereafter cited by file, CC/PGoC, RG 199.

32. Taft to Roosevelt, September 22, 1906, Taft-Bacon *Report,* pp. 471–72.

33. Taft-Bacon *Report,* p. 460; Taft to Roosevelt, September 23, 1906, Taft-Bacon *Report,* p. 472; McCoy to Wood, October 18, 1906, Wood Papers.

34. Taft to Roosevelt, September 21 and 22, 1906, Taft-Bacon *Report,* pp. 470–72; Taft-Bacon *Report,* pp. 460–62.

35. Taft to Roosevelt, September 22, 1906, Roosevelt Papers. This paragraph was edited out of the version published in the Taft-Bacon *Report.*

36. Roosevelt to Taft, September 22, 1906, Taft-Bacon *Report,* p. 472.

37. Roosevelt to Taft, September 21, 1906, Taft-Bacon *Report,* p. 471.

38. Taft-Bacon *Report,* p. 461. The Liberal position is given in detail in a statement by Zayas, Exhibit 10, Taft-Bacon *Report,* pp. 507–8. Zayas believed that even if Estrada Palma resigned, a provisional president or committee could be chosen by the congress.

39. Statement of Dr. Domingo Méndez Capote, Exhibit 9, Taft-Bacon *Report,* p. 506. The Nationalists (Nuñezistas) agreed. See Exhibit 11, Taft-Bacon *Report,* pp. 508–9.

40. Taft-Bacon *Report,* p. 462.

41. Three cablegrams, Taft to Roosevelt, September 24, 1906, Taft-Bacon *Report,* pp. 472–73.

42. Taft to Roosevelt, September 25, 1906, Taft-Bacon *Report,* pp. 474–75.

43. Roosevelt to Taft, September 22, 1906, Taft-Bacon *Report,* p. 472.

44. Roosevelt to Taft, September 20, 1906, Taft-Bacon *Report,* p. 469. The insurgents' funds, estimated at $1 million, were raised by the Liberals as graft while in office, by voluntary subscription, and by blackmail and extortion from Spanish and Cuban planters. One contribution of a few hundred dollars was traced to the American colony on the Isle of Pines. Memo by Frank S. Cairns on source of funds, September 22, 1906, Roosevelt Papers.

45. Roosevelt to C. W. Eliot, September 22, 1906, Roosevelt Papers.

46. Joseph B. Foraker to Roosevelt, September 27, 1906, and Roosevelt to Henry Cabot Lodge, September 27, 1906, Roosevelt Papers.

In a Chicago speech opening the Republican Congressional campaign in the Midwest, Beveridge said that intervention would bring annexation; it was destiny and a welcome return to the "traditional American doctrine" that "wherever the flag is raised it never shall be lowered." *Washington Post,* September 23, 1906.

47. *Times* (London), September 15, 1906. Lodge agreed with the *Times* that neither party was likely to get much of an issue out of the Cuban civil war. Lodge to Roosevelt, September 29, 1906, Roosevelt Papers.

48. Lord Acton, British minister to Spain, to Sir Edward Grey, September 19 and 22, 1906, FO 371–56, PRO.

49. Lord Acton to Grey, September 24, 1906, FO 371–56, PRO. American annexation of Cuba, according to diplomats Acton talked with, "would mean the admission of an alien race into the Commonwealth and the presence of Spaniards in Congress with an indirect share in the Government of the United States, without bringing with it material advantages in the shape of an accretion of revenue to the Federal Treasury," all of which made annexation distasteful to the Americans and therefore unlikely.

50. Chapman, *A History of the Cuban Republic,* p. 210.

51. Roosevelt to Taft, September 20, 1906, Taft-Bacon *Report,* p. 471.

52. Three cables, Roosevelt to Taft, September 25, 1906, Taft-Bacon *Report,* pp. 473–75.

53. Taft to Roosevelt, September 26, 1906, Taft-Bacon *Report,* pp. 475–77. For the Liberal position on September 26, see Zayas' letter to the peace commissioners, Exhibit 14, Taft-Bacon *Report,* pp. 514–16.

54. Roosevelt to Taft, September 26, 1906, Taft-Bacon *Report,* pp. 477–78.

55. Roosevelt to Taft, September 26, Taft-Bacon *Report,* p. 478.

56. Taft to Roosevelt, September 26 and 27, 1906, Taft-Bacon *Report,* pp. 478–80.

The British assessment was the same. G. W. E. Griffith to Grey, September 27, 1906, FO 371–56, PRO.

57. Roosevelt to Taft, September 28, 1906, Taft-Bacon *Report*, p. 480.

58. Roosevelt to Taft, September 28, 1906, Taft-Bacon *Report*, p. 481.

59. Taft to Roosevelt, September 28, 1906, Case 244/300, *Num. File, 1906–1910*, Vol. XXXVII, RG 59.

60. Sworn statements of Frank M. Steinhart, Maj. E. F. Ladd, and Gen. A. Rodríguez, September 28 and 29, 1906, Case 18730, General Classified Files, 1898–1945, Records of the Bureau of Insular Affairs, U.S. War Department, National Archives, Record Group 350. Hereafter cited as General Classified Files, BIA, RG 350.

61. Taft to Roosevelt, September 28, 1906, Taft-Bacon *Report*, pp. 483–84.

62. William Inglis, "The Collapse of the Cuban House of Cards," *Harper's Weekly*, L (October 20, 1906), 1505. Substantially the same account appeared in the *New York Times*, September 29, 1906.

63. Ferrer, *Con el rifle al hombro*, p. 204.

64. Proclamation of September 29, 1906, Taft-Bacon *Report*, p. 486.

65. Roosevelt to Kermit Roosevelt, September 30, 1906, Roosevelt Papers.

66. Roosevelt to Henry Cabot Lodge, October 1, 1906; Roosevelt to Albert C. Beveridge, October 5, 1906, Roosevelt Papers.

67. Durand to Grey, October 8, 1906, FO 371–56, PRO.

68. Root to Gonzalo de Quesada, October 1, 1906 *Foreign Relations, 1906*, p. 487.

69. "Speech of Wm. H. Taft, Provisional Governor of Cuba, at the Opening Exercises of the National University of Habana, October 1, 1906," Exhibit 26, Taft-Bacon *Report*, pp. 540–42.

*Le Temps* (Paris) observed that Taft's speech was politically wise, for Washington had no desire to annex Cuba or lose "the moral authority" cultivated by Root's good-will trip to South America. *Le Temps* doubted that any "durable solution" to Cuba's problems would be found. Sir Francis Bertie, British ambassador to France, to Grey, October 3, 1906, FO 371–56, PRO.

70. Memo for Brig. Gen. G. F. Elliott, Commandant, U.S. Marine Corps to the Secretary of the Navy, based on a telegram from Col. L. W. T. Waller, October 12, 1906, Case 24111, General File, 1897–1926, General Records of the Navy Department, National Archives, Record Group 80. Hereafter cited as General File, RG 80.

71. 1st Lt. W. P. Upshur, USMC, to Dr. and Mrs. John N. Upshur, October 5, 1906, General William P. Upshur Papers, Southern Historical Collection, University of North Carolina Library.

72. Upshur to Dr. J. N. Upshur, October 24, 1906, Upshur Papers.

73. Taft-Bacon *Report*, pp. 464–65.

74. Reports of the Disarmament Commission, October 9—November 8, 1906, Exhibit 22, Taft-Bacon *Report*, pp. 521–33.

75. *New York Times*, October 15, 1906; Taft-Bacon *Report*, p. 526.

76. Report of secret service agent to Taft, October 5, 1906, Taft Papers.

77. *New York Times,* October 1, 1906.

78. Taft to Roosevelt, October 7 and 8, 1906, Taft-Bacon *Report,* pp. 488–89; Maj. E. F. Ladd, Report of the Disarmament Commission, November 8, 1906, Exhibit 22, Taft-Bacon *Report,* pp. 530–32; Provisional Governor (PG) C. E. Magoon to Brig. Gen. J. F. Bell, November (?), 1906, and Report of the Arms Commission, November 22, 1906, and February 4, 1907, File 009, CC/PGoC.

The Arms Commission estimated that "nearly every house outside of the larger cities has an arm of some kind." Governor Magoon urged General Bell to get what arms he could with persuasion and money, but would not permit forcible searches.

79. Taft to Roosevelt, October 6, 1906, Roosevelt Papers.

80. Taft to Roosevelt, October 7, 1906, Taft-Bacon *Report,* p. 488; Funston to Taft, October 13, 1906, Taft-Bacon *Report,* pp. 521–22. For a copy of the certificate, see the Taft-Bacon *Report,* p. 533.

Major Ladd thought the Cubans had arranged to have the phrase omitted, but Taft told E. F. Atkins that Funston made a mistake in the translation. Ladd to Taft, October 9, 1906, Taft-Bacon *Report,* p. 526; Atkins, *Sixty Years in Cuba,* p. 339.

81. Funston to Taft, October 13, 1906, Taft-Bacon *Report,* p. 522.

"Unanimous opinion board that they (horse certificates) largely aided in disbanding rebel forces . . ." Ladd to Secretary of War, October 25, 1906, Case 2102, General Classified Files, BIA, RG 350.

Colonel James Parker found Funston amused by the horse controversy and unrepentent. To Parker, Funston said he purposely left the horses in rebel hands. Parker, *The Old Army,* p. 398.

82. Taft to Roosevelt, October 7, 1906; Roosevelt to Taft, October 7, 1906, both Taft-Bacon *Report,* pp. 488–89. Taft believed that $500,000 would be necessary to make reparations; actually the cost was $296,508. Magoon to Taft, June 24, 1907, Case 2102, General Classified Files, BIA, RG 350.

83. Taft to Roosevelt, October 6, 1906, Roosevelt Papers; Martínez Ortiz, *Cuba: los primeros años de independencia,* II, 753.

84. Wood to McCoy, October (?), 1906, General Frank R. McCoy Papers, Library of Congress; *Army and Navy Journal,* October 13, 1906; *New York Times,* October 5 and 18, 1906.

85. William Inglis, "The Last Act of Cuba's Tragi-Comedy of Insurrection," *Harper's Weekly,* L (October 27, 1906), p. 1526.

86. *Independent,* October 25, 1906, p. 959; *New York Times,* October 24, 1906.

87. Taft to Roosevelt, October 10, 1906, and Amnesty Proclamation, October 10, 1906, both Taft-Bacon *Report,* pp. 490, 533–34. The revolt's principal victim, Tomás Estrada Palma, left Havana with his family on October 2 and returned to his modest home near Bayamo (Oriente). There he died in political exile on November 4, 1908.

88. Taft to Root, October 4, 1906, Root Papers.

89. Taft to Charles P. Taft, October 4, 1906, Taft Papers.

90. Taft to Roosevelt, October 3, 1906, Roosevelt Papers. The official account of the intervention was that Taft and Roosevelt realized compromise with the rebels would strengthen them and sanctify rebellion, but the alternative, war, would destroy the island's economic wealth and chance for peaceful development. It was Estrada Palma's stubbornness that forced the United States to occupy the island. Under the circumstances Cuba deserved one more chance as an independent country. *New York Times,* October 19, 1906.

91. McCoy to Wood, October 18, 1906, Wood Papers. McCoy wrote substantially the same account to another Old Cuban Hand, Colonel Hugh L. Scott. McCoy to Scott, October 18, 1906, Scott Papers.

92. McCoy to Wood, October 18, 1906, Wood Papers; Taft to Roosevelt, October 6, 1906, Roosevelt Papers; *Times* (London), October 6, 1906; *North American Review,* CLXXXIII (October 16, 1906), 812–15.

The idea apparently was Root's and from the appearance of the marginal notes and blue-penciled marks in the manuscripts, it appears as if the Secretary of State personally did the editing. As a result of the disclosures, Méndez Capote and Juan O'Farrill fled to New York.

93. Chapman, *A History of the Cuban Republic,* p. 219; Fitzgibbon, *Cuba and the United States, 1900–1935,* pp. 119–20; David A. Lockmiller, *Magoon in Cuba* (Chapel Hill, N.C., 1938), pp. 58–63; Albert G. Robinson, *Cuba Old and New* (New York, 1916), pp. 159–61; Carleton Beals, *The Crime of Cuba* (Philadelphia, 1933), pp. 203–7; Leland H. Jenks, *Our Cuban Colony* (New York, 1932), pp. 87–95; Howard C. Hill, *Roosevelt and the Caribbean* (Chicago, 1927), pp. 88–105; Dana G. Munro, *Intervention and Dollar Diplomacy in the Caribbean, 1900–1921* (Princeton, N.J., 1964), pp. 125–40; Ralph Eldin Minger, "William Howard Taft and the United States Intervention in Cuba in 1906," *HAHR,* XVLI (February, 1961), pp. 75–89; Leo J. Meyer, "Relations between the United States and Cuba, 1898–1917" (unpublished Ph.D. dissertation, Clark University, 1928); Dexter Perkins, *The United States and the Caribbean* (Cambridge, Mass., 1947), p. 127; Philip G. Wright, *The Cuban Situation and Our Treaty Relations* (Washington, D.C., 1931), pp. 31–33; Johnson, *The History of Cuba,* IV, pp. 260–64; Chester Lloyd Jones, *The Caribbean Since 1900* (New York, 1936), pp. 40–42; W. H. Callcott, *The Caribbean Policy of the United States, 1890–1920* (Baltimore, 1942), pp. 231–35.

Whether the Constitutional Army would have fought the Americans is a moot question. In an interview with Lockmiller in the 1930's, Guerra and Asbert said they would not have fought; Irene Wright, Willis Fletcher Johnson, and Sir William Van Horne agree.

94. M. J. Manduley to Sir William Van Horne, September 15, 1906, Case 244/277, *Num. File, 1906–1910,* Vol. XXXVII, RG 59; Enrique Collazo, *Cuba intervenida* (Havana, 1910), pp. 121, 128–30; Enrique José Varona, *Miranda en torno,* pp. 23–24; Alexander Gonzalez to Wood, November 19, 1906, Wood Papers.

Manduley feared the United States would negotiate away its influence: "There is an old Spanish proverb which says: To dog and woman, show them bread with the left hand and a stick with the right one. The same combination of energy and benevolence is what our people need. Either method, if used separately, would simply mean failure."

95. Enrique Collazo, *La revolución de agosto* (Havana, 1906), p. 7. Alvaro Catá in *De guerra á guerra* (Havana, 1906), p. 76, pointed out that Estrada Palma's government used its power to subvert Cuban morality. He cited a popular jingle of the time:

> La Senorita Asunción,
> guapa y su reputación,
> en su destino ha cambiado:
> estaba en Gobernación
> y dicen . . . que esta en Estado.

96. Roque E. Garrigó, *La convulsión cubana* (Havana, 1906), p. 16.

97. Enrique José Varona, "El talon de Aquiles," written September 26, 1906, in *Mirando en torno*, pp. 23–27. The original article appeared in *El Figaro* (Havana) on September 30, 1906.

98. Martínez Ortiz. *Cuba: los primeros años de independencia*, II, 737–50; Emilio Roig de Leuchsenring, *El intervencionismo, mal de males de Cuba republicana* (San José de Costa Rico, 1931), pp. 11–12; Portell Vilá, *Historia de Cuba*, IV, 442–43, 474–75, 520.

Portell Vilá placed particular responsibility on fomenting revolt to J. M. Ceballos and Company, a Spanish-American real estate, sugar and financial holding company based in New York, and one of its officers, Manuel Silveira, "El Morgan Cubano." Silveira was supposed to have fallen out with Estrada Palma and financed José Miguel Gómez, then to have supported the government until he fled on October 2. His action coincided with the financial collapse of Ceballos and Company. *New York Times*, October 11–17, 1906.

# CHAPTER FOUR

# THE UNITED STATES ARMY PACIFIES CUBA

W HEN political events in Havana suggested the resignation of the Estrada Palma government, the United States Army prepared its expedition to Cuba. Warned by the War Department on September 25 that intervention was imminent, the General Staff, using its Cuban war plans as a basis, began to organize the expeditionary force. The Ordnance and Quartermaster Departments had announced the readiness of supplies in mid-September; now they prepared to purchase additional munitions and horses and charter transports.

The basic task organization, in line with the General Staff's earlier estimates, was modified only slightly and orders were dispatched to the units tabbed for Cuban service on September 29, after the intervention became official. The expeditionary force consisted of five two-battalion infantry regiments (Fifth, Eleventh, Seventeenth, Twenty-seventh, Twenty-eighth), two two-squadron cavalry regiments (Eleventh and Fifteenth), one light artillery battery (Fourteenth Field Artillery), two mountain batteries (Seventeenth and Eighteenth Field Artillery), the Second Battalion of Engineers, the Signal Corps' Company I, and the Hospital Corps' Companies A and B. The War Department prescribed a division level staff for the expedition, including seven members of the General Staff Corps. The port-of-embarkation was Newport News, Virginia. Thirty days' supplies would be loaded out with the troops, and units were to embark with full equipment for field service.[1]

From posts as far distant as Fort Russell (Wyoming), Fort Snelling (Minnesota), Fort Des Moines (Iowa), and the

Presidio (California), the units of the expeditionary force moved toward Newport News. Fresh from summer maneuvers, many of the troops had scarcely unpacked. The news of the move was not entirely welcome; desertions in the Eleventh Infantry rose when the men learned fever-famous Cuba was their destination. To bring two battalions to nearly full strength, each regiment stripped its third battalion to fill its ranks. Officers were ordered back to their commands from the Infantry and Cavalry Schools (over the Commandants' protest) and from other detached duty. Three instructors at West Point departed, though Colonel Hugh Scott, the Superintendent, tried to save his football coach. General Bell's reply was crisp:

> If West Point has come to that frame of mind where it thinks that coaching a football team is sufficient excuse for keeping a captain away from his troops when it is ordered to a foreign country for possible war service, then the Chief of Staff feels that the time has come for him to weep. I am certain . . . that others have over-persuaded your judgement.[2]

The command and the title of the force moved about as rapidly as its troops. Frederick Funston officially commanded the force as of October 2, 1906, although he was unaware of his appointment and hardly had time for it anyway. On October 4, Secretary Taft ordered General Bell to Cuba to assume command, which Bell did on October 10. Bell held the post until the end of the year when he returned to Washington. His replacement, Brigadier General Theodore J. Wint, lasted until February 25, 1907, when illness forced the sixty-one year old cavalryman to retire. Brigadier General Thomas H. Barry, previously head of the Army War College and acting Chief of Staff in Bell's absence, then commanded the Cuban force until the end of the intervention. The command itself was first called the First Expeditionary Brigade. As the troops arrived in Cuba, Taft named the expedition the Army of Cuban Intervention, but, reconsidering the political wisdom of that title, he redesignated the force the Army of Cuban Pacification on October 15. Such it remained.

As well as the General Staff had been warned and as expeditiously as the Army sailed from the United States, the five-thousand-man expeditionary force took a month to assemble in Cuba. There a thousand waiting Marines joined it. The movement, nevertheless, was a notable achievement in Army history, for the rapidity and efficiency of the deployment, planned and supervised by the General Staff, demonstrated the value of contingency planning and the improved readiness of the Army.[3]

The Fifth Infantry arrived first in Havana on October 6, having left New York City five days earlier aboard the Army transport "Sumner." Meanwhile at Newport News, the quartermasters built an embarkation depot at the end of a spur of the Chesapeake and Ohio Railroad. In the next two weeks, sixteen merchant vessels under government contract sailed with troops for Havana. The press of the ships at Newport News (first come, first contracted) slowed the movement, for each had to be inspected and, in some cases, modified to meet Army regulations. The loading of supplies was not well organized and much equipment was lost. Still the expedition began to leave Newport News on October 10 and the deployment was completed by the end of the month. In Havana the transports were unloaded at the Western Railway wharf, where lines of khaki-clad Americans queued down the gangplanks to the waiting trains which carried them to Camp Columbia west of the city. With the Marines no doubt commenting freely on the Army's "speedy" reaction, the soldiers then headed inland to their posts. By October 29, the Army of Cuban Pacification (which included the First Provisional Marine Regiment) garrisoned the island with six thousand men. The second military occupation of Cuba had begun.[4]

## Cuba Pacified

The Army of Cuban Pacification was the muscle and steel behind the Provisional Government, and from the outset its mission was to deter insurrection in Cuba. Roosevelt hoped the Army would not become involved in law enforcement per se. This was the task of the civil government and the Cuban Rural Guard. Writing Taft, the President was insistent that the Army's role be passive. Although it would provide the "moral force" behind the civil administration, the Army must hold itself aloof from Cuban affairs:

I feel it is most important that if any bloodshed occurs it should be between Cubans and Cubans, not Americans and Cubans. Please have the strictest instructions issued. . . . In the event of disorder, the American troops should not be called upon until the last resort. . . . I am most anxious that there should be no blood shed between Americans and Cubans.[5]

Taft interpreted Roosevelt's instruction for the Army in a circular issued October 12, 1906. The Provisional Governor reiterated the President's orders to avoid conflict with the Cuban people. The Army was to "exert every effort to manifest all the courtesy possible to Cubans of all parties." The soldiers must remain orderly and inconspicuous (a goodly assignment for so many red-blooded American boys) and responsive to the wishes of the Provisional Governor. Diplomacy and discipline were to be the watchwords; there would be no repetition of the rowdiness which enflamed the Filipinos. As the troops fanned out along the island, General Bell personally visited each post to lecture his officers and men on "the peculiar circumstances of their service." His indoctrination program was swift and effective.[6]

Bell had had his doubts in September about the Army's role in any intervention, but Taft made clear that the Army of Cuban Pacification would be under the orders of the Provisional Governor and, through him, responsible to the administration in Washington.[7] The civil authority, as in the United States, would dictate policy for the Cuban bureaucracy and the Army alike.

Roosevelt's goal, the creation of a new Cuban government by free elections, demanded that the island be rid of violence. Though the Army's presence was a positive factor in the Provisional Government's plans, the Army's mission, as defined for it, looked essentially passive. As defined by General Bell, however, the Army's role was seen as mediative as well as deterrent:

> Troops are . . . not expected to take part in an active way in the suppression of disorder unless an extreme emergency arises in which it is absolutely necessary for them to protect life and property. Their duties should be generally limited to tendering their good offices in preventing friction between conflicting elements. Their presence in a community should create such a sense of security that the Rural Guards and local police should be able to suppress disorders. To this end all officers and enlisted men of this command will exert every effort to manifest all the courtesy possible to Cubans of all parties. They will particularly avoid taking sides with any party or faction.[8]

The Army high command in Cuba recognized that much of its influence depended on the troops' good behavior and its own responsiveness to the needs of the Provisional Government. Yet its own definition of "moral force" (at least that of its commanding general) was more than the naked threat of armed power. Pacification, in the Army's experience, was to a degree a process of assuming moral leadership. The presence of large numbers of Americans made this inevitable. The Army, which "though small in numbers . . . has nevertheless shown itself everywhere and has quietly covered every nook and corner of the entire island," could serve by its example as a representative American institution.[9] This aspect of the occupation was explicit in General Barry's message of June 26, 1907. Congratulating his men on their "self-restraint, good judgement, sound discretion, and intelligent appreciation of the purposes of our government," Barry pointed out that the Army of Cuban Pacification had an obligation that transcended its use as guarantor of peace:

> The duty of the Army here, as elsewhere, is to give effect to the policies of our Government, and if, in carrying out such policies, the principles of liberty, independence, and self government, as set forth in "The Declaration of Independence" and exemplified in that national life of our country, are so demonstrated, it is believed that one of the essential objects of our presence here will have been accomplished.[10]

Such a high call to duty was part of the Army's tradition, earlier applied in the Philippines and Cuba, and it is likely that General Barry's sentiments were shared by his fellow officers. One, Lieutenant Colonel Robert L. Bullard, writing in the *Journal of the Military Service Institution*, stated that the Army was playing a positive role in the regeneration of the Cuban people by its moral example.[11]

Many officers in the important staff and command positions of the Army of Cuban Pacification had had ample experience in military government in Cuba and the Philippines. Ten principal staff officers and regimental commanders had Philippine service behind them; three others had played important roles in the Military Government of Cuba. Colonel William Pitcher, Twenty-seventh Infantry, for example, bore the sobriquet "Ten Dollars or Ten Days" Pitcher from his tour as Havana chief of police and police judge. Although the influence of Leonard Wood's protégés was greater in the Provisional Government than in the Army of Cuban Pacification, several officers had served with him in Cuba and the Philippines. It seems likely that the Army's leadership shared Bullard's view that the Army's position could not be neutral on questions of public order, justice, and tranquillity.

Whatever the views of its officers on the nature and aims of the occupation, the Army of Cuban Pacification was essential in reducing political unrest and public insecurity.[12] Throughout the twenty-eight months of the occupation, the Army of Cuban Pacification carried out a program for preventing insurgency. The major phases of pacification were: (1) the physical occupation of Cuba's population centers and communications network; (2) the use of practice marches to intimidate the rural population; (3) the establishment of a nationwide network to collect, analyze, and distribute military and political intelligence; (4) the preparation of a detailed topographic map to aid future counter-guerilla/bandit operations; and (5) active participation in a road-building program. In all these activities the Army of Cuban Pacification was successful enough to establish the surface tranquillity

Sugar Mills, 1907

Pinar del Rio—6

Havana—22

Matanzas—57

Santa Clara—76

Camaguey—6

Oriente—30

Sugar Mills •

ACP Garrisons ☆

MAP 2.—MAJOR SUGAR MILLS AND ARMY OF CUBAN PACIFICATION GARRISONS, 1907

the Provisional Government required to accomplish its political objectives.

The geographic pattern of the garrisons established by the Army of Cuban Pacification provides insight into the military aspects of the occupation and the political and economic requirements of American policy. Throughout October, 1906, the Marines and the first Army units to arrive were dispatched to places where large numbers of rebels and militia were being disarmed or where foreign owned sugar *centrales* were endangered. Subsequently some of these units, mostly Marine and infantry companies, were transferred. By November, with the complete assembly of the American troops, a basic pattern for Cuba's physical occupation emerged.[13]

The Army of Cuban Pacification was deployed geographically to occupy the major population centers judged to be politically restless, to control Cuba's rail and coastal shipping system, and to protect the island's economic wealth, particularly the sugar business. The troops' supply requirements and the possibility of active field operations also influenced the occupation. Garrisons were placed in twelve of the fourteen Cuban cities with populations over ten thousand. Of the Army's remaining fifteen posts (of a total of twenty-seven with an additional Marine company on the Isle of Pines) six more were in towns of five thousand or more.[14] Seven posts were established near *centrales* in Santa Clara province. The remaining two posts were at Ciego de Avila in Camaguey (site of the Stuart Sugar Company) and at Neuvitas, a small Camagueyan port.

The garrisons also controlled Cuba's transportation system by occupying a line that approximately bisected the country along its railroad nets, running west to east: Pinar del Rio, Guanajay, Guines, Santa Clara, Placetas, Sancti Spiritus, Ciego de Avila, Camaguey, Holguín, Santiago de Cuba. The Havana area was controlled from Camp Columbia, the Army's headquarters and largest garrison. Occupied coastal towns were (in addition to Havana and Santiago) Cienfuegos, Matanzas, Trinidad, Caibarién, Manzanillo, Cárdenas, Neuvitas, and Baracoa.

Another of the multiple factors which influenced the physical occupation was the geographical origins of the August Revolution. A province-by-province breakdown (by troop strength and number of posts) reveals that of the three most rebellious provinces (Pinar del Rio, Havana, and Santa Clara), Santa Clara represented the Army of Cuban Pacification's major provincial investment. There was both a political and economic reason for this pattern. In area Santa Clara was as large as both Pinar del Rio and Havana, about 8,300 square miles. The four garrisons in Pinar del Rio and Havana (Pinar del Rio, Guanajay, Guines, Camp Columbia) could adequately perform their jobs because of the area's good railroad net. In Santa Clara, the Army of Cuban Pacification high command placed fourteen posts, manned by four Army battalions and five companies of Marines. Discounting headquarters, artillery, and service troops at the Army headquarters, the number of combat units in Santa Clara equalled those in Pinar del Rio and Havana together. A major reason for this troop concentration in Santa Clara is that it was the territorial base of José Miguel Gómez and his most ardent Liberal supporters, who were particularly numerous and violence-prone in the Cienfuegos area. A politico-economic explanation for the large number of posts is obvious upon examining the Military Information Division's 1907 map of Cuban sugar mills: Santa Clara was the site of the greatest concentration of sugar mills, many foreign-owned. As an epilogue to the August Revolution, the *centrales* "Constancia" and E. F. Atkins' "Soledad" got a troop of cavalry each.

The possibility of active operations in Cuba dictated the types of units occupying the Cuban posts. The provinces torn by rebellion in 1906 were garrisoned by the Army's four cavalry squadrons with infantry support. All battalion-squadron posts had pack trains. This organization provided for both mobile operations and base security. The Army of Cuban Pacification headquarters kept a reserve of combined arms (infantry, Marines, cavalry, artillery, and support troops) concentrated at Camp Columbia near Havana. This force, centered in the troubled western provinces, had good railroad and water connections with most of the island's population and agricultural centers.

Before passing from the manner in which the Army of Cuban Pacification established its posts, it must be noted that however inconspicuous the soldiers were supposed to be, they were generally garrisoned inside each city proper (except in Havana), often in the old Spanish barracks.

The Army of Cuban Pacification used practice marches by its scattered units to impress the *campesinos* with the potential of American arms. Each garrison commander was ordered to keep at least one column constantly on the move about the countryside.[15] The explicit purpose of the marches was to demonstrate "to the lawless that order must be maintained and to assure the people that they will be protected from robbery and disturbances."[16] Acknowledging his commanders' complaints that the burden of the marches on men, animals, and equipment was becoming intolerable, General Barry, in the spring of 1907, modified the march orders. March schedules were reduced to allow more time for garrison duties, marksmanship, and field exercises. The number of marches was decreased, but their duration was increased up to three weeks.

When the marches began there was some fear in the United States, reflecting widespread misconceptions about climate and human physiology, that too rigorous exercise would exhaust the soldiers' "store of power," the danger to the white man in the tropics. A *New York Times* editorial gently criticized the Army for believing men could become acclimatized, warning against "native foods" and too much labor in the sun.[17] The marches, however, did not bring the Army to physical ruin. To dramatize his men's hardiness, General Barry ordered two troops of the Eleventh Cavalry to make a forced march back to their post from maneuvers near Havana in April, 1908. The force, in close order and full equipment, rode 110 miles in thirty hours without losing a trooper or mount.

The practice marches continued until the end of the occupation. In 1908, the Army made ninety-two marches covering 5,300 miles. During October and November, at the height of the rainy season, the Army had all its units out on two consecutive twenty-one day hikes with all animals, guns, and transport. Under the existing weather conditions " . . . the natives believed it impossible to carry on operations," but the soldiers negotiated the sticky roads and swollen streams " . . in such a manner as to amaze the populace." [18]

The Army of Cuban Pacification had brains as well as feet, and it put great emphasis on creating a nationwide intelligence system. Even before the occupation was underway, General Bell tried to collect information by asking the Disarmament Committee to compile complete rolls of all the insurgents to incude names, homes, physical descriptions, and types and numbers of arms. This intelligence, Bell stressed, "may prove of extreme value." [19] Recognizing the importance of an effective intelligence program to the pacification of Cuba, Bell sent two officers (Major D. D. Gaillard and Captain John W. Furlong) of the General Staff's Military Information Division to Havana. Based at Marianao, Gaillard and Furlong were assisted by Captain Dwight E. Aultman, a Wood veteran who spoke fluent Spanish and who had visited Cuba in early September. These officers were functioning as the Army of Cuban Pacification's Military Information Division by October 11.

The Military Information Division organized the country into twenty-six intelligence districts, coinciding with the garrisons outside Havana.[20] With the exception of the numerous Santa Clara stations, whose officers reported to a provincial supervisor, Major William D. Beach, each district had an intelligence officer to collect and forward information to Havana. Throughout the occupation, the Military Information Division supervised mapping, compiled an extensive file of photos and personality sketches, and wrote extensive descriptions of the terrain, towns, and communications system.[21] It employed Cuban agents and spent liberally (more than $1000 monthly) for information. Its original allowance, provided from the War Department's Emergency Fund (created by

Congress in 1899), was $20,000. During the Second Intervention, the Military Information Division provided the Provisional Governor with much of the political intelligence he received, and, as his files show, he relied heavily upon its analysis of Cuban political developments.[22]

Among the methods used to maintain peace in Cuba, the Army attached great importance to mapping the island. General Bell regarded the mapping as absolutely essential to the pacification operations and began the work in October, 1906.[23] Although the Military Government had started mapping Cuba in 1899, it had not finished the task. The Spanish maps were inaccurate; only the railroad surveys were dependable. Because of such difficulties, General Bell asked for and got an additional engineer battalion (the Third) which arrived in February, 1907. The Army's Chief Engineer supervised the work (assisted by the Military Information Division) and fully employed his men, but more than half the mapping was done by line units. Reconnaissance parties (one officer, four to seven enlisted men) did the leg work, sketching all topographic features.[24] The sketches were rough and emphasized roads, trails, old Spanish fortifications, and landmarks. The completed map, finished in the spring of 1907, was detailed beyond complete belief. The master copy is composed of seventy sheets, each sheet 32 by 35 inches. Reproduced for field use, the map was distributed to the troops in 1908, and corrections were continuously made. If even close to accurate, the map would have been an invaluable aid in military operations.[25]

The reconnaisance parties were seen throughout Cuba and the result of their work was publicized to reassure some and discourage others. One officer wrote General Bell that the map was good, a vast improvement on the Spanish maps. The officer admitted the map had errors, but through personal use he had found it basically accurate.[26] A New York *Sun* dispatch praised the map as crucial in preventing or defeating revolts. Refuting claims that Cubans could still go into the hills and confound American troops, the *Sun* retorted:

The Americans have mapped the country thoroughly—every hill, ravine, swamp, thicket, watercourse and trail. Cuba has no topographical secrets for the General Staff; it knows the island better than all the *practicos,* or guides, in existence, and there is no maze an American officer with a map in his pocket could not thread, no camp he could not find.[27]

Lieutenant Colonel Bullard, in an interview, emphasized the map's deterrent value. The Army's exploration of the island, he said, had impressed the Cubans and they now realized that the soldiers knew the countryside better than they. Bullard concluded that "if the Army can but get past the term of pacification without firing one hostile shot. it is probable that we shall thereby have already accomplished the conquest of future revolution."[28]

The mission of the Second Battalion of Engineers when it was assigned to the Cuban expeditionary force was to handle map making and, in case of hostilities, provide engineer support for the Army of Cuban Pacification. At the Provisional Governor's request, the engineers became involved in building roads. General Bell originally sold the road-building program to the Chief of Engineers as a military necessity, but this argument was secondary to providing jobs for the unemployed during the rainy season and to open markets to Cuban farmers.[29] The engineers worked on four roads in western Pinar del Rio which were to link the towns of Guane and Pinar del Rio with the lines of the Western Railway and the coast. The Corps of Engineers, not accepting the military rationale for these public works projects, withdrew five companies of engineers after the mapping was finished. Nevertheless, by the end of 1908, Army engineers had graded ninety-two kilometers of new road and macadamized sixty-nine, at a cost of $1.6 million. Much of the expense, reported the Army of Cuban Pacification's Chief Engineer, Major Mason M. Patrick, was due to working in the rainy season and the high wages paid native labor.[30] The engineers' contribution to the Provisional Government's road-building program, however, represented a fraction of the total effort of construction.

## The Army and Cuban Policy

In reviewing the several phases of the Army's pacification program, it is clear that the internal security that the Army of Cuban Pacification maintained was essential to American goals in Cuba and gave the Army commander and his subordinates an important voice in the execution of American policy. There is no significant evidence that the Army abrogated a major political role to itself during the occupation, but because its officers, in both the Army of Cuban Pacification and the Provisional Government, shared common experiences and values, it had a cohesiveness of opinion and certainty of judgment that influenced the Provisional Governor's political program.

On the whole, the officers of the United States Army serving in Cuba believed that the longer and stronger the American influence over Cuban affairs, the better the island's chances for peace and prosperity. Reduced to the simplest ideological terms, the officers believed that race and tradition rendered the Cubans unfit for self-government until they learned American ways: individual moral responsibility, private enterprise in economic matters, fair play in all private and public associations, truthfulness, tolerance for others and discipline for one's self, and obedience to the law and to the constituted government. In terms of Cuban politics, the officers, according to Lieutenant Colonel Bullard, were sympathetic to the old Moderates. This attitude was rooted in the revulsion the Americans felt toward rebellion of any kind; the officers, however, generally refrained from direct intervention into local matters.[31]

There is evidence of frustration and ambivalence in the officers' reaction to the eccentricities of Cuban life. Around them they saw poverty, ignorance, sickness, and purposelessness spawning the disorder they were supposed to prevent. Describing a fight between American soldiers and some Rural Guards in front of a house of prostitution, one regimental commander drew a sharp picture of Cuban life:

> The occurrences in themselves between Rural Guards and soldiers have been of little importance and were it not for the attitude of the hoodlum and vagrant element who congregate in and around houses of ill-fame, cantinas and cafes, always armed with knives and generally with revolvers and who are against constituted government in any form and who urged on the recruit rural guards by taunts of cowardice and vile epithets to engage in combat with American soldiers, the slight ill feeling engendered would have promptly died out. . . . In any communities [sic] of the Island if a man stubs his toe or a dog fight occurs the majority of the population, men, women and children, especially the vagrant class, flock to the scene, blocking the way, talking, gesticulating and producing veritable pandemonium.[32]

More discouraging to the officers than the irresponsibility of the poor Cubans and their demagogic leaders was the attitude of the well-to-do. Although the Cuban people were unfit to manage a stable government, Major Francis J. Kernan wrote, "this does not mean that there are not honest and able men in Cuba." It did, however, mean that propertied Cubans as a class held themselves absolutely aloof from governmental service and political parties. They were "as unavailable to lend character to the Cuban government as if they dwelt in China." Cuba had two alternatives, armed autocracy or American tutelage, Major Kernan concluded, and "we might as well count on Cuba as a field for tropical service indefinitely."[33]

The administration's policy of playing down the Army's role in the occupation apparently worried the officers, for such a decision deprived them of the authority they had enjoyed under General Wood's government, and they believed it hurt their status in Cuban eyes. The *Army and Navy Journal* reported that the officers feared that the Cubans did not believe the soldiers would fight to keep order.[34] Another observer, however, believed that the common people "desired no further trouble with the Americans whom they consider 'merciless,' and that war with the American forces would be one of extermination and absolutely fatal to Cuba."[35] In any case, the Army's inclination was to draw out the occupation as long as possible, hoping that the "better elements" could be persuaded to enter politics; those Cubans now interested in politics, Army officers in Havana told junketing Republican congressmen, were unfit to manage public affairs.[36] Still the American goal was only to find honest leaders, insure republican government, and keep peace so that Cuba might prosper. As one colonel put it:

Every year that passes by brings new prosperity to Cuba. Cuba is for the One Hundred Millions Americans [*sic*] a wonderful, beautiful and charming country which lies at its door. She is the sleeping beauty waitting [*sic*] the kiss of love. . . . It will not be many years before Cuba will be the delight, the paradise of the western hemisphere. Once the Cubans are rich, prosperous and happy they will forget talking conspiracy.[37]

Havana's English-language press seized upon the Army's malaise to agitate for continued occupation and to threaten potential rebels. The newspapers told their readers that the Army of Cuban Pacification chafed for action. The *Havana Post* declared that the soldiers ("who have not had the scent of blood since a year ago") would welcome a fight; revolution in such an atmosphere was foolhardy.[38] The *Havana Daily Telegraph*, mourning the eventual withdrawal of the American troops, urged them to stay on, for "revolution is racial in Cuba and it will take several generations to bring the people to the point where they can govern themselves."[39]

The Army's stay in Cuba, including its relations with the Cuban people, was more than an experience in alienation and disgust. First the soldiers had some physical discomforts to surmount. The major inconvenience was the hurricane of October 18, 1906. Sweeping out of the Gulf of Mexico (where it had already pounded Biloxi and Pensacola), the storm devastated the western end of Cuba. For forty-eight hours, Havana was a slice of the Inferno—trees ripping from the ground, live wires sparking in the sheets of rain, roof tiles winging down flooded streets. Down came Camp Columbia's tent city; down came the Havana telephone and power lines; and partially down went two transports in the harbor, drowning two hundred Army mounts. For Cuba the hurricane was as great an economic disaster as the August Revolution, but the Army of Cuban Pacification quickly repitched its shelters, restacked its supplies and went on with the occupation.

By December, 1906, the Army headquarters staff was caught in the business-as-usual problems of military administration. The Judge-Advocate juggled court-martial percentages to prove that Marines were more unruly than soldiers; the Chief Quartermaster worried about the semi-monthly supply ship from Newport News and the distribution of $200,000 in stationery and blank forms (triplicate). The Chief Commissary struggled to find refrigeration for the frozen beef sent from the United States (cost: nine cents a pound), hoping that the price of Cuban beef would drop. The Medical Department dealt with periodic yellow fever scares and fought the more immediately dangerous typhoid. As a medical commentary on Cuban-American relations, it should be noted that medics treated nearly 10 per cent of the command for assorted venereal diseases, which had a higher incidence than diarrhea-dysentery. In January, 1907, company venereal disease inspections began on a weekly basis.[40] Then, having interfered with one off-duty diversion, the Army acted further to protect the troops' health:

Respectfully referred to the Commanding General, Army of Cuban Pacification, with the information that the views of the Surgeon General are concurred in by the Acting Secretary of War, who directs that the sale of Coca-Cola by the post exchange be discontinued.[41]

At Camp Columbia the occupation had a style rare in the other garrisons. There the men were comfortably quartered, well fed, given excellent medical attention, and barred from many of the Havana fleshpots. The officers could join the American Club of Havana as non-dues-paying members and officers' families could have hotel accommodations and fares

at half-price, courtesy of the Cuban railways. Summer recrea-
tion at Camp Columbia, announced General Barry, included
polo, boating, and bathing.[42] And then there was the great
Cuban Olympiad of June 29–July 4, 1908. Involving 1,300
participants and designed to impress the Cuban spectators,
the Army held games "to develop the resourceful brain, the
accurate eye, and the spirit of courage." The athletic and
military competitions, in General Barry's perishable prose,
were a great success:

> On the green-clad parade, rising high above the blue waters of the
> gulf and swept by breezes, with all the colors of the different arms of
> the service blowing from the brawny breasts of the soldier-athletes, the
> scenes and events of this first Olympiad of Cuba formed a brilliant
> background for its distinguishing spirit of achievement and good will.[43]

The Cubans' reactions were not reported.

In the provinces, occupation duty was hot, monotonous
and hard.[44] In addition to the practice marches, the soldiers
had to bear the normal garrison instruction, inspections,
equipment upkeep, and police of buildings. Finding pure
water was a continuing problem. The rations were dull, as
usual, and not so good, the Marines griped, as the chow fur-
nished by the Navy. Social contacts in the occupied community were generally limited to other Americans, hucksters,
and the skin-traders. An inspecting officer left this description
of Ciego de Avila, the worst of the battalion posts:

> The town . . . is the most unattractive station for troops that I have
> yet seen. The streets are dirty and unpaved, and in the whole town there
> are but three buildings with a second story to them, and they are
> small. The hotel is vile and dirty. . . . There are no means of enter-
> tainment or diversion. The result of this condition is evidenced among
> the men by the fact that at my inspection, there were fourteen prisoners
> in the guardhouse, many of them on account of over-indulgence in
> liquor.[45]

However routine the occupation became for the American
troops, their presence contributed to the economic welfare
of the communities which housed them and incidentally con-

tributed to the island's pacification. The funds spent locally by the Army came from two sources, individual pay and goods and services purchased by the garrisons. In the twenty-eight months of the occupation, paymasters counted out some $4 million in pay to bored and thirsty soldiers, and it is fair to guess that much of this money ended in Cuban hands. Secondly, the Provisional Government paid for a host of items out of the revenues of the Cuban Treasury: rent for quarters and property, maintenance and repairs, water, sewage disposal, construction materials and labor, and sanitation services. Total disbursements for these items was $850,000. When local prices permitted, in addition, the Chief Commissary authorized the purchase of ice, beef, forage, and perishable foods by individual posts. The Chief Quartermaster, too, spent $4 million during the occupation, much of it in Havana.[46] In fact, James L. Rodgers, Steinhart's successor as Consul-General, reported that American spending supported the Cuban economy through a world recession in 1907 and a glutted sugar market in 1908; Rodgers specifically mentioned the local impact of Army funds for spreading the prosperity throughout the population.[47] Though the expenditures of the Army represented only a fraction of the sums spent by the Provisional Government to bolster the Cuban economy, they made, nonetheless, a substantial contribution to the stability the Army was assigned to maintain.

The Army of Cuban Pacification's influence on American policy in Cuba was based on its military responsibilities on the island and the attitudes of its officers. Though it remained responsive and obedient to civil direction, the Army, by counseling caution and by stressing the political unrest its intelligence officers reported, contributed to the progressive lengthening of the occupation. The Army's sympathies and rational preferences were to expand American control of Cuban affairs. Though its political orientation by implication favored the alien business class, the Army was not as committed to economic imperialism as it was to benign paternalism. It was most interested in improving education and public health, in curbing social and political exploitation of the common people, and in eliminating violence.

However favorably disposed it might have been to increasing American influence in Cuba, the Army did not take the part of the annexationists. Indeed, its own institutional self-interest demanded that it halt any political agitation which might lead to rebellion. Cuban problems might come and go, but the Presidency and the Congress went on forever, and another war of pacification on the Philippine model could hardly be to the Army's advantage. There was more to this consideration than political expediency, for the Army regarded the new extracontinental possessions as strategic aberrations. There were plenty of big-power competitors to worry Army planners and too few forces to squander on more unpleasant campaigns in the Indies and Pacific isles.

The Army's own inherent value system committed it to law and order in Cuba just as surely as its belief in disciplined democracy made further tutelage attractive. In reading the Military Information Division's reports, one cannot help seeing that violence and anarchy for whatever purpose (and however inconsequential) horrified the American officers. The irony of the Cuban situation was that only another general insurrection between 1906 and 1909 would have given Roosevelt the justification to establish a clear-cut protectorate over Cuba. The Army of Cuban Pacification, which best recognized the long-range benefits that complete American political control of Cuba could bring the common people, saw to it that such a revolt never occurred.

1. The original task organization is given in a memorandum from the Office of the Chief of Staff, September 22, 1906, Doc. File 1168303, FG 94. Subsequent modifications were the substitution of Company I for Company B, Signal Corps, and the addition of two Hospital Corps companies, one of which returned to the United States at the end of November. "Report of the Adjutant General," U.S. War Department, *Annual Reports, 1906–1907*, I, 207–11.

2. Brig. Gen. J. F. Bell to Col. H. L. Scott, October 1, 1906, Doc. File 1169753, RG 94.

3. *Army and Navy Journal,* October 13, 1906; Maj. Gen. Otto L. Nelson, Jr., *National Security and the General Staff* (Washington, 1946), pp. 101–2.

4. "Record of Events," a hand-written chronology appended to "Return of the Army of Cuban Pacification, October, 1906," in *Inspection Reports, Department of Cuba and Cuban Posts, 1903–1912,* Records of the Office of the Inspector General, U.S. Army, National Archives, Record Group 159. Hereafter cited as RG 159.

Also Maj. T. H. Slavens, QM, USA, "Report of the Embarkation of the Expedition for Cuban Intervention from Newport News, Va. between the dates of September 29, 1906 and October 19, 1906," Doc. File 1219504, RG 94; Maj. W. A. Mann to Military Secretary, ACP, November 16, 1906, and Maj. C. B. Baker to Brig. Gen. J. F. Bell, November 19, 1906, in "Collation of Reports of Various Staff Officers with Expedition of the Army of Cuban Pacification," Appendix 6 to Army War College Serial 11, "Cuba," AWC Doc. File, RG 165.

The staff officers' major suggestion was politically obtuse: that in case of future expeditions advance parties be sent ahead to prepare for the troops' arrival.

5. Roosevelt to Taft, October 2, 1906, Taft-Bacon *Report,* p. 487.

6. Circular No. 1, October 12, 1906, *Cuba: General Orders, Circulars, and Special Orders, Headquarters, First Expeditionary Brigade . . . 1906,* RG 350; Magoon, *Report, 1906–1907,* p. 86.

In dealing with the Cubans, Bell found "my Philippine experience very valuable." Bell to Taft, November 16, 1906, Taft Papers.

7. Bell to Maj. E. F. Ladd, September 25, 1906, Doc. File 1170541, RG 94.

8. General Order No. 17, November 3, 1906, *Cuba: . . . General Orders, Circulars and Special Orders, Headquarters, Army of Cuban Pacification, 1906,* RG 350.

9. "Report Army of Cuban Pacification," U.S. War Department, *Annual Reports, 1906–1907,* III, 314.

10. General Order No. 84, January 26, 1907, *Cuba: General Orders, Special Orders and Circulars, Headquarters, Army of Cuban Pacification, 1907–1909,* RG 350.

11. "Cubans" and "The Army in Cuba," manuscripts in the Bullard Papers. The latter was printed in the *Journal of the Military Service Institution,* XLI (September, 1907), 152–57. Colonel Bullard served as Magoon's personal agent, traveled throughout the island, and was close to the political scene.

12. Memorandum, Chief of Staff, ACP, to Commanding General, ACP, October 24, 1906, Case 244/341–349, *Num. File, 1906–1910,* Vol. XXXVII, RG 59; G. W. E. Griffith, British Minister to Cuba, to Sir Edward Grey, January 11, 1907, FO 371–242, PRO.

13. In this statistical and geographic-strategic analysis the author used the following materials: The General Cartographic Records of the Army of Cuban Pacification and the map records of the Military Information Division, Army of Cuban Pacification, both collections in the Carto-

graphic Branch, NA, particularly maps of Cuba showing the railroad and steamship connections and the garrisons of the ACP and a map showing the sugar mills of Cuba, indicating ownership and location (1907); Gannett and Olmstead, *Cuba: Population, History, and Resources, 1907,* pp. 233–34; "Report Army of Cuban Pacification," U.S. War Department, *Annual Reports, 1906–1907,* III, 313–58; "Roster and Directory: United States Troops Comprising the Army of Cuban Pacification," in *Inspection Reports, Department of Cuba and Cuban Posts, 1903–1912,* RG 159.

14. Cities garrisoned were Havana, Santiago, Pinar del Rio, Cárdenas, Santa Clara, Camaguey, Cienfuegos, Manzanillo, Sancti Spiritus, Trinidad, Sagua la Grande and Matanzas. Posts in towns of more than 5000 were located in Guines, Holguín, Placetas, Caibarién, Baracoa, and Guanajay. In these cities, thirteen of the posts were of battalion size, representing the bulk of the ACP's strength.

15. General Order No. 24, November 15, 1906, *Cuba: . . . General Orders, Circulars and Special Orders, Headquarters, Army of Cuban Pacification, 1906,* RG 350.

16. E. V. Morgan, Minister to Cuba, to Root, November 6, 1906, Caso 1852/31, *Num. File, 1906–1910,* Vol. CCI, RG 59.

17. *New York Times,* November 14, 1906.

18. "Report of the Army of Cuban Pacification," U.S. War Department, *Annual Reports, 1908–1909* (Washington, 1909), III, 242–43.

19. Memo by the Chief of Staff and cable to Maj. E. F. Ladd, October 2, 1906, Doc. File 1169916, RG 94.

20. Maj. D. D. Gaillard to Col. R. D. Potts, Chief, Military Information Division, Nov. (?), 1906, AWC Doc. File 1452, RG 165.

Maj. D. D. Gaillard to Military Secretary, ACP, October 26, 1906, Appendix 6 to Army War College Serial 11, "Cuba," AWC Doc. File, 165.

21. A sanitized edition of Captain Furlong's study of Cuba was published as *Military Notes on Cuba, 1909* (Washington, 1909). This War Department publication omits all of Furlong's analysis of guerrilla warfare and Cuban political behavior. His original manuscript is in AWC Doc. File 4352, RG 165. Another book put together by the MID, ACP, was *Road Notes, Cuba . . . 1909* (Washington, 1909).

22. For examples, see Files 013 (political affairs in Matanzas), 014 (political affairs in Santa Clara), 031 (political conditions in Caibarien), 040 (investigation of political conditions), 096 (conditions in Pinar del Rio), CC/PGoC, RG 199.

23. Bell to the Military Secretary, October 15, 1906, Doc. File 1175353, RG 94.

24. General Order No. 28, November 23, 1906, *Cuba: . . . General Orders, Circulars and Special Orders, Headquarters, Army of Cuban Pacification, 1906.* RG 350; "Report Army of Cuban Pacification," U.S. War Department, *Annual Reports, 1906–1907,* III, 336.

25. The author has examined the map and sample sketches in the Cartographic Branch of the National Archives.

26. *Army and Navy Journal*, May 4, 1907.

27. Reprinted in the *Army and Navy Journal*, May 25, 1907.

28. *Army and Navy Journal*, September 7, 1907.

29. Magoon to Brig. Gen. Clarence R. Edwards, Chief, Bureau of Insular Affairs, June 24, 1907, File 134–1, CC/PGoC, RG 199.

30. "Report Army of Cuban Pacification," U.S. War Department, *Annual Reports, 1907–1908*, III, 315–16; Lt. Col. Mason M. Patrick, "Notes on Road Building in Cuba," *Professional Memoirs*, II (July–September, 1910), 263–84.

31. Bullard notebooks, entry for March 22, 1907, Bullard Papers. *Cf.* Bullard, "The Army in Cuba," *passim.* Here Bullard states: "Let the American people take note that to the core their army is loyalist and everywhere hates the name of rebel and insurgent."

32. Report of Col. E. D. Thomas, Eleventh Cavalry, March 25, 1907, File 096, CC/PGoC, RG 199.
Major (politically significant) incidents of violence between Americans and Cubans were limited to a fight between Cuban police and a liberty party from the cruiser "Tacoma" in Santiago on July 30, 1907, and the killing of two Cuban boatmen by three American soldiers near Coloma (Pinar del Rio) in March, 1908. In the latter case, a court-martial acquitted the accused, which outraged Cuban editorial opinion. Magoon disapproved the court's findings, but the ACP discharged the men administratively rather than retry them. On the whole, though there were numerous minor incidents, American troop behavior was good.

33. *Army and Navy Journal*, August 17, 1907.

34. *Army and Navy Journal*, July 13, 1907.

35. Lt. Cmdr. C. D. Stearns, USN, CO, USNS, Guantanamo Bay, to the Assistant Secretary of the Navy, August 9, 1907, File 146–12, CC/PGoC, RG 199.

36. J. Hampton Moore, *With Speaker Cannon through the Tropics* (Philadelphia, 1907), p. 325.

37. *El Liberal* (Havana), September 28, 1907, quoting Col. James Parker, File 096–23, CC/PGoC, RG 199.

38. *Havana Post*, quoted in the *Army and Navy Journal*, October 5, 1908. The reference is to the Masso Parra conspiracy in 1907.

39. *Havana Daily Telegraph*, July 31, 1908.

40. "Report Army of Cuban Pacification," U.S. War Department, *Annual Reports, 1906–1907*, III, 326–33.

41. Circular No. 38, June 18, 1907, *Cuba: General Orders, Special Orders and Circulars, Headquarters, Army of Cuban Pacification, 1907–1909*, RG 350, NA. The order was revoked in November, 1907, as a result, no doubt, of irresistible political pressure and public demand.

42. *Army and Navy Journal*, November 24 and December 1, 1906, and April 27, 1907.

43. General Order No. 153, July 5, 1908, *Cuba: General Orders, Special Orders and Circulars, Headquarters, Army of Cuban Pacification, 1907–1909*, RG 350. "Report Army of Cuban Pacification," U.S. War De-

partment, *Annual Reports, 1907–1908*, III, 325–26; *Army and Navy Journal*, July 18, 1908.

44. The best picture of the occupation duty in Cuba is contained in the reports of Maj. Charles G. Treat, Inspector General, ACP, found in *Inspection Reports, Department of Cuba and Cuban Posts, 1903–1912*, RG 159.

45. Maj. Charles G. Treat to the Military Secretary, ACP, February 6, 1907, "Report of Inspection Post at Ciego de Avila," Doc. File 401–22, RG 94.

46. "Report of Chief of Bureau of Insular Affairs," U.S. War Department, *Annual Reports, 1908–1909*, VII, pp. 26–27. In all, the "extraordinary expenses" of the intervention to the War Department were $6.5 million.

47. James L. Rodgers, "Report on the Commerce and Industries of the Republic of Cuba for the Calendar Year of 1908," No. 202, *Dispatches*, U.S. Consul General, Havana, 1909, General Records of the Department of State, Record Group 59, National Archives, RG 59.

# CHAPTER FIVE

# THE POLITICS OF THE CUBAN OCCUPATION

THE ESTABLISHMENT of an American army and government in Cuba reopened the whole problem of Cuban-American relations. Roosevelt insisted publicly that American intervention had occurred through the acts of Cubans, especially the Estrada Palma administration; the goal of the intervention was simply to restore representative government in Cuba, for there had been no basic alteration of the Cuban-American relationship outlined in the Platt Amendment. Roosevelt introduced this view of view in his open letter to Gonzalo de Quesada, and it was repeated by Taft in the proclamation which established the Provisional Government on September 29:

> The provisional government . . . will be maintained only long enough to restore order and peace and public confidence, and then hold elections as may be necessary to determine those persons upon whom the permanent Government of the Republic should be devolved.[1]

Roosevelt spelled out the purpose of the intervention and the goal of the occupation in his sixth annual message to Congress, December 3, 1906. He took this opportunity to reassure Americans that the intervention was not an administration-inspired act to annex Cuba, nor was it solely to protect foreign investments. His discussion of the Cuban situation ended with a warning to the Cubans that they could not indefinitely count on the United States to referee their political squabbles without risking permanent occupation. In the first objective of his statement, to silence domestic criticism of the intervention, Roosevelt was successful. His good intentions seemed clear enough: the Provisional Government would only " . . . administer the island for a few months" until there was enough peace to hold an election and form a new Cuban government. His sermon to the Cubans, the veiled threat to act "right" or else, left the weaknesses in Cuba's political system still unfaced:

> The United States wishes nothing of Cuba except that it shall prosper morally and materially, and wishes nothing of the Cubans save that they shall be able to preserve order among themselves and therefore to preserve their independence. If the elections become a farce, and if the insurrectionary habit becomes confirmed in the Island, it is absolutely out of the question that the Island should continue independent; and the United States, which has assumed sponsorship before the civilized world for Cuba's career as a nation, would again have to intervene and to see that the government was managed in such orderly fashion as to secure the safety of life and property.
>
> The path to be trodden by those who exercise self government is always hard, and we should have every charity and patience with the Cubans as they tread this difficult path. I have the utmost sympathy with, and regard for, them; but I most earnestly adjure them solemnly to weigh their responsibilities and to see that when their new government is started it shall run smoothly and with freedom from flagrant denial of right on the one hand, and from insurrectionary disturbances on the other.[2]

Privately, Roosevelt weighed the ramification of the new intervention, his promise to sponsor a new Cuban government, and whether such a course held any real hope for Cuban stability. He remained concerned about the possible reaction of American voters to any other policy but the announced one, and he believed that his administration had barely escaped major criticism for the intervention itself. His attentions in the fall of 1906, too, were on more important subjects: the Congressional elections, the gubernatorial race in New York, his forthcoming trip to Panama, The Hague Conference, the Algeciras negotiations, and tensions with Japan. In the moments when he considered the Cuban problem, he found that he still had lingering doubts about Cuban independence. He concluded that one more revolt in Cuba would force a more permanent occupation.[3] Roosevelt, however, would not support a policy of acquisition under the circumstances of 1906–7:

> There can be no talk of a protectorate by us. Our business is to establish peace and order on a satisfactory basis, start the new government and then leave the island. . . . I will not even consider the plan of a protectorate. . . . The good faith of the United States is a mighty valuable asset and must not be impaired.[4]

Both Root and Taft shared Roosevelt's view that the Cuban government should be restored. Root, unhappy with the intervention's effect on the new American image he had cultivated in Latin America, opposed any acts by the Provisional Government that would antagonize the Cubans or prolong the occupation. Taft, more doubtful about the next Cuban government's chances for survival, nonetheless agreed with Roosevelt and Root that the primary objective of the occupation should be to reshape the Cuban electoral process. The component parts of this mild electoral reform were to give the Cuban municipalities more legal autonomy, establish laws which would insure honest elections run by non-partisan officials, create a civil service system which would protect government employees from dismissal on political grounds, and make the Cuban judiciary independent.[5] Taft was, nevertheless, skeptical about whether such American grafts on the Cuban body politic would flourish long; the Provisional Government faced "a very heavy task," he wrote his brother Charles. The situation in Cuba was appalling:

> . . . the bitterness of political rancor, the absence of patriotism and moral courage, the aloofness of the conservative and property holding classes, the peeping out of racial and class differences . . . the venality and corruption that permeates the municipal and central government so far as the legislature is concerned are calculated to make a man who seeks to set up self government feel as he is making bricks without straw.[6]

In Taft's opinion election frauds had caused the Cuban revolt. Elihu Root shared this assessment. The Secretary of State was in favor of doing no more during the occupation than tightening up the electoral laws and getting the economy going. Writing Leonard Wood, Root stressed the limited goal of the intervention: to make the minimum constitutional changes necessary to insure orderly elections. The problem, Root stated, was that the Cuban congress had not passed the laws necessary to execute the Constitution of 1901, laws which would provide for the peaceful transfer of political power through "a reasonably fair sort of election." The Cubans, of course, had forced the United States to intervene, but Americans must be patient with them. After weighing the alternatives, the United States realized that " . . . the only thing to do was to go in and set them up and give them another chance."[7]

In replying to a letter from James H. Wilson (who again advocated free trade as the way to stabilize Cuba), Root wrote that he had been trying to arrange a more favorable tariff for Cuba. From such a treaty, "I hope to get some material advance in the direction of greater freedom of reciprocal trade." Root had found Congress stubborn: without annexation there would be no free trade. Even a new tariff was unlikely. Root himself believed that annexation was out of the question, and unwise: "I think it is much better for Cuba to govern herself than it is for us to try to govern her. The sooner we can get them going again and get out, the better I shall be pleased."[8] To a wider audience Root emphasized his opposition to annexation. In a speech on January 14, 1907, to the National Convention for the Extension of the Foreign Commerce of the United States, the Secretary of State denied that annexation was the best policy for Cuba: "Never! So long as the people of Cuba do not themselves give up the effort to govern themselves."[9]

The Roosevelt administration stressed the temporary nature and the legality of the occupation. The official interpretation was that Cuban sovereignty was unimpaired because Article III made intervention part of Cuba's constitutional system. Root believed the Provisional Government was, therefore, the legitimate government of Cuba and should govern in accordance with Cuban organic law.[10] Following Root's reasoning, the *American Journal of International Law* concluded that "Cuba is in possession of its own government and is not occupied by the United States."[11] To heighten the illusion, Cuba carried on formal diplomatic relations (even with the United States) as a sovereign nation during the occupation, and the Cuban flag was flown. The administration, by such acts, pacified Congress as well as Cuba; in voting a supplemental appropriation for the Army of Cuban Pacification, the Senate hardly murmured.[12]

The Roosevelt administration had no intention of making the Provisional Government a political issue in the United States, either by antagonizing the Cubans to the point of revolt or by encouraging any Congressional debate on the temporary administration of the island. The Army of Cuban Pacification was crucial to the first problem, and the Provisional Government to both. Roosevelt, with Taft's and Root's concurrence, decided to use a civilian governor in Cuba, supervised by Taft through the Bureau of Insular Affairs. Analyzing Roosevelt's efforts to balance political control of the Provisional Government against Cuban sensitivity, the *Times* of London observed that "red tape is to be lavishly used in the attempt to bind the wound that Cuban independence has suffered."[13] Whatever Leonard Wood's virtues (or those of any other general), Roosevelt wanted a responsive civilian managing Cuban affairs, someone skilled in compromise and personal diplomacy, someone knowledgeable in Hispanic law and of unquestioned loyalty to the administration's goals, a man who understood the relationship of administration in Cuba to politics in the United States. Roosevelt's choice, at Root's suggestion, was Charles Edward Magoon.

## Magoon and Wood in Cuba

In the selection of a civil governor, Roosevelt was limited by the fact that the United States had no real colonial civil service outside of the Army. The only two available candidates with the requisite knowledge and sensitivity to policy were Beckman Winthrop, governor of Puerto Rico, and Charles E. Magoon, former governor of the Canal Zone and minister to Panama. Taft wanted to send Magoon to the Philippines, but Root convinced the President that Magoon was the man for Havana. Magoon, a Nebraska lawyer who had earned Root's admiration for his researches on the Hispanic codes, had been Law Officer of the Bureau of Insular Affairs. His Panama service had proved him to be good at pacifying the Corps of Engineers and Latin Americans. Root described him to Taft as "large and serene, like some others of my acquaintance, of sound judgement, good temper, never fears responsibility and perfectly adapted to control excitable elements which have to be dealt with."[14]

Tactful to the point of pliancy, honest, congenial, unimaginative, Charles E. Magoon had been an able administrator in Panama though he spoke little Spanish and had not the slightest touch of brilliance. His forte was paperwork, compromise, and untangling the cobwebs of the law. A bachelor of forty-five, physically cut from the same portly pattern as Taft, Magoon looked exactly what he was: a prosperous, hardworking country lawyer. He enjoyed a good table, and his favorite exercise was riding in an automobile. He was a "solid type." The virtues which made him Roosevelt's man in Havana, however, proved to be weaknesses when seen in Cuban eyes. That Magoon was not a military man (was not, in fact, Leonard Wood), that he was unflamboyant, uninspiring, and conciliatory, damaged his effectiveness in Cuba. Most of the criticism leveled at him by Cubans stems from the policy he was executing, and he has borne the historical burden. According to Cuban tradition, he invented *botellas* (soft jobs) and graft, took bribes, favored American businessmen, and was "a lazy, miserly, good-for-nothing slob."[15] To govern Cuba, where personal appearances were everything, Roosevelt selected a man who was a hopelessly conventional American civilian, and a bureaucrat at that. Magoon was all the things Leonard Wood was not. As governor of a land populated with military heroes, Magoon was incongruously pacific. By selecting a passive executor of admin-

istration policy, Roosevelt sacrificed the potential effectiveness of an American Governor-General surrogate. Much Cuban
resentment and frustration over the occupation was bound to
focus on the person of the governor. The chief casualty was
Magoon's character, but the morale and influence of the Provisional Government must also have diminished with the
Governor's reputation. Many of Magoon's problems in his
relations with the Cubans would have been lessened if he
had worn a uniform and acted as the Cubans thought a ruler
should.

From the day of his assumption of office, Magoon left no
doubt about how he had been ordered to handle the "Cuban
problem." The Provisional Government had to protect "life,
property, and individual liberty" (which had been accomplished), and then "restore the ordinary agencies and methods
of government" under the existing laws and general provisions
of the Cuban Constitution.[16] In terms of day-to-day administration, Magoon approached his task as an exercise in partisan
politics. He agreed that it was "necessary to have good laws,"
but the heart of his task was to promote party cohesion in
Cuba, and patronage was his chief instrument.[17]

Roosevelt and Taft saw the problem in the same way; they
had started the Provisional Government on this path before
Magoon arrived in Havana. Taft had already promised the
Liberals that he would see that vacancies in the bureaucracy
would go to qualified Liberals in order to balance out the
Moderate domination in the executive departments.[18] To
further pacify the insurgents, Magoon restored Liberal administration in twenty-two of the thirty-two municipalities where
the Liberals claimed the Moderates had arbitrarily removed
their partisans in 1905 and 1906. To aid in the selection of
Liberal officeholders, Magoon worked with the Liberal Committee, composed of the leading members of the Revolutionary Committee and "heroes" of the August Revolution. The
Committee (known to the Liberals as the Committee for
Appointments) was formed to make the Liberals speak with
one voice on patronage problems. Its original members were
Pino Guerra, Eduardo Guzmán, Ernesto Asbert, Alfredo

Zayas, José Miguel Gómez, Tomás Recio, Demetrio Castillo Duany, José de Jesus Monteagudo, Juan Gualberto Gómez, and Carlos García Vélez.[19]

Staffing the executive departments of the Cuban government presented a different problem to the United States policy-makers, for they wanted close fiscal control and an American-oriented administration. The Moderate secretaries had resigned with Estrada Palma. Rather than appoint new men for such politically sensitive posts, Taft, during his brief tenure as provisional governor, made the chief clerks (also Moderates) acting secretaries. To insure that the departments functioned effectively Taft assigned four Army officers as advisers to the secretaries of five key departments: Colonel Enoch H. Crowder, Departments of State and Justice; Lieutenant Colonel Edwin St. J. Greble, Department of Government; Lieutenant Colonel William M. Black, Department of Public Works; and Major Jefferson R. Kean, Department of Sanitation.

Although Major Eugene F. Ladd returned to the United States after his audit of the Treasury, an American Treasury official, J. D. Terrill, served as adviser to the Department of Hacienda. Major Herbert J. Slocum was detailed to assist the commanding general of the armed forces. Major Frederick S. Foltz served as chief of the Provisional Governor's office and, later, supervisor of the Havana police. Lieutenant Colonel Robert L. Bullard and Captain James A. Ryan became Magoon's aides and political agents. Major Francis J. Kernan and Captain George W. Read headed the American representatives on the Cuban Claims Commission, which settled claims arising from the insurrection; they had six American officers as assistants, all of whom spoke Spanish. Eight more officers went to the Rural Guard as advisers. Four engineers went to the Department of Public Works; four Army doctors joined the Department of Sanitation, and three officers, the Department of Government. By the end of 1908, the Army had fifty-eight officers serving with the Provisional Government.[20] Only the Department of Agriculture, Industry, and Commerce remained solely in Cuban hands; even the Department of Public Instruction temporarily went under American control in 1908 when Lieutenant Colonel Bullard became acting secretary. As for the role of the officer-advisers, one American observed that

. . . they are de facto secretaries. Of course, to placate the Cubans,— and it does seem as we are afraid of them, strange as it may seem,— or else diplomacy is the fetish just now,—there must be acting secretaries, but they simply sign papers and do what the advisors tell them.[21]

Secretary Taft personally selected the department advisers, and his criteria for appointment, understandably, was prior experience in Cuba or the Philippines in civil government.[22] His chief advisers in the selection process (which began on September 27, 1906) were Captain Frank R. McCoy, Leonard Wood's trusted aide, and Frank Steinhart, consul-general and former chief clerk of the Military Government. Thus it is not surprising that most of the officers detailed to the Provisional Government had a striking common denominator: they had been effective administrators in Leonard Wood's Cuban government.[23] Those who were not part of Wood's coterie had seen equally extensive service in the Philippines. A survey of the officers who played major roles in the Provisional Government indicates the breadth of their experience in pacification operations and colonial administration:[24]

*Colonel Enoch H. Crowder.*—Military Secretary and Legal Adviser to the Military Governor of the Philippines. Judge Advocate General, Department of the Philippines. Associate Justice, Supreme Court of the Philippines. 1898–1901.

*Lieutenant Colonel Edwin St. John Greble.*—Adjutant General, Department of Matanzas-Camaguey. Superintendent, Department of Charities and Corrections, Cuba, 1899–1902.

*Lieutenant Colonel William M. Black.*—Chief Engineer, City of Havana. Chief Engineer, Department of Cuba. Supervisor, Department of Public Works. Cuba, 1899–1902. "Good record and has confidence of Cubans."

*Lieutenant Colonel Robert L. Bullard.*—Service in the Philippines in posts from regimental commander to provincial governor, 1899–1904. With Wood on Sulu, 1902–3.

*Major Jefferson R. Kean.*—Medical Department. Associated with Gorgas, Carroll, and Lazear on the Yellow Fever Commission. "Succeeded Greble as superintendent of hospitals and charities; excellent man in any kind of duty." Cuba, 1898–1902.

*Major Herbert J. Slocum.*—Adviser, Rural Guard. Cuba, 1899–1902.

*Major Frederick S. Foltz.*—Provost marshal of Havana. Chief, Cuban secret service. Captain of the Port of Havana. Cuba, 1899–1902.

*Major Francis J. Kernan.*—Military government in Cuba, 1800. Aide to General Arthur MacArthur, Military Governor and Commanding General, Department of the Philippines, 1900–1902.

*Captain George W. Read.*—Military government in the Philippines, 1900–1902.

*Captain James A. Ryan.*—Provost marshal and provost judge in the Philippines, 1900–1903.

Leonard Wood's influence in the Second Intervention was present from the start. Steinhart played a crucial role in Havana, and McCoy and Ladd were the military advisers in the Taft-Bacon Mission. Wood himself wanted to return to Cuba; when Roosevelt turned down his request, he was comforted by the thought that so many of his old comrades had returned to Havana.[25] Steinhart, in particular, was to have a major influence on Magoon, for he became the Governor's principal adviser on Cuban politics. Steinhart, McCoy wrote Wood, "has done you credit. He has your administration and policy always in his mind's eye."[26]

How did the veterans of Wood's regime react to Magoon's charitable treatment of the Cuban *políticos*? They could not help but measure the new policy against the acts of the Military Government. Steinhart, called the "Prime Minister" by the officers, described his part in Magoon's government in a revealing letter to his former general. Steinhart told Wood that he was "the Cabinet and considering the balance of the Cuban Generals, I think I am well fitted for the position—at least they could not have selected a worse Mikado." He was running a "general employment agency," Steinhart wrote. The Liberals were fighting each other for offices while the conservatives and Americans harassed Magoon from the sidelines. The former insurgents had noticed the Provisional Governor's capacity for leniency and would probably soon "go to the woods," not for revolution, "but to make an honest dollar stealing without committing murder." The commercial interests were advocating tariff revision, on the principle of "to hell with the public," to increase their own profits. Assessing Cuban affairs after a year of American occupation, Steinhart could see no constructive outcome to Magoon's policy:

> Were I competent to put it [Cuban politics] clearly before you I could make a fortune as a riddle solver. The man who can see the end ought to be the head of a star gazing brigade and should be able to tell the color of the hair on the lady in the moon. . . . "Doctor Time" is the one who can help this country . . . the Presidential election is as far off now as it was then [January, 1907] . . . if held now [October, 1907] it is nothing less than an international crime.[27]

The Army officers in the Provisional Government were not in sympathy with Roosevelt's permissive treatment of the Liberals or with Magoon's attempt to strengthen the Cuban political system by encouraging cohesive parties. Instead, they saw their task in pragmatic and humanitarian terms, but restricted by politics. They were there "trying to reconstruct the Republic of Cuba with the back ground [sic] of a strong military intervention, made necessary by the existence of disturbing elements."[28] To accomplish the betterment of the Cuban people, the United States, instead of banking on the *políticos*, should establish, as Major Slocum put it, "a superior resident control" because the Cubans now despaired of ever managing self-government. Slocum put it bluntly to Colonel Hugh L. Scott:

> They [the Cubans] say that their dream, their hope, their sentiment for which they and many others fought for, has been accomplished, and they have failed beyond doubt. They have had their independence; they have demonstrated that they cannot have it without a controlling influence in the hands of our government; I entirely agree with it.[29]

Lieutenant Colonel Greble, adviser to the Department of Government, shared Slocum's views on Cuba's unfitness for self-government or partisan politics. He disapproved of Magoon's failure to attack Cuba's social ills. American policy, he wrote Colonel Scott, "seems to be the idea . . . to interfere as little as possible with existing conditions." [30] In writing General Wood, Greble questioned the wisdom of the occupation's goals:

> . . . . It seems to me that the whole thing resolves itself into an attempt to re-establish a government, the best possible, which will protect the foreign interests in this Island, and such policy is being pursued. There is no doubt that we can establish a government and there is not much doubt in my mind that such government won't last very long . . .[31]

Eighteen months later, Greble saw no reason to change his opinion that the United States government had taken an expedient, but unwise, course by establishing a civil government in Cuba. "I've spent a lot of time in half dreams," he wrote Wood, "of the old days in Cuba with you and perhaps whole dreams of what would have happened had the old crowd been here again." Greble assured Wood that the elections would go all right in form, but there would be no change in the people's voting habits; they would vote for local protection and favors, for the candidate most likely to win. The Cubans were still unfit to govern: "There will be no trouble while we are here," but a new Cuban government "will not last without an active intervention of the U.S. or some force strong enough to make the malcontents behave." [32]

For Major Jefferson R. Kean, M.D., adviser of the Department of Sanitation, Magoon's sensitivity to Cuban political pressures handicapped the humanitarian work he was doing through the public health services. Only Steinhart's influence kept Magoon from interfering with the Army's work, Kean wrote Wood. He reported that "things are not exactly the same as in the other Intervention. It seems to me there is not so much zeal, and there is certainly more pessimism and more politics. . . . "[33] The Provisional Government was too political and its favoritism to the Liberals had made Kean revise his hopes that the Republic would survive. The "best people" were uninterested in politics, and "without some restriction of suffrage, I think the future of the Republic is hopeless. . . . "[34] The conduct of the Provisional Government had made efficient, just and humane administration so difficult that the Army officers' morale was sinking: "The Cubans are probably being pacified all right, but I think there may be an uprising at any time among the advisors." [35]

In examining American policy in Cuba, Lieutenant Colonel Bullard believed it was based on ignorance, "though we do it with intentions that would honor angels." The dilemma in Cuba was that the Cubans were "a people of monarchial habit, tradition, customs . . . and even genius . . . with republican, constitutional ideals and aspirations." The Cubans had become addicted to violence, but were still willing to bear the oppression of authoritarian government, high taxes, and local *jefes*. America should either provide tutelage or not interfere at all, but repeated interventions and the sponsorship of the *políticos* was fruitless. "Time, time will be needed for adjustment here." [36]

On the whole subject of Cuban politics, the Army officers probably shared the frank analysis of Captain Andrew G. Dougherty, an adviser to the Rural Guard:

I have spent four and a half months in the Province of Santiago [Oriente], horseback, living and talking with these people . . . there are no two men or group of men in the Province of Santiago, or for that matter in all Cuba, who can . . . speak for the "people of Santiago" or any considerable part of them.[37]

Whatever their disenchantment with Roosevelt's policy to create a viable party system, the officers in the Provisional Government did not attempt to appeal their case to political pressure groups in the United States or ally themselves with the alien-conservatives in Cuba. None of them had the force or political stature of Wood or Wilson; the restraints upon them in terms of their professional self-image and their careers were real and assertive. That they questioned the essential wisdom of occupation policy is certain. That they obstructed it is less so. Yet the longer the occupation lasted, the more complex the political problems became and the more intense the pressure upon Magoon, largely from his officers and the business elite, to increase American control for the purpose of making lasting changes in the island's institutions. The officers' influence upon Magoon depended largely upon how accurate he believed their assessment of conditions in Cuba to be, and he relied on them heavily. In retrospect the officers' contempt for politics Cuban-style was justified in terms of the political events they witnessed, for the act of intervention itself made it more difficult than ever to identify party alignments in Cuba.

## The Political Residue of the Intervention, 1906–1907

As the work of disarming the insurgents and militia progressed, as the Claims Commission began to pay for damages, and as *la zafra* put the people to work, Magoon tackled the reconstruction of the Cuban political system. He found the Liberals ascendant and the Moderates moribund. Each group presented different problems, similar only in their complexity, and complex because neither of these loose personal alliances was a political party.

The Liberal party in the first six months of the occupation fell completely apart. In September and October, 1906, the Liberal leaders were given a façade of solidarity when the Revolutionary Committee, which had bargained with Taft, was institutionalized as the Liberal Committee. This committee was to advise the Governor on the Liberal position on controversial issues and suggest candidates for appointment. Its membership (by agreement of the Liberals themselves) reflected the rapid rise in the Liberal ranks of the military leaders of the August Revolution: Pino Guerra (president), Eduardo Guzmán (vice-president), and Ernesto Asbert (secretary). Only Enrique Loynaz del Castillo was excluded. The committee also included the prerevolt Liberal notables, but they were temporarily eclipsed.

October, 1906, was the Liberals' honeymoon month. For two weeks they promenaded, dined, and orated in Havana, and capped the celebration with a victory rally at the Payret theater on October 15. They considered the insurrection successful and their influence with the Provisional Government strong.[38] They would not have been so jubilant had they known that Taft had instructed Magoon that American policy was to "neutralize" and "prevent" Liberal efforts to dominate the next elections.[39] Unaware of this instruction, the Liberals pushed Magoon on the question of patronage, telling him that Taft had promised them that Liberals would replace all the "undesirables" in the administration. They held to their argument that they stood for honest government, impartiality in the appointment of officials, and free elections. Juan Gualberto Gómez reminded Magoon that Cubans would not tolerate further injustice:

. . . A country never has a revolution without it is necessary. A mob or street disturbance is brought about by half a dozen people, but for a revolution it is necessary that the whole people participate. . . . When the people have been impelled to revolution it is a mistake to impede the development of that idea of revolution, because in such case what is done is to prepare a second revolution. That is what we wish to avoid here.[40]

Magoon, however, held firm to his position that no new secretaries would be chosen, that only qualified men would be appointed to other positions, that the congress would remain in recess, and that the Liberals would not control Cuban politics.

By mid-winter the leading Liberals had fallen out among themselves. Part of the power struggle stemmed from the popularity of the military chieftains of the August Revolution and the conflicting views on the presidential nomination for the promised elections. Another factor was traditional personal and regional rivalries. One more divisive influence was the struggle for the patronage which Magoon, in the name of fair play and party harmony, had promised to distribute. As early as January, 1907, the Liberal Committee was internally split over patronage control and the presidential nomination. The leading contenders, José Miguel Gómez and Alfredo Zayas, were soon trying to line up supporters, and the Liberal party dissolved into two shifting factions.[41]

The Liberal split complicated what might have been a ludicrous issue: the repeal of the laws banning cock-fighting. In February, acting on a Zayista tip, the Havana police broke up a private *pelea de gallos* arranged for some American officers and arrested José Miguel Gómez and Pino Guerra. Their arrest sparked a mass rally, organized by Monteagudo, in Havana and a mob of fifteen thousand demonstrated in front of the national palace for repeal of the ban. Impressed by the crowd's reaction, the Miguelistas made repeal a campaign issue, which angered the Havana SPCA and the conservatives. Although Magoon believed Wood's law ill-advised, he (on Taft's advice) declined to rule on the problem. Privately he was dumfounded at the furor such an incident could create.[42]

By the spring of 1907, the Liberals were completely divided into Miguelistas and Zayistas on national matters, while strong men held local power in the provinces. In anticipation of elections to be held in June, two separate slates of candidates were prepared by the factions. The Military Information Division gave Gómez the balance in Pinar del Rio and Camaguey (thanks to Loynaz del Castillo and Cisneros Betancourt). Zayas held the city and province of Havana (his home) and Oriente, where he was supported by Juan Gualberto Gómez and Castillo Duany. Provincial *jefes* Generals Eduardo Guzmán and José Luis Robau held Santa

Clara, once Gómez territory, and were uncommitted. Only in Matanzas did the conservatives have a chance; to win elections elsewhere they would need the potential alien vote. Summarizing the situation, Captain Furlong believed the Zayistas more stable than the "military" Liberals, but pictured both groups as incurably radical and incapable of honest, peaceful government.[43]

To encourage a party differing with the Liberals, Magoon turned to the wreckage of the Moderate party in an effort to salvage a conservative opposition. The Moderates, however, were finished as a unified party. The Moderates' immoderate behavior in the 1905 elections and during September, 1906, ended whatever popular appeal they once had. The Roosevelt administration itself administered the coup de grâce by publishing the diplomatic correspondence with Palma, Sleeper, and Steinhart and the Taft-Bacon *Report*; both sets of documents clearly put the onus of the intervention on the Moderates.[44]

Following the establishment of the Provisional Government, the Moderate leaders met in Havana and formally dissolved their party on November 3. As one Cuban wit observed, the Moderates were simply disposing of "a corpse that has been unburied for some time and exposed to the sun." At the final Moderate meeting, however, General Juan Ríus Rivera proposed the formation of a new conservative party with a far-reaching program. He advocated the redrafting of the Constitution to include a six- or eight-year presidential term, new procedural rules for the congress, the extension of the suffrage to propertied foreigners, and greater central control over provincial and municipal government. He also proposed the creation of a five thousand man regular army.[45] Two weeks later Ríus Rivera abandoned his attempt for lack of support. The American minister reported that the new party had been obviously an alliance of sugar planters and cigarmakers working for a protectorate, and the Cubans had realized immediately that it was a façade.[46]

Discouraged by the Moderate's failure to regroup, Magoon called in a number of conservatives and assured them that the Provisional Government had not capitulated to the Liberals. He told them that the Liberals had regained the positions denied them by fraud and that if the Moderates would select a group like the Liberal Committee, they too could have a voice in the patronage. The purpose of Magoon's offer was "to see the Moderates reorganized and begin to sit up and take notice as otherwise they will continue their present agitation that moral peace is as far off as ever."[47] Magon found, however, that the former Moderates could not agree among themselves. Their anger at being blamed for the intervention and the temporary nature of the occupation divided them into three groups. The first favored no dealings at all with the Provisional Government. Another was allied with the Nuñezistas of Havana and was awaiting a Liberal split. This group was unified by its hate for Zayas and was sympathetic to José Miguel Gómez. A third faction, Magoon reported, wanted to compel a long intervention by fomenting unrest. This faction included many office-holders and was agitating among the dissatisfied Negroes.[48]

By March, 1907, however, Magoon wrote Taft that the ex-Moderates would soon form a new conservative party, which had a good chance of success at the polls if plural voting, the alien franchise, and proportional representation were adopted. Magoon thought the conservatives would participate even if only proportional representation was enacted.[49]

### Secretary Taft Visits Havana: Cuban Policy Revised

Although Roosevelt and Taft had planned to hold Cuban elections in June, 1907, the disarray of Cuba's political parties forced them to reconsider their timing. In April, 1907, Taft visited Havana for four days (April 7-10) and reviewed Cuban problems with Magoon, the Army officers in the Provisional Government, the leaders of the Liberal factions, conservatives, and alien businessmen. At that time, Roosevelt was still firm that the American intervention should be terminated as quickly as possible, but he was acutely aware that withdrawing too hastily could bring even greater disaster than the United States had coped with the previous year.[50]

From Washington, British ambassador James Bryce reported that the administration believed there was little desire among Americans to annex Cuba. Indeed, Bryce observed, Roosevelt thought his handling of the Cuban situation had won general approval. Repeated, endless intervention, in the administration's view, was preferable to annexation. The administration believed that the difficulties in the Philippines had created an underlying public aversion to more colonial experiments, while travelers from Cuba said that only the larger planters and commercial elite there favored annexation.[51]

It was against this background that Taft returned to Cuba. During his stay in Havana, he sampled enough conflicting opinions to become convinced that the date of the elections should be postponed, but also that the promise of elections should be reinforced by positive action for their accomplishment.[52] Taft's decision to recommend postponement was based on several factors. First, he found the Liberals, particularly the "military faction," eager (perhaps too eager) to hold elections sometime in 1907. One of the Liberals' fears was that if elections were not held shortly there would be a revolt which would force an American protectorate. The Liberals believed a national census, judged essential by the Provisional Government for fair elections, could be carried out in four months. Taft, however, thought their fears exaggerated and their desire for speedy elections offset by their trust in American policy. The Liberals had "blind confidence in the United States" and would take postponement peacefully.[53]

The rise of a conservative opposition party under the leadership of Rafael Montoro, former minister to Great Britain and onetime autonomist, also influenced the decision to ask for postponement.[54] Taft's goal was not necessarily to favor a conservative party (though emotionally he probably did), but to give Cuban voters some choice other than the candidates of the Miguelistas and Zayistas. Talking with conservatives (whom he called "Conservatives," though the party had not yet been formed officially), Taft found them willing to accept an indefinite postponement. The Havana bankers, seconded by the Chamber of Commerce, stated that they needed at least one year's notice of the withdrawal in order to stave off a financial collapse.[55]

Governor Magoon had believed as early as January that the weakness of the political parties made it unwise to hold elections until 1908.[56] His position on the timing of elections was shared by Colonel Crowder, adviser to the Departments of State and Justice and president of the Advisory Law Commission. As a result of the Commission's review of the Cuban constitutional system, Crowder already had reported to Taft that the whole electoral system needed drastic revision and that a national census was essential.[57] Crowder was no advocate of hasty reform of the law; indeed he recognized that Cuba needed its entire criminal and civil codes revised as well as its political legislation modified.[58] Magoon and Crowder, lawyers both, were concerned that the Provisional Government should have enough time to draft new laws, which they hoped would lessen the chance of election injustices and unrestrained spoils politics.

For a number of reasons, then, Taft drew up a plan outlining the preconditions for American withdrawal. They were (1) the drafting and declaration of a new electoral law, (2) the completion of an accurate census, (3) the holding of municipal and provincial elections after a voter registration based on the census, and (4) six months later, the holding of national elections. The elections would be closely supervised by the Provisional Government. The American withdrawal would come some three months later when the new president was inaugurated. The Provisional Government, however, would follow this loose timetable only if the country remained peaceful.[59] Taft cabled Roosevelt for his decision and the President replied simply, "I approve."[60] By the time Taft left Havana the understanding was that the census would take a year and that the first elections would follow in the *tiempo muerto* of 1908.[61]

Taft's Havana visit was a major event in the conduct of the occupation, for it reassured the Cubans that the United States fully intended to leave the island in the forseeable future. His open letter explaining the election plans to Governor Magoon was circulated throughout the island. It was a clear pledge of withdrawal, with the proviso that there be no violence in Cuba. This proviso, that "the carrying out of this plan is of course strictly dependent on the tranquillity of the country," may have had a sobering effect on the *políticos*, but it also meant that the annexationists within Cuba were offered one last chance to provoke a protectorate and avoid a repetition of "the Crime of 1902." In the complex and confusing events that troubled the *tiempo muerto* of 1907, Magoon, the officers of the Provisional Government, and the Army of Cuban Pacification were to experience their most trying moments.

1. Taft-Bacon *Report,* p. 463.

2. James D. Richardson (ed.) *A Compilation of the Messages and Papers of the Presidents, 1789–1908* (Washington, D.C., 1910), X, 7436–37.

3. Roosevelt to Sir Edward Grey, February 28, 1907; Roosevelt to William Coolidge Lane, April 15, 1907, Roosevelt Papers.
To his son Kermit, Roosevelt wrote of his talks with Taft and Bacon that "they said they never could tell when those ridiculous dagos would flare up . . . and start cutting one another's throats."

4. Roosevelt to Taft, January 22, 1907, Roosevelt Papers.

5. Taft-Bacon *Report,* p. 468; Taft and Bacon to Estrada Palma, September 24, 1906, in Taft-Bacon *Report,* p. 509–11.

6. Taft to Charles P. Taft, October 9, 1906, Taft Papers.

7. Root to Wood, October 31, 1906, Wood Papers.

8. James H. Wilson to Root, October 18, 1906, and Root to Wilson, October 24, 1906, Root Papers.

9. Bacon and Scott (eds.) *Latin America and the United States,* p. 275.

10. Root to Magoon, December 16, 1907, Root Papers.

11. Editorial, "The Nature of the Government in Cuba," *American Journal of International Law,* I (January, 1907), 149–50. For a concurring opinion, see David A. Lockmiller, "La base legal de la intervención de los Estados Unidos en Cuba en 1906," *Revista bimestre cubana,* XXXVIII (September–December, 1936), 268–81.

12. *Congressional Record,* 59th Con., 2d Sess., XLI, 849–50, 2638–40. Senator Shelby Cullom stated that the occupation was an administration responsibility, and that the Committee on Foreign Affairs was not in-

volved. Ben Tillman criticized Taft for following a radical policy (i.e, giving horses to the insurgents) which endangered the right of property and encouraged Negroes to leave the sugar plantations.

In newspaper interviews, eight congressmen agreed that order must be kept in Cuba, but were split (4–4) on the advisability of annexation. They all agreed that annexation would be of questionable popularity. *New York Times,* September 30, October 3 and 4, 1906.

13. *Times* (London), October 12, 1906.

14. Root to Taft, October 2, 1906, Case 244/269, *Num. File, 1906–1910,* Vol. XXXVII, RG 59.

15. The question of Magoon's character is most carefully studied in Chapman, *A History of the Cuban Republic,* pp. 230–36, and David A. Lockmiller, *Magoon in Cuba* (Chapel Hill, N.C., 1938), pp. 70–78, 213–21. The single most significant source of evidence on Magoon's personality is the Crowder-Chapman Correspondence, Enoch H. Crowder Papers, Western Historical Manuscript Collection, University of Missouri Library. The consensus was that Magoon was an honest man who remained that way while governor.

16. Magoon, *Report, 1906–1907,* p. 9.

17. Magoon to Taft, November 29, 1906, Taft Papers; Magoon to McCoy, December 10, 1906, McCoy Papers.

18. Taft-Bacon *Report,* p. 466.

19. Magoon, *Report, 1906–1907,* pp. 16–17. Portell Vilá criticizes Magoon for dealing with Cuban politicians devoid of "true patriotism," ignoring men "dedicated to the cause of national regeneration." Portell Vilá, *Historia de Cuba,* IV, 535.

20. U.S. Congress, House, Charles E. Magoon, *Report of the Provisional Governor of Cuba, December 1, 1907–December 1, 1908,* 60th Cong., 2nd Sess., House Doc. 1457, pp. 147–53. Hereafter cited as Magoon, *Report, 1907–1908.* The officers were distributed as follows: Executive branch, Office of the Provisional Governor: 8; Departments of State and Justice, Election Bureau: 16; Department of Government: 6; Department of Public Works: 16; Department of Sanitation: 4; Armed Forces: 8.

This breakdown included acting governors and election supervisors, public works supervisors, and the officers-in-charge, national insane asylum and boys' correctional school. Officers were not customs collectors as they had been under the Military Government.

21. Mrs. L. L. Beckwith, secretary in the Secretaria de Hacienda (Treasury), to Gen. Leonard Wood, January 3, 1907, Wood Papers; also Maj. F. S. Foltz to Col. H. L. Scott, November (?) 1906, Scott Papers; Portell Vilá, *Historia de Cuba,* IV, 535.

22. Memorandum, September 27, 1906, drafted by Captain Frank R. McCoy, listing officers recommended for service in Cuba, McCoy Papers.

23. McCoy to Wood, October 18, 1906, Wood Papers.

24. Biographical data from McCoy's memo, previously cited, and Edward S. Holden and Wirt Robinson (eds.), *General Cullum's Bio-*

*graphical Register of the Officers and Graduates of the U.S. Military Academy Supplement, 1900–1910* (Saginaw, Mich., 1910). See also Bangs, *Uncle Sam Trustee, passim.*

25. Wood to McCoy, September 24, 1906, Wood Papers; Wood to de Armas, January 18, 1907, Wood Papers; McCoy to Wood, October 18, 1906, McCoy Papers. Among the Wood Papers is a "hello . . . wish you were here" telegram sent from Havana by Steinhart, McCoy, Black, Greble, Foltz, and Ladd.

26. McCoy to Wood, October 18, 1906, McCoy Papers. "Undoubtedly he (Steinhart) was a man of great influence with the Wood Administration. In the second intervention, he actually controlled Magoon and was the invisible government." E. H. Crowder to Henry P. Fletcher, October 29, 1921, quoted in Robert F. Smith, *The United States and Cuba* (New York, 1960), p. 25.

27. Steinhart to Wood, October 27, 1907, Wood Papers. Steinhart hoped that Congress would discuss making Cuba a protectorate. Steinhart to McCoy, December 31, 1906, McCoy Papers.

28. Crowder to Maj. Gen. J. F. Bell, May 20, 1907, Crowder Papers.

29. Maj. H. J. Slocum to Col. H. L. Scott, December 15, 1906, Scott Papers.

". . . there are many hours when General Rodríguez and myself and Other people here look back to those days under General Wood's control." Slocum to McCoy, June 6, 1907, Wood Papers.

30. Lt. Col. E. StJ. Greble to Scott, October 10, 1906, Scott Papers.

31. Greble to Wood, January 4, 1907, Wood Papers.

32. Greble to Wood, June 7 and July 31, 1908, Wood Papers.

33. Maj. J. R. Kean to Wood, January 9, 1908, Jefferson R. Kean Papers, Manuscript Division, University of Virginia Library. The Kean Papers, which include Kean's official and personal correspondence and letters received while adviser to the Department of Sanitation, are a valuable source on the occupation, public health affairs in Cuba, and the Army's attack on tropical diseases.

34. Kean to Maj. M. W. Ireland, April 7, 1907, Kean Papers.

35. Kean to Ireland, October 19, 1907, Kean Papers.

36. Entry for November 30, 1907, Notebook 10, Bullard Papers. See also Robert L. Bullard, "How Cubans Differ from Us," *North American Review,* CLXXXVI (November, 1907), 416–21.

Magoon was highly displeased with an earlier Bullard article on the lack of political opportunity for the Cuban Negro, also published in the *North American Review.* He considered it too sensitive politically. When Bullard learned his second article was published, therefore, he purchased most of the November issues of the magazine when they reached Havana to prevent their circulation.

37. Capt. A. G. Dougherty to Capt. J. A. Ryan, August 8, 1907, File 146–9, CC/PGoC, RG 199.

38. E. V. Morgan, Minister to Cuba, to Root, October 17, 1906, Case 244/334, *Num. File, 1906–1910.* Vol. XXXVII, RG 59.

Morgan rode out Roosevelt's wrath and stayed in Cuba. His reports are a valuable "control" on the Provisional Government's assessment of Cuban political conditions.

39. Taft to Magoon, October 31, 1906, File 005, CC/PGoC, RG 199.

40. "Report of Conference between the Provisional Government and Commission of the Revolutionary or Liberal Party, November 9, 1906," File 008, CC/PGoC, RG 199.

41. Charles Hernández to McCoy, December 8, 1906, McCoy Papers; G. W. E. Griffith, British Minister to Cuba, to Sir Edward Grey, January 11, 1907, FO 371–242, PRO; Martínez Ortiz, *Cuba: los primeros años de independencia,* II, p. 401.

42. Magoon to Taft, February 25, 1907 and reply, File 076–076–2, CC/PGoC, RG 199.

43. MID to Chief of Staff (C/S), ACP, March 30, 1907; April 23, 1907; April 26, 1907, File 100–100/2–12, CC/PGoC. The British minister largely concurred with the MID. Griffith to Grey, February 26, 1907, FO 371–242, PRO.

44. In Cuba, press reaction to the disclosures was varied. The *Havana Daily Telegraph* reported (December 20, 1906) that Cuban reaction ranged from outrage to despondency; it took the position that the reports proved the Cubans unfit for self-government and urged a protectorate. *La Lucha* (October 23, 1906) said that the diplomatic revelations proved "Messrs. Roosevelt, Taft, Bacon and Magoon are not novices. They know politics as an art and as a science."

45. Morgan to Root, November 7, 1906, Case 1943/2–7, *Num. File, 1906–1910,* Vol. CCV, RG 59; *Independent* (November 8, 1906), pp. 1078–79.

46. Morgan to Root, November 20, 1906, Case 1943/19–21, *Num. File, 1906–1910,* Vol. CCV, RG 59.

47. Magoon to McCoy, December 10, 1906, McCoy Papers.
Individual conservatives, Magoon wrote, gave welcome advice freely but distained taking leadership in a political party.

48. Magoon to Taft, December 25, 1906, File 017, CC/PGoC, RG 199. "My own idea is to occupy it three months each year (during the winter months)." Magoon to Taft, December 18, 1906, Crowder Papers.

49. Magoon to Taft, March 4, 1907, File 081, CC/PGoC, RG 100.

50. During the winter of 1907 Roosevelt received long, thoughtful memos on Cuban affairs from Gustavus Bock of the American Tobacco Company, a forty-three year resident of Havana, and from William E. Curtis, author, journalist, and former official of the Pan American Union. By implication both Bock and Curtis favored continued occupation and political supervision of Cuban affairs. Roosevelt sent the memos to Taft. Taft-Roosevelt Correspondence, 1907, Taft Papers. See also Magoon, *Report, 1906–1907,* pp. 24–25.

51. James Bryce, British ambassador to the United States, to Grey, April 18, 1907, FO 371–242, PRO. Colonel Bullard would have agreed with Bryce. Bullard to Magoon, reports of February 6 to April 8, 1907, File 066–66–3, CC/PGoC, RG 199.

52. The findings and recommendations produced by Taft's visit are contained in the Secretary's open letter to Magoon, reprinted in Magoon, *Report, 1906–1907*, pp. 23–26.

53. Memoranda of conference held with Faustino Guerra, José Miguel Gómez, José de Jesus Monteagudo, and Enrique Loynaz del Castillo, April 8–10, 1907, File 078, CC/PGoC, RG 199. Guerra recommended that the Army of Cuban Pacification stay on six months after the new government was inaugurated and that Magoon appoint the President-elect's cabinet choices to insure a smooth transition.

54. Taft press conference as reported in the *New York Times*, April 11, 1907.

55. *New York Times*, April 9 and 11, 1907.

56. Magoon to Taft, January 20, 1907, Taft Papers.

57. Col. E. H. Crowder to Taft, January 12, 1907, Crowder Papers.

58. Col. E. H. Crowder, "Report of Department of State and Justice," in Magoon, *Report, 1906–1907*, pp. 119–39. For a summary of Crowder's service in Cuba, see David A. Lockmiller, *Enoch H. Crowder: Soldier, Lawyer, Statesman,* University of Missouri Studies No. 37 (Columbia, Mo., 1955), pp. 107–20.

59. Taft to Roosevelt, April 10, 1907, Roosevelt Papers; Magoon, *Report, 1906–1907*, pp. 214–26. The three month period (i.e., 100 days) from the election of the president to his inauguration conformed with the Cuban Constitution.

60. Roosevelt to Taft, April 10, 1907, Roosevelt Papers.

61. *New York Times*, April 10, 1907; Chapman, *A History of the Cuban Republic*, p. 260; Lockmiller, *Magoon in Cuba*, pp. 174–75.

# CHAPTER SIX

# THE ANNEXATIONISTS AND MASSO PARRA: THE REVOLT THAT NEVER WAS

Dᴜʀɪɴɢ the confused and dangerous days of September, 1906, there had been a brief annexationist boom in the United States and Cuba. American sugar planters and financiers, Spanish businessmen in Cuba, the New York press, and some European journals agreed that the Cubans had had their independence and forfeited it.[1] While Roosevelt and Root discouraged the agitators in the United States with public statements condemning annexation, the alien and conservative business groups in Cuba clung to the faint hope that American protection would not be withdrawn.

Taft found during his brief tour as Provisional Governor that the businessmen of Havana, nearly all annexationists, were as troublesome as the *políticos*. Though the Spanish seemed incapable of organizing opposition to the United States goals, the American adventurers in Cuba posed a real threat to peace. Writing his brother Charles, Taft described the American agitators as "the yellow dog type, not business men, who are also strongly in favor of annexation and who are equal to stirring up trouble just for the purpose of bringing about annexation."[2]

Charles Magoon quickly learned upon taking over the governorship that the "business interests," favoring annexation or an American protectorate, were unconvinced that there was peace in Cuba. In order to prolong the United States occupation, these men (many of them ex-Moderates or non-party types) were perfectly capable of secretly financing a revolt by Cuban dissidents. American citizens were a vocal minority among the agitators, Magoon wrote Taft. Their alarms to the contrary, peace prevailed in Cuba, Magoon insisted. As for the annexationists, the Governor believed that their efforts would be futile; they were, nonetheless, a dangerous nuisance:

> Eventually no good will result from such misrepresentation and they are playing with fire in their endeavor to keep up public excitement and magnify unimportant incidents into important and alarming events.[3]

Magoon's lack of sympathy with the annexationists, who plagued him daily with plans to establish a permanent protectorate, soon turned them against the Provisional Government. They remained militantly opposed to the restoration of a Cuban government. Focusing their ire on the Governor, they wanted to secure his removal, Magoon thought.[4] Although the Governor was sensitive to criticism, he was no paranoid. One Cuban annexationist, José de Armas, was already in touch with Taft. Believing him sympathetic with the Cuban conservatives, Armas implored the Secretary to keep Roosevelt from returning the island to the "Cuba Libre politicians." The annexationists could not organize a political party, Armas said, because such open opposition to Cuban independence would only stimulate the nationalists. Only Washington could help the annexationist cause.[5]

Sugar planter Edward F. Atkins wrote Taft that "a general feeling of unrest" prevailed in Cuba because of the high cost of living and low sugar prices. He knew Taft was aware that the businessmen, storekeepers, merchants, and planters wanted the United States to stay on, but Atkins wondered if the Secretary realized that such desires were common among the Cubans themselves:

> I find that an almost universal sentiment exists on the part of the Cuban country people who have any interest at stake however small, that some form of control by the United States is desirable and necessary, and this feeling, I understand, extends to the more industrious of the black population, the class opposed to such a course being those who seek minor offices and those who seek benefit through any dis-

turbed conditions, among them large numbers of the irresponsible blacks without families or property.[6]

Havana was the seat of annexationist agitation and criticism of the Provisional Government. Among the Americans there, James Runcie, a former Army officer and one-time Wood confidant before he embarrassed the general with his annexationist propaganda, formed the Good Government League. The goals of the League were unclear. The American minister admitted that Runcie could be simply trying to interest businessmen in politics, but he thought it more likely that the League was a cover for the annexationists.[7] The Americans were reluctant to sponsor a conservative party because they feared that the emergence of such a party would speed the withdrawal of American troops. The Army's continued presence was essential if a protectorate was to be established.[8] The Spaniards, on the other hand, worked to discredit the Provisional Government by accusing it of ignoring the advice of the Havana financiers and merchants, and all those of "pure Latin stock." [9]

If the annexationist spirit or the dissatisfaction it fed upon had been limited to the salons and counting houses of Havana, Taft and Magoon easily might have coped with it. Troubling reports from other parts of the island, however, flowed into the Governor's office. After returning from a trip through Cuba in December and January (1906-7), the Reverend Albion W. Knight, Episcopal Bishop of Cuba, told Magoon of conditions and attitudes much like those Atkins reported to Taft. The Americans he had seen, Bishop Knight said, favored annexation or a protectorate, but stood aloof from politics. Bishop Knight characterized the typical American's attitude:

He does not hesitate to express his opinion, but he does not assert or inject his activity into the situation. He leaves the matter in the hands of the Government and the Cuban people. I do not mean to state that it is due altogether to indifference or to delicacy of feeling, but more to a well grounded belief that to leave the people of the Island to adjust their own affairs will more quickly bring about annexation or a Protectorate.[10]

Bishop Knight hastened to add that the Cubans themselves wanted peace and independence, in that order. Their greatest concern was to avoid the economic catastrophe of another revolt. Although they were not sympathetic to annexation, they valued the security provided by the American troops.

From widely scattered Army stations, the Military Information Division received reports from its intelligence officers that the talk of revolt was more than idle gossip. Caches of weapons, used or recently smuggled, were constantly being reported, and often linked with foreign property owners.[11] Sometimes the reports proved false or exaggerated, but the rumors heightened the sense of insecurity the annexationists were cultivating. When Colonel John Van Orsdale of the Seventeenth Infantry told the Military Information Division that two thousand new English rifles from Jamaica had been smuggled into Camaguey, Captain C. I. Crockett looked into the matter and found it a hoax. The Englishman who convinced Crockett that the arms had never landed admitted, however, that "it is necessary to show the Americans that they must remain in Cuba."[12] After an investigation in Oriente, Captains Charles F. Crain and Andrew G. Dougherty agreed with an English hotel owner they interviewed that the planters in the province would eagerly contribute $50,000 to any aspiring rebel. The planters' motive was to fight the United States into annexation.[13] The Military Information Division found substantially the same rationale behind a report by a Mr. Barker, merchant of Havana, that nine thousand new rifles had been landed at Mariel Bay for Pino Guerra.[14]

The false alarms did not obscure a very real need to disarm the Cubans. Lieutenant Colonel Bullard, for example, learned that General José Luis Robau had eight hundred thousand cartridges stored in Santa Clara and a large number of rifles. He warned the *jefe* that any uprising would be crushed quickly, and promised more public works for the province.[15] Bullard thought Robau's war-talk was simply part of the

Miguelistas and Zayistas' strategy to extort extra jobs from the Provisional Government. The trouble was that one never knew when a fanciful revolt might become real. The Military Information Division did what it could to track down weapons, and its undercover agents paid seven dollars for a voluntary turn-in. The agents also bought arms by posing as revolutionaries, but the American officers were aware that the arms they received were a small percentage of those in Cuban hands.

Much of the frustration, vindictiveness, and passion which the annexationists hoped to exploit dissolved after *la zafra* of 1906–7 began and American troops had occupied the trouble spots. As the harvest progressed, Magoon's personal agents and the officers of the Military Information Division agreed that, despite the alarms, most of Cuba was at work, business was good, and violence was limited to banditry and factional name-calling.[16]

Even during *la zafra*, however, economic insecurity in Cuba troubled the Provisional Government and the *tiempo muerto* promised to be worse. Rumors of revolt jarred the domestic price structure and credit system. During February when an uprising was feared in Camaguey, *campesinos* flooded the market with cattle, driving beef prices down as much as 30 per cent. The profit-makers were the cattle buyers, who, not incidentally, started the talk.[17]

At other levels of competition, as Magoon learned, unrest was profitable; some Americans talked rebellion in order to discourage German sellers of sugar refining machinery.[18] The sugar planters themselves faced fires in their ripe cane fields from two sources. First, there were professional arsonists who threatened the fields and extorted money from the planters or sinecures from the local officials.[19] Secondly, the cane-cutters would fire the fields, for, being paid by the weight of the cane they cut, they could harvest enough burned cane to earn $3.50 to $4.50 a day. Working on the tough green stalks, they could earn only $1.50 to $2.00 for the same work.[20] Arson in the cane and tobacco fields caused the tension and the number of armed men in the provinces to increase. To protect their fields, the planters armed their own excitable retainers or hired gangs provided by the local *alcalde*.[21] Another predictable reaction to arson came from the Spanish financiers who, upon news of violence, cut off the cash advances the planters needed to pay their laborers.[22] It took no genius to guess what the unemployed laborers would then do. As for the planters, there always seemed to be someone eager to buy their land at depressed "unrest" prices.

Faced with economic conditions for which they could offer only palliatives and fearing the political implications of the annexationist movement, Magoon and his advisers also had to entertain a group of junketing Republican congressmen in March, 1907.[23] The attitudes of these visitors illuminates the Congressional restraints on Roosevelt's Cuban policy. At the head of the delegation was none other than Joseph G. Cannon, the powerful and autocratic Speaker of the House. His entourage was the cream of the Republican "regulars": Senator-elect Charles Curtis of Kansas; Representatives James S. Sherman (N.Y.), chairman of the Republican Congressional Campaign Committee and chairman of the Committee of Indian Affairs; James A. Tawney (Minn.), chairman of the Appropriations Committee; Henry C. Loudenslager (N.J.), chairman of the Committee on Pensions; J. Van Vechten Olcott (N.Y.); James R. Mann (Ill.); William B. McKinley (Ill.); and J. Hampton Moore (Pa.).

This group of investigators sailed into Havana aboard a German steamer and there saw the ubiquitous gunboat *"Panther"*, all of which moved "Uncle Joe" Cannon to worry about European influence in the Caribbean and German sea power in particular. J. Hampton Moore also noted that thirty-three vessels of the United States Navy were in port. Ashore, where Moore marveled at the children playing baseball under the Spanish-language Lydia Pinkham billboards, the delegation was greeted by Magoon, Steinhart, Morgan, Governor Núñez, and Mayor Cárdenas of Havana. The congressmen soon met representatives of the American Club, German Club, Spanish Club, the Cuban clubs, the Chamber of Commerce, and several "financial institutions." Cannon was not very impressed with the conservative businessmen: "These rich fellows are too cowardly to fight their own battles."[24] The Speaker was most unhappy with the way America's Cuban policy was working. It was based on "the very sublimity of altruism," but American capital (which "induced improvement" wherever it went) would not benefit Cuba unless American control was increased. Didn't the Cubans realize the Reciprocity Treaty was costing the United States $10 million annually, Cannon asked? As Moore summarized the Speaker's assessment of the Cuban problem:

> We had found the baby on our door-step and the spirit of father-hood required that we should put it asleep o' nights and provide for its maintenance. We were doing something for the baby, but its appetite was enormous and its disposition to cry at unseemly hours was characteristic. Indeed, the baby seemed to be getting the best of the bargain all the way through, for it was still doing business for itself under the protection of its new-found parent.[25]

Cannon, according to Moore, told his Havana audience that although the American people would not now accept involuntary annexation, "it is not unnatural, however, that we should look forward to the time when Cuba will become a part of the United States, and when the other islands of the Caribbean Sea shall be so regarded."[26] No doubt the Speaker's words heartened the "professional Cubans . . . men of refinement and property" whom he addresesd. At the conclusion of their visit, the congressmen generally agreed that they supported Roosevelt's course in Cuba. If there was one more revolt, however, "may not the American people fairly insist that the time has come to protect Cuba against her foes, within or without, by annexation?"[27] As Moore saw the Cuban problem:

> . . . Shall we continue to govern her by proxy at our own expense and annoyance, or shall we end the trouble once and for all in the way the United States may be trusted to end it—firmly, but with justice and humanity, and with due regard to the right of Cubans to the pursuit of life, liberty and happiness.[28]

And back to New York sailed Speaker Cannon and his friends, while Magoon and his advisers must have wondered what the visit had done to their efforts to hold the annexationists at arms-length and pacify the *políticos* as the *tiempo muerto* approached. Already, Magoon had word from Santa Clara that a drought had caused considerable suffering; food prices were going up, and only immediate public works employment could head off the growing lawlessness.[29]

At this critical time, Secretary of War Taft suggested in a speech in St. Louis that "we may not have committed ourselves to a policy best adapted to the welfare of the Cubans." Taft's speech, published by the conservative *Diario de la Marina* the same day it was delivered, moved José de Armas to write the Secretary that his words had heartened the annexationists.[30] Taft might have given Magoon encouragement rather than the annexationists, for at the time of the St. Louis speech, the Governor faced banditry in Santa Clara and Oriente, a cigar workers' strike in Havana, and a growing yellow fever epidemic. The Provisional Government could (and did) act decisively in these cases, but the general political situation posed a different and potentially more serious danger to the peace.

The split of the Liberal party into Miguelistas and Zayistas meant that all over Cuba a reorganization of the personal factions was necessary. Local uprisings or the threat of revolt were an intrinsic part of this process. In Pinar del Rio, for example, Pino Guerra, considered by Magoon to hold the balance between Gómez and Zayas, was at odds with the Paez brothers, his former supporters.[31] To prove their ascendency over one another, the two groups were raising funds through fraud (e.g., forged horse certificates), blackmail, and extortion. Each faction threatened revolt to demonstrate the strength of its popular appeal. The Paez brothers accused Guerra of being too co-operative with the government. To increase their own following, they encouraged anti-Americanism with popular ditties: "The little American rooster is crowing now but keep quiet, brothers; gather your tobacco, and when our work is done he will crow no more."[32]

In Havana and Matanzas, Liberal groups loyal to the "half-crazy" Loynaz del Castillo had formed paramilitary organizations called the "Constitutional Militia" in the spring of 1907. While their announced purpose was to deter the conservatives from trying to incite violence, the units constituted a shadow army available to the highest bidder.[33] In Oriente, the Miguelistas considered a revolt to impress Gómez with their potential voting strength, and at the same time hoped the Provisional Government would buy them off with work.[34]

Partially screened by the sound and fury of the Miguelista-Zayista reorganization, another political movement gathered strength in the summer of 1907: an all-Negro party. Whether such a racially-based party might have developed without the American occupation is problematical, but the Negro movement began only after the intervention. The organizers' motives were mixed, but dissatisfaction with their share of Liberal patronage and confidence that the Negroes would be fairly treated by the Provisional Government seem to have been among the more obvious reasons for the movement's rise.[35] In March, 1907, the Negro movement started rumors among the whites of a race war in Cuba, and the rumors persisted throughout the summer.[36] Upon closer investigation the Military Information Division discovered that the Negro movement was not simply another political faction. In various provinces under such names as "Unión Social," "Gran Coalición Social de Occidente," "Antonio Maceo Association," and the "Camaguey Directory," the Cuban Negroes attempted to institute a broadly based, reform-oriented mass social movement. The Negroes' goals included the reorganization of the economy, moral regeneration, the elimination of discrimination in the courts, free public instruction, and full political participation.[37] The Negro associations, the basic units in the movement, were regionally based; their major figures, Evaristo Estenoz and Luis Pena, were former insurgent officers.

The Negro associations were vigorously opposed by the leading Liberals, white and Negro, including Pino Guerra,

Juan Gualberto Gómez, and Martín Morúa Delgado. The Liberals' concern is understandable because the Negro movement endangered the Liberal patronage system. The Negroes' case against the Liberals was made clear in the Lajas Declaration, signed by twenty-three Negro leaders in Santa Clara:

> If the title of revolutionist will get one public positions, we Negroes are revolutionists, too; and if it is necessary to be capable, we Negroes have ability also; and just as a white man goes to fill a position without any experience and acquires his knowledge while in that office, the colored people can do the same.[38]

The Provisional Government's concern with the Negro movement was as great as that of the *políticos*, but it was not certain what the Negroes' goals were or how they would try to achieve them. The movement, however, could not be ignored, and it formed an essential part of the pattern of tension that held Cuba in the *tiempo muerto* of 1907. Strikes, unemployment, drought, yellow fever, high prices, rumors of revolt, the political factions in flux—all threatened to shatter the surface tranquillity. The central question that bound the interests of the government, the *políticos*, and the annexationists was: Would there now be a real, general insurrection?

### The Masso Parra Conspiracy

On June 22, 1907, the man who would attempt to turn Cuban anxiety into a bloody revolt against the Americans walked into the Cuban consulate in Port-au-Prince, Haiti, asked for the news from Havana, and then announced he was returning "home." [39] His name was Juan Masso Parra and his business was insurrection. Son of a Spanish merchant in Manzanillo, Masso Parra fought on the insurgent side of the revolt against Spain until January 19, 1898. On that day he and his entire battalion of 107 men defected to the Spanish, and resumed fighting, against the insurgents, as merciless guerrillas. Masso Parra later explained his treachery as disgust with the Cuban generals, but he was also paid handsomely to change sides. As a result of his change of allegiance, he became one of the most hated men in Cuba; he returned Cuban hostility full measure with a notorious book, *Masso Parra contra Cuba.* He often said, his father reported, that nothing would please him more than to fight Cubans again.[40] Masso Parra made his headquarters after 1898 on the island of Curaçao. He boasted that both Colombia and Venezuela paid him not to ply his trade within their borders. Twice he tried to return to Cuba, but General Wood and Estrada Palma refused to let him land. In late July, 1907, inexplicably, he was allowed to return to Cuba, where he immediately began to behave like an active conspirator.[41]

Apparently rebuffed by the Liberal factions, Masso Parra turned to individual radicals with no apparent common interest except political conspiracy per se. One was Juan Ducasse, the only Negro general linked with the conservatives; he was former *colono* who had lost his land for debts to the Cuban Land and Leaf Tobacco Company, a subsidiary of the American Tobacco Company.[42] Masso Parra also enlisted José Lara Miret, white, a Liberal, a veteran, and a former Rural Guard officer dismissed for defecting to the Constitutional Army in 1906. Since then Lara Miret, a protégé of Loynaz del Castillo, had been active in organizing the subrosa Constitutional Militia.[43]

During August Masso Parra met with leaders of almost every identifiable political group in Cuba. The theme of his interviews apparently was that the Cubans should attack the Americans and destroy foreign-owned property. Among those he approached with this appeal were the Zayistas (who defended him in the press), the Miguelistas (who denounced him), Evaristo Estenoz of the Negro movement, Spaniards, conservative planters, local *jefes* of every affiliation, and foreign businessmen.[44] To complicate matters for the Provisional Government, which was trying to sort out the conspiracy, the Bureau of Insular Affairs forwarded a bulky file implicating Masso Parra with the civil war in the Dominican Republic. Magoon, however, was convinced that Cuba was

Masso Parra's major interest, and that his conspiracy involved the Negro associations of Havana and Pinar del Rio.[45]

By mid-September Masso Parra's contacts had narrowed to two distinct groups, Spanish and Cuban businessmen and representatives of the Negro associations.[46] Rumors of an anti-American rising grew in western Cuba. The Havana press reported fresh plots every day, and several intelligence reports linked Masso Parra with the Tobacco Trust.[47] The Military Information Division alerted Magoon that the plans for a revolt were set, arms were cached and that only last-minute complications kept violence from beginning in Pinar del Rio. The major complication was Pino Guerra, who was persuading the Cubans involved that a revolt would mean annexation. Guerra's own interest, Captain Furlong believed, in quelling the revolt was to win favor with the government, perhaps even to being named commanding general of Cuba's armed forces.[48]

Magoon's own conviction was that Masso Parra was the agent of financial interests fomenting revolt to bring on annexation. Masso Parra himself admitted this much to a secret service agent.[49] On the basis of the intelligence reports of September 22 and 23, Magoon acted to break the conspiracy before the rising, supposedly scheduled for September 27, could begin. Among his first moves was to cable Frank Steinhart, who was in New York negotiating another Cuban loan with Speyer and Company. Magoon told Steinhart that revolt was imminent, that he must return at once. Steinhart wired back: "Coming soon as steam can carry me. Keep stiff upper lip. We will lick them sure." In another cable, Steinhart sent advice rather than encouragement: "Tell Hill [George S. Hill, a Havana financier] name of Steinhart that he is making trouble for himself."[50] Magoon wired back that some eleventh hour negotiations in Havana promised success:

Have had several interviews with party you name. He is active and believed honest efforts counteract movement. Chiefs both parties active and energetic. News received this afternoon encouraging. Efforts behalf Government producing good results.[51]

The conspiracy itself began to unravel as it became apparent in Havana that the Provisional Government was aware of the plot, but not panic-stricken. In the towns of Pinar del Rio, San Juan y Martinez and Consolación del Sur, the local *políticos* hastily denied complicity and pledged their loyalty to the Provisional Government.[52] Both the Zayistas and Miguelistas were loud in their condemnation of Masso Parra. At the heart of their denunciations, the Military Information Division reported, was their fear of a Negro revolution. On the other hand, Cuban conservatives, the Spaniards, and the Germans hoped a Negro revolt would break out because it would force the United States to establish a military government and end the "Negro problem" and "the chance of Negro control" of an independent Cuba.[53] Since these views were widely publicized, the Negro associations, the suspected backbone of the revolt, must have had some second thoughts. Signs of panic among the probable backers of the revolt, the annexationists, appeared in a news release drafted by the Havana Merchant's Association and published by the New York *World*. The *World* article pictured Cuba as on the brink of a great antiforeign rebellion caused by Magoon's leniency with the Cuban radicals and the reduction of the Army of Cuban Pacification to three thousand men. Cuba, the *World* reported, was near chaos, and its credit was ruined.[54]

In Havana, Magoon, upon learning that the leaders of the plot were assembled for the last time before going off to the countryside, ordered their arrest. Under the direction of Captain James A. Ryan, the Havana police on the morning of September 26 arrested seven men; Masso Parra, Lara Miret, and Juan Ducasse were among them. They were charged and indicted for conspiring "to burn property of foreigners, excepting Spaniards" and to revolt.[55] In Pinar del Rio a troop of the Eleventh Cavalry patrolled the towns the plotters had visited and found them tranquil.[56]

With the arrest of Masso Parra and his associates, the conspiracy collapsed. The comparative ease with which it was broken and the improbable violence of Masso Parra's plans gave the whole episode an unreal quality. Magoon was undecided whether the Masso Parra affair constituted a dangerous threat to peace. In his first report to Taft after the arrests, he described the plotters as the agents of persons who wished to provoke annexation and discredit the Roosevelt administration. Masso Parra's acts had been enigmatic: "the pure cussedness of the traditional bad man explains his conduct but does not account for money he spent."[57]

A week later Magoon wired that all the evidence pointed to an alliance-of-convenience between the annexationists and some Cuban radicals, that the plot might have been backed by Roosevelt's enemies in the United States who had sizable business interests in Cuba. On the island itself, Magoon said, Masso Parra had no backing except from criminals: "I am entirely satisfied that this conspiracy found no favor with the inhabitants of Cuba."[58] By the time he submitted his annual report two months later, Magoon was ready to believe that the "attempted conspiracy was brought about solely by the instrumentality of Masso Parra, whose life has been devoted to rebellion."[59] Masso Parra and his fellow plotters, abandoned by all but their families, were subsequently sentenced to three year prison terms and forgotten. More importantly Magoon found himself flooded by expressions of loyalty from the *políticos* and the Cuban press.

However fantastic in conception and execution, the Masso Parra conspiracy was something more than the fanciful posturing of a handful of radicals. The contemporary evidence (and subsequent Cuban history) suggests that it was the only threat, however small, to Roosevelt's plan to restore the Cuban government. Though the plotting ended on September 26, the anti-American feelings and unrest on which the conspirators hoped to capitalize did not.[60] In Havana, for example, although most Cubans viewed the whole affair as an annexationist plot, the secret service agents who revealed the conspiracy were called traitors. Captain Furlong also found that the radical "Constitutional Militia" was still active after the abortive revolt, and arms continued to arrive in Cuba.[61] Among the *políticos*, Zayas and José Miguel Gómez took the government's part only at the last minute, although both knew of the plot. Pina Guerra's help, on the other hand, had been crucial to checking revolt in Pinar del Rio. To the surprise of the grateful Military Information Division, he did "excellent work for the government."[62]

As for the Negro associations, they too continued to grow, and were organized in the same year as the Independent Party of Color. For the next five years (1907–12), this third party tried to arrange patronage for the Negroes by promising block votes to whomever offered the most favors. The party was outlawed by a 1910 bill prohibiting racially based parties. In 1912, in an effort to continue in office, José Miguel Gómez planned a "little" revolt with Evaristo Estenoz, but the affair flamed into a full race war in which three thousand Negroes were finally killed by the Cuban Army before the fighting ended.[63]

The basic human material for a revolt was present in 1907, as in 1906, and the annexationists were convinced, after Taft's April visit, that 1907 might be the last time Cuban tranquillity could be sufficiently disturbed to prolong the American occupation. Clearly they had sufficient motive to stir up at least the illusion of rebellion. The statements made by Roosevelt, Taft, and Cannon suggested that the administration was still not thoroughly convinced that Cuba was ready for self-government. All business and political logic demanded continued American occupation. Even if the rebellion threatened their properties, the business elite was willing to gamble that the Army of Cuban Pacification could smash the rebels quickly. At least active fighting might persuade Washington to replace Magoon with a general and a military government. This change might have both increased the revolt (and the chances for annexation) and destroyed the government's liaison with the Cuban radicals. Even after 1907, the American annexationists continued to protest the anticolonial trend in the United States foreign policy, and they were men with a cause:

While the other nations of the earth have fought tooth and nail to add to their domains, in all lands and in all ages territory being considered a most desirable possession, we Americans lie awake night painfully planning how to rid ourselves of the additions to our greatness, resulting from our prowess or from Providential causes.

Is it not time for us to abandon this childish shrinking from mixing in the world with other grown up nations?

What would Travis and Crockett and Houston, the men who wrung the huge State of Texas from the Mexicans, and added it to the Union, think of the timid, not to say cowardly, conduct of their descendants who pulled down the flag of the United States in Honolulu and in Cuba, and would pull it down in the Philippines.[64]

In the balance, the Masso Parra conspiracy appears to have been exactly what the Provisional Government first suspected it was: an alien-conservative attempt to provoke annexation by encouraging Liberal dissidents and the Negro associations to revolt. The Military Information Division, whatever Magoon's disclaimers, remained convinced that Masso Parra was financed by Spaniards who desired some sort of permanent intervention, if not American, then British, French, or German. The Spanish wanted a strong government which would provide absolute security for their property interests, "not one like the United States, which plays to the common people and makes their [the businessmen's] interests secondary to politics in the United States."[65] Masso Parra, aware of the conservatives' wishes, "considered a movement that appeared to be war against the Americans, a means to the ends desired."[66]

The plan failed for several reasons. First, the Miguelistas and Zayistas believed they could turn their support of Magoon into more government patronage and halt a challenge to their political hegemony at the same time. Both factions feared that a revolt would endanger the plans to restore the Cuban government, although such a realization was made only after each faction decided it could not pin the onus of the conspiracy on the other. In addition, the Provisional Government, through its public works projects and the Army's practice marches, made clear to the Cuban people that rebellion was unnecessary to get work and unhealthy at best: "As long as they have work and money to support their families they will be peaceable, and the politicians will find it difficult to stir them up. This is one reason why some politicians are antagonistic to public works."[67] Within the conspiracy, the plotters and their financial backers failed to make the revolt credible in their anxiety to create the illusion of a great anti-American rising. Masso Parra may have worried Magoon, but he did not really shake the Army's grip on the situation.

Ironically, the conspiracy's failure may have given impetus to Cuba's Conservative party and the presidential candidacy of Mario G. Menocal, sugarman, peacemaker, and respected general of the Army of Liberation. Menocal was solidly backed by the same people interested in annexation: dissident "Liberals, Conservatives, Spaniards, Americans, and all other commercial and producing classes of the island."[68] With the alternative of annexation denied them, the conservatives turned to party politics. The Provisional Government, by pinching off the Masso Parra conspiracy in 1907, destroyed the last, desperate attempt to join Cuba to the United States and helped create the organized conservative opposition party which American policy needed.

1. Lockmiller, *Magoon in Cuba*, pp. 69–70; Portell Vilá, *Historia de Cuba*, IV, 527–28.

2. Taft to Charles P. Taft, October 9, 1907, Taft Papers.

3. Magoon to Taft, November 29, 1906, Taft Papers.

4. Magoon to Taft, January 20, 1907, Taft Papers.

5. José de Armas to Taft, December 27, 1906, Taft Papers.

6. Atkins to Taft, January 19, 1907, Taft Popers.

7. E. V. Morgan to Root, October 22, 1906, Case 1943–1, *Num. File, 1906–1910,* Vol. CCV, RG 59.

8. E. V. Morgan to Root, December 29, 1906, Case 1943–43, *Num. File, 1906–1910,* Vol. CCV, RG 59.

9. Editorial, *La Unión Española,* October 24, 1906.

10. "Report of the Very Rev. Albion W. Knight, Episcopal Bishop of Cuba," File 056–056–1, CC/PGoC, RG 199.

11. Capt. C. F. Crain to MID, December 13 and 14, 1906, File 017, CC/PGoC; MID to C/S, ACP, December 21, 1906, File 032, CC/PGoC; Maj. W. D. Beach to C/S, ACP, June 4, 1907, File 063/19, CC/PGoC;

MID to C/S, ACP, December 10, 1906, File 021, CC/PGoC; Capt. Carl Reichman to MID, January 11, 1907, File 014–6, CC/PGoC; Capt. A. J. McNab, Jr., to MID, February 28, 1907, File 079, CC/PGoC; Maj. M. W. Day to MID, December 26, 1906, File 014–2, CC/PGoC; MID to C/S, ACP, January 15, 1907, File 047, CC/PGoC, RG 199. Captain Furlong estimated that perhaps 10 per cent of the weapons used in the August Revolution had been confiscated.

12. Col. J. T. Van Orsdale to Military Secretary, ACP, December 8–19, 1906, File 020–020–4, CC/PGoC; Capt. C. I. Crockett to Maj. H. J. Slocum, January 19, 1907, File 020–7, CC/PGoC, RG 199. These particular reports were forwarded all the way to Secretary Taft.

13. Capt. C. F. Crain to MID, February 2, 1907, File 017–9, CC/PGoC, RG 199.

14. MID to C/S, ACP, December 10, 1906, File 021, CC/PGoC, RG 199.

15. Maj. F. P. Fremont to Military Secretary, ACP, December 7, 1906, File 015–1, CC/PGoC; Lt. Col. R. L. Bullard to Magoon, December ?–21, 1906, File 015–2 to 015–6, CC/PGoC, RG 199.

16. MID to C/S, ACP, March 18, 1907, File 022–1, CC/PGoC; Maj. M. W. Day to MID, ACP, January 1, 1907, File 014–5, CC/PGoC; Lt. Col. R. L. Bullard to Magoon, December 21, 1906, File 033, CC/PGoC; "Report of the Very Rev. Albion W. Knight," previously cited.

17. Maj. W. D. Beach to C/S, ACP, February 9, 1907, File 063–6, CC/PGoC, RG 199.

18. Magoon to Taft, March 4, 1907, File 082, CC/PGoC, RG 199.

19. Reports of Capt. D. E. Aultman to MID, December 7, 1906, to January 2, 1907, File 023–023–3, CC/PGoC; Sr. I. Sobrado, Governor of Pinar del Rio, to Magoon, April (?), 1907, File 096–5, CC/PGoC, RG 199.

20. Fuentes, secret service agent, to MID, January (?), 1907, File 052, CC/PGoC, RG 199.

21. MID to C/S, ACP, March 28, 1907, File 96–4, CC/PGoC; "Notes of Capt. C. F. Crain on conditions in Matanzas, December 13, 1906," File 017–017–3, CC/PGoC, RG 199.

22. Col. O. J. Sweet to MID, December 19, 1906, File 013–2, CC/PGoC, RG 199.

23. The account of the Republicans' Cuban inspection is from J. Hampton Moore, *With Speaker Cannon through the Tropics,* pp. 291–340. Moore was recorder of unforgettable phrases for the party and a Cannon protégé.

24. *Ibid.,* p. 333.

25. *Ibid.,* p. 305.

26. *Ibid.,* p. 313.

27. *Ibid.,* p. 407.

28. *Ibid.* Andrew D. White, former president of Cornell University and ambassador to Germany, visited Cuba at the same time and, upon his return, posed the dilemma: Cuba was incapable of self-government,

but annexation was impossible because of racial and cultural differences. *Harper's Weekly,* LI (April 20, 1907), 561.

29. 1st Lt. Ben Lear, Jr., supervising officer, MID, Santa Clara, to C/S, ACP, May 2, 1907, File 063–18, CC/PGoC, RG 199.

30. José de Armas to Taft, June 1, 1907, Taft Papers.

31. Magoon to Taft, July 21, 1907, File 2102, RG 350, 1st Lt. T. W. Brown to MID, March 18, 1907, File 097, CC/PGoC; Capt. S. G. Jones to MID, August 16, 1907, File 096–11, CC/PGoC, RG 199.

32. 1st Lt. T. W. Brown to MID, April 24, 1907, File 097–3, CC/PGoC, RG 199.

33. Capt. A. J. McNab, Jr., to MID, March 2, 1907, File 017–15, CC/PGoC; MID to C/S, ACP, March 21, 1907, File 017–17, CC/PGoC, RG 199.

34. MID to ACP, July 9, 1907; Capt. A. G. Dougherty to Maj. Gen. A. Rodríguez, July 9 and 10, 1907; Capt. A. G. Dougherty to Maj. H. J. Slocum, July 15, 1907, all File 146, CC/PGoC, RG 199.

35. Col. G. F. Chase to Military Secretary, ACP, December 30, 1906, File 034, CC/PGoC; Capt. H. C. Smither to MID, January 5, 1907, File 044–1, CC/PGoC, RG 199.

36. Brig. Gen. T. H. Barry to Magoon, March 5, 1907, File 013–3, CC/PGoC; MID to C/S, ACP, March 24, 1907, File 096–3, CC/PGoC; MID to Magoon, September 17, 1907, File 014, CC/PGoC; Col. O. J. Sweet to MID, September 25, 1907, File 013–12, CC/PGoC, RG 199.

37. Brig. Gen. T. H. Barry to Magoon, September 25, 1907, File 14–20 (Negro manifestos enclosed), CC/PGoC; José Jerez Varona, chief of secret police, to Maj. F. S. Foltz, August 6, 1907, File 159, CC/PGoC; MID to C/S, ACP, August 11, 1907, File 159–1, CC/PGoC, RG 199.

38. Enclosure to MID to C/S, ACP, September 13, 1907, File 014, CC/PGoC, RG 199.

39. Memo, Dept. of State and Justice, to Provisional Governor, July 31, 1907, File 158, CC/PGoC, RG 199.

40. Reports assembled by E. V. Morgan, U.S. Minister to Cuba, for Magoon, February 25–June 18, 1907, File 072—072–13, CC/PGoC; Emerterio S. Santovenia, *Un día como hoy* (Havana, 1946), pp. 43–44.

41. MID began to tail Masso Parra immediately, and he made no attempt to hide his activities, which no doubt was part of his purpose. MID to C/S, ACP, July 31 and August 2, 1907, File 158, CC/PGoC, RG 199.

42. *Havana Post,* September 27, 1907; MID to C/S, ACP, October 4, 1907, File 096–27, CC/PGoC, RG 199.

43. MID to C/S, ACP, August 5, 1907, File 158–3, CC/PGoC; MID to C/S, ACP, December 27, 1907, File 17–40, CC/PGoC, RG 199.

44. MID to C/S, ACP, August 5, September 1, 1907, File 158, CC/PGoC, RG 199.

45. Magoon to Maj. F. MacIntyre, September 15, 1907, File 2102, General Classified Files, BIA, RG 350. File 2102 contains the reports of investigations by Treasury Department agents, photostats of letters by

Dominican conspirators to Masso Parra, and correspondence with the Provisional Governor.

46. MID to C/S, ACP, September 7, 16, 18, 19, 21, 1907, Files 158 (15–25) and 096 (14–19) with enclosures, CC/PGoC, RG 199.

47. MID to C/S, ACP, September 20, 1907, File 158–23, CC/PGoC; Col. J. Parker to C/S, ACP, September 20, 1907, File 096–13, CC/PGoC, RG 199.

48. MID to C/S, ACP, September 22, 1907, File 158–28, CC/PGoC; Capt. S. G. Jones to Col. J. Parker, September 25, 1907, File 096–17, CC/PGoC, RG 199.

49. Magoon to Taft, September 26, 1907, File 017–26, CC/PGoC; MID to C/S, ACP, September 23, 1907, File 158–28, CC/PGoC, RG 199.

50. Magoon to Steinhart, September 23, 1907; Steinhart to Magoon, September 23, 1907, File 017–23, CC/PGoC, RG 199.

51. Magoon to Steinhart, September 23, 1907, File 017–23, CC/PGoC, RG 199.

52. Col. J. Parker to C/S, ACP, September 29, 1907, File 096–21, CC/PGoC; Sr. I. Sobrado to Magoon, September 30, 1907, File 096–22, CC/PGoC; MID to C/S, ACP, File 096–25, CC/PGoC, RG 199.

53. MID to C/S, ACP, September 26, 1907, File 017–27, CC/PGoC, RG 199.

54. Maj. F. MacIntyre to Magoon, September 26, 1907, File 017–23, CC/PGoC. The *Havana Post* ran almost the same story on September 27.

55. Memo, Manuel Landa, Secretary of Justice, to Col. E. H. Crowder, October 1, 1907, File 199, CC/PGoC, RG 199.

56. Col. J. Parker to C/S, ACP, October 2, 1907, File 096–26, CC/PGoC; *New York Times*, September 27 and 28, 1907.

57. Magoon to Taft, September 26, 1907, File 017–26, CC/PGoC, RG 199. General Barry believed the business connections with the revolt were real. Barry to Magoon, October 10, 1907, File 096–22, CC/PGoC, RG 199.

58. Two telegrams, Magoon to Taft, both October 2, 1907, File 199–1, CC/PGoC, RG 199.

59. Magoon, *Report, 1906–1907*, p. 91. His official summary of the incident is printed on pp. 89–92. Magoon also asked the Bureau of Insular Affairs to continue the investigation of Masso Parra's New York connections. Magoon to MacIntyre, October 10, 1907, File 2102, Classified General Files, BIA, RG 350.

60. MID to C/S, ACP, September 30, October 2, October 8, 1907, File 017, CC/PGoC, RG 199.

61. MID to C/S, ACP, December 27, 1907, File 017–40, CC/PGoC, RG 199.

62. MID to C/S, ACP, October 5, 1907, File 195–4, CC/PGoC, RG 199.

63. Chapman, *A History of the Cuban Republic*, pp. 308–13.

64. *Havana Daily Telegraph*, July 13, 1908.

65. MID to C/S, ACP, February 1, 1908, File 203, CC/PGoC, RG 199.

66. MID to C/S, ACP, October 18, 1907, File 202, CC/PGoC, RG 199.

67. MID to C/S, ACP, September 2, 1907, File 100–16, CC/PGoC, RG 199.

68. MID to C/S, ACP, October 18, 1907, File 202, CC/PGoC, RG 199.

# CHAPTER SEVEN

# THE PROVISIONAL GOVERNMENT
# AND CUBAN STABILITY

WHEN Charles E. Magoon replaced Taft as Provisional Governor in October, 1906, the general guidelines for his administration had been well established by the Secretary of War. In his proclamation of September 29, Taft assured the "people of Cuba" that the Provisional Government, though temporary and under the authority of the United States, would be "a Cuban Government conforming . . . to the Constitution. All the executive departments and the provincial and municipal governments, including that of the City of Havana, will continue to be administered as under the Cuban Republic." The courts would function normally and the laws remain in effect. As soon as peace and stability returned (which presumably meant when violence was reduced to non-political proportions) and a representative Cuban government elected, the Americans would withdraw.[1]

However "Cuban" the Provisional Government was supposed to be, it was, at the level of administrative policy-making, distinctly American-conservative. It was not a businessmen's government in the sense that the requirements of the large sugar and tobacco planters and the banking and commercial institutions in Cuba received highest priority. Rather it was a government of lawyers, judges, bureaucrats, and soldiers ruling, largely, by balancing what they conceived to be in the national interest of Cuba with the demands of American foreign policy. Between these two there was a division caused, on the one hand, by Cuba's need for revolutionary changes in its economic and social structure and, on the other, by the short-term needs of Roosevelt's Caribbean policy. Magoon, despite his power to rule by decree, was caught between his allegiance to Washington and his ambiguous instructions to govern in Cuba's interest. In two different ways he was restrained from working meaningful reforms in Cuba: his decrees had to be cleared with Taft as consistent with American policy and had to be compatible with his own assumptions about the proper role of government per se. These restraints limited his activities within Cuba.

At the same time, Magoon had to contend with demands for "more" government from two intrinsically hostile groups, the American officers on his staff and the Cuban *políticos*. These two groups were not as concerned with the short-range aims of Roosevelt's Cuban policy as they were with conditions in Cuba itself. Naturally, their own prescriptions for Cuba's ills differed widely in both means and ends, but in their own way the officers and the *políticos* spoke for Cuba rather than the United States. While the *políticos* were to a large degree excluded from the highest administrative decision-making elite, the American officers dominated the day to day activities of the Provisional Government.

The influence of the United States Army in the Provisional Government grew during the occupation. American officers became increasingly important in politically sensitive posts, not only in national government, but in provisional and municipal government as well. From Magoon's viewpoint, the Army men offered unquestionable advantages over the Cubans: they were quick to act, incorruptible, trained in effective administration and loyal. Whether he realized their basic lack of sympathy with Roosevelt's Cuban policy is uncertain.

In addition to staffing the executive departments, the Rural Guard and the Governor's office, Army officers held other important posts. Colonel Black, Colonel Greble, and Major Kean, for example, composed an *ad hoc* Board of Municipal Aid, which passed on most municipal expenditures.[2] In the Department of Justice, Captain T. B. Steele headed the politically powerful Bureau of Pardons. Three other officers in the Department of Government handled the administration of Cuba's correctional school, insane asylum, and charity hospital.[3] In April, 1908, when the terms of the provincial governors and councilmen expired, Magoon appointed six officers (either Rural Guard advisers or supervisors from the Military Information Division) to serve as governors through the next elections.[4] Since these officers did not relinquish their military duties, they were in a strong position to insure peaceful elections.

Magoon strengthened the executive branch with five distinctly political appointments in 1907. The Liberal Justo García Vélez became Secretary of State; his brother Carlos was named Inspector of Prisons. The conservative Judge Manuel Landa joined Crowder in the Department of Justice. Demetrio Castillo Duany, a Liberal leader, was appointed chief of the National Penitentiary, and Colonel Charles Hernández, a popular veteran, became Director of Posts and Telegraphs. All five men had reputations for effective public service under Wood; Judge Landa, former Chief Justice of the Audiencia of Havana, was a close friend and frequent correspondent of Wood's.[5]

In terms of domestic reform, Magoon's understanding of Cuba's problems was more comprehensive than his instructions from Roosevelt to re-establish a new government. After successfully completing the first order of business, "to allay or turn into proper channels the political strife which had divided the inhabitants into two hostile camps . . . ," Magoon examined and listed for Taft and Roosevelt the problems that had to be dealt with if Cuba was to be truly stable. It is unclear if the list was prepared in descending order of priority. Its comprehensiveness, however, indicates that the Provisional Governor was aware of the magnitude of the task facing any Cuban government:[6]

1. public health
2. employment during the *tiempo muerto*
3. lack of roads and harbor facilities
4. the high cost of transportation

5. the high cost of the necessities of life: food, clothing, shelter

6. the small margin of profit on sugar and tobacco

7. high interest rates

8. low wages for labor

9. extortion of wage earners by lenders

10. unjust restrictions upon commerce and shipping imposed by customs regulations

11. the need for a banking law to protect savers

12. the need for a national currency

In his annual report for 1908, Magoon made clear that Cuba would remain unstable until some revolutionary changes were made in its national life. Although he did not presume to tell Roosevelt that the United States was responsible for effecting these changes, Magoon clearly described the enormity of the needed changes:

1. To induce the floating population to select a permanent abiding place, build habitations and make it their home.

2. To develop and expand industries so that a larger proportion of the inhabitants may secure employment and incomes for twelve months in the year.[7]

Colonel Enoch H. Crowder, the senior and most influential of Magoon's officer-advisers, went further than the Governor in committing the Provisional Government to the cause of national reconstruction. In a letter to General J. Franklin Bell, he pointed out that the Cuban episode was but another in a long line of Army nation-saving experiences. The work was "closely allied" to that of Wood's government and "substantially identical" to the Army's postwar duties in Mexico and the South. It was as demanding as the tasks facing administrations in Puerto Rico and the Philippines. The effective fulfilment of the Provisional Government's domestic program had great significance for both the United States and Cuba:

"Upon the success with which we build depends, in my judgement, the avoidance of a more serious military problem than we have yet encountered in Cuba."[8]

The restraints upon the Provisional Government in its programs were several. While Magoon had ample legal power, he was mindful that Cuban disapproval of his government could endanger the peace and American policy. The expectation of the Roosevelt administration was that Magoon respect the Cuban Constitution and organic law while making acceptable (to both the United States and Cuba) reforms within it. He had to govern efficiently within his revenues and stabilize the Cuban electoral system and the political parties. At the same time Magoon had to adjudicate several important legal disputes between the Cuban government and some American contractors and the Catholic church. To put the nation's credit on a firm basis, all claims against the government arising from the August Revolution had to be settled and political prisoners released. In addition, the yellow fever problem needed more attention. These issues, however tangential to the basic problems of Cuban political and economic development, absorbed much of the Provisional Government's energies.[9]

Magoon found that administration in the colonial style kept him rooted to his desk in the national palace. His routine work load was immense. He had to give the final approval of the appointments for all political, judicial, and bureaucratic personnel, including municipal judges, notaries, court clerks, professors and teachers, and the cleanup crew of the congressional offices. He authorized all expenditures, franchises, concessions, pardons and amnesties, and approved petitions for private relief. He reviewed and ruled on all judicial decisions appealed through the national court system. In his first year in office he published over a thousand decrees.[10]

The Cuban Treasury, a major American concern, weathered the August Revolution and a series of post-intervention economic setbacks.[11] An ambitious public works program voted by the Cuban Congress in 1906 and the August Revolution turned Estrada Palma's treasury surplus into an estimated deficit of $4 million. When the government's obligations were balanced against the cash surplus of $13.5 million, it looked as if the government would end fiscal 1907 in the red.[12] In his October, 1906, report to Magoon, Major Eugene F. Ladd estimated that if Magoon paid for the revolt and carried out the programmed Cuban budget, the government would spend $31 million and receive $26.8 million. (By comparison, Estrada Palma's government had spent $26 million in fiscal 1906.) By July, 1907, however, the economy had revived enough to bring revenues to $41.2 million of which the Provisional Government spent $39.6 million.[13] In the following year, an economic decline caused by a weak harvest and the Panic of 1907 reduced Magoon's revenues to $34 million, but he increased the government's expenditures to $44.5 million.[14] Although Magoon budgeted only $23.3 million for fiscal 1908, he found it necessary to offset a general economic decline with increased government spending.

The cost of pacifying Cuba came high, and subsequent Cuban presidents made expenditures under the same economic logic, though not as reluctantly as Magoon. Government spending in times of low sugar prices was the easiest alternative to economic collapse or public violence. When Magoon relinquished the Treasury in 1909, he turned over a cash surplus of only $2.8 million and obligations for fiscal 1909 totaling between $6 and $8 million.[15] While many of the Provisional Government's expenses were determined for it by Taft (e.g., claims settlement, census) and Root (e.g., yellow fever eradication) and thus open to question, the bulk of the costs of the occupation came from providing much-needed services and employment which, whatever Magoon's motives, were necessary for good health, education, economic growth, justice and order.

The August Revolution itself created an immediate financial strain on the Cuban Treasury, which Magoon could not correct simply by canceling public works projects. The establishment of an American-controlled government set off a wave of claims for damages and expenses caused by the revolt. The claimants' expectations that the Americans would settle quickly were realized. While the settlements did not come close to the amounts claimed, the total cost of the revolt ($8.6 million) and the amount granted for private claims ($1.3 million) was an added burden to the Treasury. The claims were adjudicated by two commissions, both controlled by American officers. The first, the Cuban Claims Commission, which settled private claims against the government, was headed successively by Major Francis J. Kernan and Captain George W. Read. Two of the three board members were always Army officers. Another commission, headed by Captain Charles F. Crain and dominated (4–3) by Americans, investigated and settled expenses and contracts incurred by Estrada Palma in fighting the rebellion.

The Provisional Government was conservative in awarding settlements. Aliens, who asked $436,000, received $179,000 in damages. Claims for lost horses brought $296,508 to their owners, who wanted $653,000. Miscellaneous claims for damages totaling more than $1 million were settled for $441,000. The costs of mobilization to the Cuban government depleted the Treasury far worse than did private claims: for guns and ammunition, $777,000; for horses, $416,788; for pay for, and upkeep of, the men added to the armed forces, $3.2 million.[16] The comparison of damages to mobilization costs amply demonstrates an integral part of the Liberal strategy: bankrupt the Cuban Treasury (a sure way to get an American response) without hurting too much private property. Taft and Magoon were sure that the financial drain of the revolt on the Treasury would discourage the Cubans from rebelling again; more probably it was an incentive for the American government to prevent another intervention of the 1906 type.

*Legal Reforms and the Advisory Law Commission*

The Provisional Government gave highest priority to a limited revision of Cuba's constitutional system. The goal of this reform, which was to be accomplished through the adoption of new laws, was to insure peaceful elections, representative government at all levels, and an honest, secure judiciary and civil service.

During the September, 1906, truce negotiations, Taft, the Liberals, and the Moderates agreed generally that four new laws were essential if the political parties and government were to function.[17] As passed on by Taft to the Provisional Government, the suggested reforms were to establish the municipal governments on a more autonomous footing, provide for elections supervised by non-partisan boards, protect minority representation in government, reorganize and free the judiciary from presidential control, and create an efficient civil service based on the merit system.[18] To study, draft and recommend the new laws, Magoon, on December 24, 1906, created the Advisory Law Commission.[19] The Cuban membership of the Advisory Law Commission was politically balanced (five Liberals, four conservatives) in order to give the three American members real control of this rump legislature.[20] These Americans were Colonel Enoch H. Crowder, Otto Schoenrich (a judge from Puerto Rico on Magoon's staff), and Major Blanton C. Winship, Judge Advocate General of the Army of Cuban Pacification.

The working procedures of the Advisory Law Commission were designed to make the new laws as palatable in Cuba as possible, but not at the expense of American control. The Commission divided into subcommittees (electoral law, judiciary law, municipal law, civil service law) where the basic research and drafting were accomplished. The subcommittee membership worked to give the American and conservative members the voting advantage. A finished law went to Magoon for consideration by the majority vote of the full Commission. Magoon then published the recommended draft for public comment, and revisions were considered before the final draft became a decree.[21] While the procedural details worked to the conservatives' advantage, the Advisory Law Commission worked under the basic assumption that it could only modify the law within the provisions of the Constitution of 1901.[22] This restriction, repeatedly invoked by the Liberals and grudgingly accepted by the Americans, placed very real limits on the kinds of reforms the Advisory Law Commission could accomplish. The Commission described its work in constitutional terms as "democratic" and "decentralizing," but in reality the laws it passed did not significantly alter the President's powers and, in some places, increased those of the national government.[23]

The work of the Advisory Law Commission, while it satisfied Magoon and Taft and did not arouse the *políticos*, did not meet Colonel Crowder's standards for meaningful reform. In his first report for the Department of Justice, Crowder recommended that the legal reforms be truly revolutionary, that they reach into all phases of Cuban life.[24] Crowder recognized that the Provisional Government was following a "conservative policy of revision" because it did not have the mandate to do more. Simply to rectify the political laws was a challenge, for they were an incongruous maze of Spanish colonial codes, Wood's decrees, acts of the Cuban congress, and decrees by Estrada Palma and Magoon. Within this system the minimum change, Crowder felt, should be to curb the President's powers. He argued, however, that it would be necessary to go far beyond revision of the political and administrative laws to bring Cuba's "monarchical" system into harmony with the ideals of the Constitution. To truly free the Cubans from authoritarian habit patterns, changes should be made in the civil codes, penal codes, criminal procedural codes, and civil procedural codes.[25] Crowder wrote:

> The legislative action above recommended is first in importance among the reconstructive measures which confront the Provisional Government and the work involved is one of great magnitude. . . . Undertaken and conducted in Cuba under most favorable circumstances, this work, in which the beginning has hardly been made, would protract itself over a period of several years. The Republic should, I think, be re-established under adequate *guarantees* [italics added] that this work, so essential to the maintenance of orderly and stable government, shall be prosecuted to as speedy a conclusion as possible.[26]

While Magoon agreed with Crowder that the sweeping changes the Colonel advocated were essential if Cuba was to progress, he did not recommend that the United States assume any more responsibility than it already had for

Cuban reforms. Rather, he adhered to the more conservative Root–Taft position, that some minimal separation and balancing of powers under the Cuban Constitution was about all the reform the Provisional Government should undertake.[27] Magoon lauded Crowder personally, but he did not support the Colonel's specific proposals for more radical legal reforms than the four laws to be drafted by the Advisory Law Commission or for post-restoration legislative guarantees.[28] The best explanation for Magoon's ambivalent position is that he was perfectly aware that Taft would not accept the diplomatic implications of Crowder's reforms. In fact, the Advisory Law Commission did draft the proposed reform codes and then passed them on to the Cuban congress in 1909, but they did not become law.

In the two years of its existence, the Advisory Law Commission drafted the four laws considered essential to the restoration of the Cuban government, wrote another regularizing the organization of the executive departments, and drafted other measures of secondary importance.[29] All were duly put into effect by decrees of the Provisional Governor. All the laws were acceptable compromises, some were well-thought out, but after the American withdrawal none worked as they were designed.

The electoral code, so devilishly complex that it took the *políticos* several months to subvert it, featured permanent, mandatory registration of all Cuban citizens, non-partisan election boards at the three political levels, and proportional representation in electing congressmen and provincial and municipal councilors. Despite conservative efforts, no changes in the franchise were adopted. The electoral machinery, while it was organized in detail so as to be uniform and honest, depended on the impartiality of those conducting the elections. The code clearly was designed on the assumption that stable, coherent political parties would dominate Cuban politics: there were detailed requirements for nominating petitions and conventions, for party representation on electoral boards, and for minority representation.

The two major aspects of the municipal and provincial laws were that the provincial and local governments were given more theoretical independence and less freedom to spend. They could budget without Treasury approval, but could not spend more than a fixed percentage of their income on personnel or exceed a limited bonded indebtedness. In a municipal tax law, the local tax base was made compatible with the national one, but was not radically changed. Irene Wright observed that the only thing the Liberals and conservatives could agree on was that they did not want tax reform.[30] The code also more or less nationalized Havana by giving the national government control of the city's police and sanitation services.

The judiciary and civil service laws protected judges and bureaucrats from arbitrary removal, fixed their salaries and reorganized the courts and the civil service system. Both laws were widely discussed in Cuba because they confirmed the current officeholders in their posts. Both were modeled in their personnel provisions after similar statutes then in force in the United States.

The Advisory Law Commission did succeed in its assigned task: making statutory modifications that would enable the United States to restore a representative Cuban government. The Commission drafted and Magoon decreed a legal, systematic basis for the peaceful transfer of political power. Nonetheless, legal reforms, however well-intentioned, politically acceptable and brilliantly wrought, were no more than palliatives. They were the Roosevelt administration's timid solutions to fundamental economic and political problems in Cuba.

Colonel Crowder pointed out the implications of such limited solutions. He emphasized that even to bring Cuba to the point where its legal system matched its Constitution, the Provisional Government would have to sponsor much more radical reform than Roosevelt and Taft were ready to approve. Crowder identified the Cuban dilemma: it could not be anything but an authoritarian or chaotic state until some radical changes were made in more than just its form of government.[31]

## The Economics of Cuban Stability

The economic situation Magoon inherited in October, 1906, was not promising. Though the Cuban economy recovered from the credit scare and hurricane of that fall, its vulnerability was a continuing problem for the Provisional Government. The United States concern was not simply to protect foreign property; Roosevelt believed that unless these interests were protected, the entire Cuban economy would crumble. Happily, the tobacco and sugar crops of 1906–7 proved profitable; agricultural and mining production picked up; and the financial situation was momentarily stabilized.[32] The Panic of 1907, which began a world-wide liquidation of credit, rocked the economy, but Magoon successfully counteracted the scarcity of funds by depositing $5 million from the Treasury in private banks. These funds gave the planters the operating capital they needed to meet their harvesting expenses.[33] Nevertheless, national income in 1908 was not as high as in 1907. By *la zafra* of 1908, however, economic indicators showed that a recovery was well advanced.

The Provisional Governor was aware of the basic instability in the Cuban economy, its political implications, and the poison it produced in Cuban–American relations. As he said in his annual report for 1908, "the industrial situation in Cuba is the same as it would be in a manufacturing community in the United States, where, each year, the mills were run to their full capacity, night and day, for six months and then closed down for six months."[34] In a long letter to Roosevelt in 1908, Magoon emphasized that political unrest was directly related to the harvesting cycle. Only government spending on public works could offset unemployment. Both employment and the government's revenues were tied inextricably to the world sugar price, which meant that public

works, essential both to internal peace and Cuba's development, would have to be financed by long-term loans to the
Cuban government. Magoon believed that although the government's bonded indebtedness was then $50.6 million, another
loan of $20–$25 million was mandatory.[35]

Early in the occupation, Magoon, at the urging of the
Cuban Chamber of Commerce, Industries and Navigation,
investigated the possibility of another, more liberal, reciprocity
treaty with the United States. Havana businessman Louis V.
Placé urged Magoon to consider a draft treaty that the
Moderates had ignored. A new treaty would benefit Cuba,
to be sure, but:

> The Cuban question, I repeat, is an economical question, and needs
> to be settled economically.
> Cuba's economical problems once settled can make Cuba sufficiently
> rich to support any political problems, for her political leaders do love
> Cuba for the fat there is in it.[36]

Magoon forwarded Placé's letter, and other opinions to
Elihu Root and asked for the State Department's view of such
a treaty. Root's reply was brusque: plans for a new reciprocity
treaty were "rejected, abandoned."[37] Some merchants and
planters turned to lobbying in Washington and agitating for
annexation in Cuba, but reciprocity remained a dead issue.[38]
With a good deal of justice, *Diario de la Marino* said that
Cubans and Americans were not ready for mutual understanding. The Cubans had wanted American assistance, but

> . . . it was not supposed that the Americans, besides shedding their
> blood and spending their money for the so-called Cuban cause, would
> change also their principle of protectionist tariffs and ruin great agri-
> cultural and industrial interests of their own, merely to make happy a
> people of such different race and mentality.[39]

Although the Provisional Government was sympathetic to
Cuban agricultural development and diversification, it did
little to alter the conditions under which Cubans farmed.[40]
The Provisional Government's major effort was in building
roads, but its motives were not entirely to stimulate produc-

tion. Magoon, advised by a fourteen-man commission from the Liga Agraria, an organization of sugar planters, put great stress on the problems of agricultural credit in his reports. Despite the urgings of the sugar planters no action was undertaken to establish a government-backed agricultural bank as then existed in the Philippines, Mexico, and France.[41] Beyond the $5 million loaned in 1907 on a one year basis, the Provisional Government did nothing to ease the sugar planters' credit problems. Magoon changed the tariff slightly to benefit the Cuban cattle business, but rejected a proposed homestead act as too radical for his government to sponsor.

In its relations with Cuban labor, the Provisional Government was far more solicitous than its predecessors, though more from a fear of labor violence than a commitment to the working man. During the occupation, a rash of strikes swept Cuba involving the unions of the cigar-workers, masons and plasterers, railway workers and trainmen, box-makers, plumbers, broom-makers, and carpenters.[42] Generally the strikers wanted a 10 per cent pay increase and an eight-hour working day. The Cuban labor movement was handicapped by the competition between the native Cubans and the Spanish immigrants, some of whom were anarchists. The strike was a favorite device of the Spaniards to clean the Cubans out of an industry; they would arouse the Cuban laborers, then take the jobs themselves after the walkout.[43] The Provisional Government blamed Spanish agitators for the few instances of violence which marred the strikes, and would not intercede for the employers. It did, however, allow railway strikebreakers to land and others to take strike-vacated jobs.[44] The Havana businessmen, particularly the Spanish and English, were highly critical of Magoon's "pro-labor" government. Some formed a "Federation of the Producing Classes of the Island of Cuba" to defend themselves from the strikers since the government was so pliant.[45] For settling the cigar-makers' strike in 1907, Magoon received congratulations from Taft and General Edwards, chief of the Bureau of Insular Affairs, but in Cuba the governor was not so well treated: "I feel it is my duty to report the existence of resentment toward me on the part of large employers of labor and that portion of the inhabitants who believe in the Spanish methods of dealing with the laboring classes."[46]

In its relationship to the Cuban economy, the Provisional Government did nothing to alter permanently the basic conditions under which Cubans worked, earned, bought, and sold.[47] What it did do was to mediate justly between the competing, economically important segments of the population. In the case of the labor movement and rural workers, the government's actions probably increased their expectations for equal treatment from succeeding regimes. Although the Cuban economy performed well during the occupation, the real key to the temporary year-long prosperity was the Provisional Government's own spending. Coupled with increased foreign investment caused by the American presence, this spending created a business upswing. In 1909, the old patterns of wealth distribution re-emerged; as the American Consul-General, James L. Rodgers, reported:

. . . The fact remains, that a good portion of the abnormal purchasing power of the people disappeared when it was seen that in the future Cuba would have to depend largely upon her own resources and that under somewhat restricted conditions.[48]

*Public Works and Good Works: Policy and Administration*

During the twenty-eight months of occupation, within the traditional spheres of governmental activity, the Provisional Government worked to improve living conditions in Cuba. While its programs had to be acceptable to the Roosevelt administration, it often planned, appropriated and administered in what it considered to be Cuba's best interests. How the civilian policy-makers defined these interests and how the American officers reacted to these definitions reveals some significant differences in policy criteria between Magoon and his advisers. In general, Magoon was aware of the political relationship of his government's activities in Cuba to his mission, the peaceful re-establishment of an elected Cuban government. Even when he attempted to provide for Cuba's future economic growth, he worked with the political context in mind.

The Army officers, on the other hand, though they were only too aware of the political situation, evaluated the government's work in terms of professional efficiency and long-range, humanitarian accomplishment. They became concerned when policy obstructed administration, and, in some cases, they recommended reforms which, in the name of efficiency and professionalism, reinforced the colonial-centralist nature of the Cuban government. In some areas the officers were in perfect agreement with Magoon's programs because they recognized the government's activities were essential to the Army's pacification plan.

Magoon's public works projects included harbor improvements, waterworks, and sewerage systems, but his major interest was in building roads. In 1906, the Provisional Governor discovered that Cuba had but five hundred miles of macadamized roads, whereas Jamaica, a smaller island, had a thousand. Because of this transportation lag, only six of forty potential ports were in use. The cart roads were atrocious, for the heavily-laden bull-carts with their canted wheels slashed the unpaved roadbeds into gullies or mudholes. In economic terms, the lack of roads meant that sugar *colonos* and other farmers had to depend on either public or company railroads, both expensive, to transport their produce.[49] To cut transportation costs and force railway rates down, Magoon planned to build a central highway across the island and to open feeder roads which would serve at least two ports (one north, one south) in every province.[50]

Magoon also believed that the road-building program was essential to Cuban pacification because it provided employment during the *tiempo muerto*. He specifically justified it this way in his first public report, and he wrote General Bell that without the new roads the United States could expect another Philippines in terms of time, lives, and cost.[51] Irene Wright seconded Magoon's views; she believed road-building in Pinar del Rio averted Masso Parra's revolt in 1907.[52]

The actual work was performed under the supervision of Army Engineers in the Army of Cuban Pacification or by officers detailed to the Department of Public Works. Because of the shortage of trained engineers in Cuba, American civil engineers were also hired. Although some of the construction was done by government workers, much of it was handled by Cuban and American contractors. A common ploy to silence potential "rebels" was for Lieutenant Colonel Bullard to see the "leader," make him straw boss, and get road work for the whole crew.[53] Only then did the Cubans learn that American officers would be in charge, an unpleasant discovery for the contractors and workers alike.[54]

Magoon's original (April, 1907) plans called for the construction or improvement of 2300 kilometers of road at a cost of $13 million. The entire public works budget was to have been $22 million, as compared with $13.8 million appropriated in 1906 by the Cuban congress. By September, 1908, the Provisional Government had built 570 kilometers of road, expected to finish 190 more before February, 1909, and had repaired 200 kilometers. The cost had been $13 million. Though Magoon's plans outstripped his accomplishments, his government doubled the mileage of Cuba's paved roads and halved the costs of transporting sugar and tobacco in the affected areas.[55]

The entire public works program, which included the improvement of harbor facilities, water and sewerage systems and the construction of public buildings, was the Provisional Government's answer to cyclic unemployment, and by this standard it was successful. In assessing the sizable investment in public works (1907—$19.5 million; 1908—$16.2 million), Magoon believed the expenditures had "greatly stimulated" trade and commerce because the money reached all sectors of the population. The Cubans agreed, for in June, 1908, when the Provisional Government announced that no new contracts would be let, the entire Cuban press predicted chaos.[56] Magoon's final judgment on his projects was more benediction than report: "I doubt if history presents an instance of more good in more ways resulting from an equal expenditure of public funds in constructing public improvements." [57]

The Department of Public Works increased both in size and in the scope of its activities during the occupation.[58] To a large degree it assumed many of the responsibilities given to local government for construction and maintenance of roads and buildings. During the first year of occupation the technical and non-technical permanent employees of the department doubled. This trend toward centralized control over public works was justified in terms of increased efficiency and achievement by Lieutenant Colonel William M. Black, the department's adviser. Black believed that the highly professional direction given public works projects by American and Cuban civil engineers provided "object lessons in ways of decreasing the cost, by introduction of modern methods of work and modern plant."[59]

Within the Department of Government, Lieutenant Colonel Greble and the secretary, Manuel Sobrado, agreed that the national government should assume greater responsibilities because local governments had not adequately provided funds and supervision for Cuba's charitable institutions.[60] During the occupation, the department assumed complete control of construction and maintenance for the public institutions under its supervision, centralized these institutions' administration, completed the nationalization of the Havana police, and broadened the powers and activities of the postal and telegraph service. The new municipal law of 1908 gave the department supervisory responsibility over all local public works projects where national funds were committed. Within the department, the secretary was given improved accounting and personnel management procedures to strengthen his own control.

In the field of public instruction, the Provisional Government did little to arrest the deterioration of Wood's school program. There was no crusade to Americanize the Cuban children or to stimulate local interest in managing the schools. The Department of Public Instruction remained under a Cuban holdover from the Wood regime, Lincoln de Zayas, whose principal concerns seem to have been the moral dangers of coeducation and the growth of "the whole child." Zayas, despondent over the Cubans' failure to accept Wood's reforms, urged that the entire public school system be nationalized, but it was not.[61] In 1908, Lieutenant Colonel Bullard became acting secretary. He was appalled at the corruption he found: sinecures, officials carrying their mistresses on the payrolls, falsified reports, kickbacks on supply contracts, promotion for sexual and political favoritism. His own mission, he guessed, was to keep the scandalous conditions hidden until the occupation ended. In public education, Bullard observed, pacification meant "dealing out the pie."[62]

### Politics and Public Health

In the eyes of Major Jefferson Randolph Kean, M.D., American policy in the area of public health was poorly conceived and not well executed.[63] In no other area did the professional-humanitarian concerns of an American adviser come into more direct conflict with the Provisional Governor's political priorities. The basic conflict lay in two areas, the United States inordinate concern about yellow fever and the necessity of using the Cuban health service as a political instrument. From Kean's point of view, the Provisional Government obstructed what he believed were programs designed to help the Cuban people. The only concession he won was an administrative one which also benefited Magoon, the nationalization of the public health service and the creation of an autonomous Department of Sanitation.

Kean's own service in Cuba dated back to the Military Government when he had been intimately involved in Wood's antidisease crusade. Although he realized that the eradication of yellow fever had been an inspiring accomplishment, he was perfectly aware that the Cubans themselves were unconcerned about the disease. They simply did not get it; the victims were nearly always non-immune Americans and Europeans.[64]

On the other hand, typhoid, malaria, cholera, and tuberculosis posed continuing, major threats to the population. In 1907 in Havana deaths from diarrhea and enteritis among children (610) outnumbered the total deaths for all other age groups from all other infectious diseases, except tuberculosis.[65] Only Havana, with lavish appropriations from the national government, had attempted to maintain the standards set by the Military Government, and it had concentrated on yellow fever control. Conditions elsewhere in Cuba can be imagined from this report from Matanzas by one of Kean's special inspectors:

Of the occupied houses only two were found to have water closets . . . the others had outhouses with earth pits, the conditions of which was nasty and foul smelling in the extreme. The patios of the *bodegas* [stores] also contained pig pens, chicken yards and stable, and there were wet areas extending under the houses, from all of which very foul odors and swarms of flies arose. The patio of Sr. Pages contained a chicken yard and a small pig tied by its leg, in the vicinity of the latter was a very foul spot from which a swarm of flies arose. A leak in a hydrant keeps part of this patio very wet in the region of the chicken yard. . . . The keeper of one of these *bodegas* and a lady who had been living for two months near the home of Sr. Pages says the number of flies is about what it has always been in this neighborhood.[66]

Whatever Cuba's health problems in general, the Provisional Government concentrated on stamping out yellow fever. This disease had reappeared in Havana in 1905 and 1906, and the Roosevelt administration became concerned lest the Army become infected, trade and credit in Cuba be hurt by an epidemic, and the disease spread to the southern United States. (As a matter of fact, the infection came to Havana from New Orleans.) Kean admitted that yellow fever did pose a threat, principally because the Cuban municipalities had neither the will nor the funds to sanitize themselves.[67] Although the Provisional Government went to work on the problem, another epidemic broke out in August, 1907, lasting until November. The concern in Washington is amply documented: the American minister in Havana submitted "sanitary reports" from Cuba every ten days, and these reports gave the prognosis for each yellow fever case. For the period of the epidemic the reports listed sixty-two new cases of yellow fever among Spanish immigrants and American soldiers. The September reports put the yellow fever problem in perspective: in that month there were 15 active fever cases, 26 typhoid cases, and 2094 active cases of tuberculosis.[68]

In 1908, another small yellow fever epidemic aroused the State Department. Writing Magoon, Elihu Root stressed that Cuba must live up to its public health pledge in the Platt Amendment:

> If there had been no intervention I should be hammering away vigorously at the Government of Cuba to require them to go on with the plan for the sanitation of Havana . . . perhaps we ought to declare war on you. You are a large mark and would be easier to hit than the average Cuban.[69]

Despite the Department of Sanitation's successful eradication of the fever, the State Department quarantined Cuba (with the exception of Havana and Marianao) in April, 1908. Major Kean called the quarantine "unreasonable," "unnecessary," and a violation of the Sanitary Convention signed by the United States and Cuba in 1905. At the time of the quarantine there were active cases in only two Cuban towns and no new cases in seven weeks, Kean stated.[70] Later in the summer, the quarantine was lifted.

The yellow fever outbreaks, the United States government's concern about them, and the generally bad condition of public health administration in Cuba convinced Kean early in the occupation that the sanitary service should be completely nationalized.[71] Under the existing conditions, Kean observed, the municipalities had too few funds and the councilors did not enforce the sanitary laws because of family and political loyalties. Official indifference was wedded to public resistance. Kean's first step to enforce the codes was to have Magoon place Army medical officers on the municipal boards of health; Kean told the Governor that American supervision was essential to yellow fever control.[72] By the summer of 1907, Kean had persuaded the Governor that if he wanted an effective Cuban sanitation program, the entire public health system must be nationalized. On August 26, 1907, citing Kean's reasons almost verbatim, Magoon created the Department of Sanitation.[73] Local sanitary officers, in lieu of municipal boards of health, under the direction of a national Chief Sanitary Officer, were introduced. The national government assumed all costs, but the municipalities had to remit 10 per cent of their annual income for public health services. At the national level, a board of distinguished doctors and public health officers would advise the Chief Sanitary Officer.[74]

The creation of the Department of Sanitation brought Kean and Magoon into conflict over the role of the department in political affairs. Part of Kean's motive in advocating nationalization was to get public health out of politics and make it responsive to his trusted Cuban associates, Drs. Carlos J. Finlay and Juan Guiteras, and to the Cuban medical profession. Because he realized that to be efficient the department would have to employ many (potentially corruptible) public health inspectors, he hoped to place it under non-partisan, professional control.[75] He clearly intended that the department should do more than police the yellow fever problem. Already Kean had four Army medical officers supervising public health work (primarily yellow fever control) and he shared their frustration at not having the money or authority to tackle the entire infectious disease problem.[76]

Magoon agreed that Cuba's good health was related to national development, commerce, immigration and foreign trade, but the Governor was not so enthusiastic about professionalizing the Department of Sanitation as was Kean. Magoon would not appoint men as sanitary officers solely on their professional qualifications as certified by the National Sanitary Board. As he told Kean, "everything in this Island is political and the political chiefs must be consulted. . . . "[77] Kean's analysis of the Governor's reasoning was that the sanitary officers would be ineffective without public support and this depended on the *políticos'* approval. Although Magoon had not appointed unfit men, Kean observed, they had been drawn totally from the political factions. Kean believed Magoon was trying to make the *políticos* dependent on him and responsible for their nominees.[78]

Magoon kept the Department of Sanitation in politics, much to Kean's disgust. In one instance, Kean found that Magoon and Steinhart had changed all the public health officers of importance in Cienfuegos without consulting him, whereupon he suggested to the Governor that the *jefe local* be changed too if the Governor wanted anything accomplished.[79] In February, 1908, Kean told Magoon that unless he approved the National Sanitary Board's nominees quickly the Provisional Government would have a yellow fever epidemic on its hands.[80] He made the appointments and got quarantined too.

The genesis of the Department of Sanitation illustrates how closely related the Provisional Government's administrative acts were to its policy of restructuring Cuban politics along party lines, and how it instead reinforced colonial patterns. The creation of the department actually forced the *políticos* to compete for posts at the national level rather than at the local level. Clearly, Major Kean's motives for nationalizing the public health service were professional from both a military and medical standpoint. He hoped that the standards of performance he and his fellow officers and physicians demanded during the occupation would continue, and that Cuba would be able to do more for its people than keep itself clean of yellow fever for the United States benefit. He underestimated the political imperatives facing Magoon and the opportunities the new Department created for the Governor's patronage policy. Both men wanted a Department of Sanitation to check yellow fever; beyond that their goals split. At the time the occupation ended, the Department was far from being the non-partisan, public-service agency Kean first envisioned.

During the course of the intervention, the Army officers in the Provisional Government carried on two separate arguments with their civil superiors. The first concerned the wisdom of trying to establish a stable government for an unstable society; the second hinged on a basic disagreement over the cures for Cuban instability itself. The officers, however disenchanted they were with the United States Cuban policy, accepted the fact that Roosevelt would leave Cuba in the hands of the *políticos* and exercise control from afar through economic policy and the Platt Amendment. They did, nevertheless, within the context of American policy, wish to continue the programs of national reconstruction begun under Wood and paralleled by themselves and others in the Philippines and Puerto Rico. They considered their qualifications for the task superior to most Cubans' and most civilians in general. The *Army and Navy Journal* presented the military assessment of the officers' work:

> Under these efficient Army officers, who are again demonstrating the wonderful versatility of their profession, Cuba is being given excellent government unquestionably superior to what she had during the period of the Republic and superior to that of the ordinary state and city governments of the United States.[81]

The weakness in the officers' ambitious plans to better Cuba (a weakness they recognized) was that there was no guarantee that the Cubans would continue their work after the American withdrawal. Yet only Colonel Crowder officially advocated increasing American control over Cuban domestic affairs so that sweeping legal reforms could be made. The officers attempted to preserve their achievements by increasing the role of the national government in the areas of their responsibility. The various reorganizations that took place and many of the new laws published illuminate this development: the establishment of the Department of Sanitation, the enlarged role of the Department of Public Works, the tightened administration of police and charities in the Department of Government, the introduction of uniform accounting and auditing practices in all departments, and the changes in provincial and municipal government made by the Advisory Law Commission. The rationale for these administrative changes, from the officers' viewpoint, was that they would add to the Cuban government's efficiency and work to make the national bureaucracy less political by putting it in the hands of a professional-technical elite.

From Magoon's standpoint this centralization of government was acceptable not only because it improved administration, but because it also furthered his political goal, the encouragement of responsible parties in Cuba. Magoon was sure that a free election would return the *políticos* to office, and he saw no reason to exclude them from a voice in his own government. He doubted that the "example" set by the American officers would have any lasting impact without a continuing, direct American presence in the Cuban government. This he knew was an unlikely development. Magoon did agree with Crowder that legal reform could leave a lasting impact on Cuba, but he differed on the extent of that reform. Magoon stopped short of directly altering any institution other than the government. On this issue, Magoon was far more conservative than Crowder, who was, in fact, suggesting basic social changes through the medium of revising the Hispanic civil and criminal codes.

Although the officers were correct in believing that Magoon's political policies and the holding of elections were a superficial answer to Cuban instability, their own prescription for change was at least equally limited. They believed that the United States intended to do more for Cuba than it did. They realized more slowly than the American political leadership that the days of civilizing backward peoples in the missionary manner were at an end. They were interested in lasting internal reform in Cuba, but the Roosevelt administration was not.

In the most important area, that of economic reform, the officers were as conservative as their civil superiors. That they were mindful of the important role an efficient, honest Cuban government could play in national development is unquestionable, but they had no other answer to Cuba's colonial economy than freer trade with the United States. This was, as Roosevelt and Root knew, impossible without annexation.

One factor that cannot be overlooked is that the officers saw internal reform in Cuba as a military imperative. They believed that a real possibility of future, more violent interventions existed and that the occupation offered them a chance to win the respect (if not the friendship) of the Cuban people. Their Philippine experiences and service under Wood had taught them the potential military benefits of winning popular support in an occupied country. If such a political relationship with the people was authoritarian, it was at least benignly so, and the officers could argue with some justification that Army rule was for the general welfare, not that of a privileged native class. The irony was that, confronted with orders to return home, the Army turned over the government to just such a privileged elite. Because of the American reforms, the governmental apparatus the officers built for their successors was a far handier tool for waste and oppression than it had been before the intervention.

1. Taft-Bacon *Report*, p. 463.

2. Magoon, *Report, 1906–1907*, pp. 52–53.

3. *Ibid.*, p. 249.

4. Magoon, *Report, 1907–1908*, p. 41. The officers were Capt. C. W. Read (Pinar del Rio), Maj. F. S. Foltz (Havana), Capt. E. Wittenmyer, (Matanzas), Maj. W. D. Beach (Santa Clara), Maj. W. O. Clark (Camaguey), and Capt. A. J. Dougherty (Oriente). They served until October, 1908.

5. Gen. Leonard Wood to Manuel Landa, March 30, 1907, Wood Papers.

6. Magoon, *Report*, 1906–1907, p. 45. Even the administration's critics admitted that Magoon grasped Cuba's economic problems, even if his measures were ineffective. A. G. Robinson to James H. Wilson, January 26, 1908, and James H. Wilson to A. G. Robinson, January 27, 1908, Wilson Papers.

7. Magoon, *Report, 1907–1908*, p. 27.

8. Col. E. H. Crowder to Maj. Gen. J. F. Bell, May 20, 1907, Crowder Papers.

9. The most satisfactory summary of these American-defined problems and the Cuban response is Lockmiller, *Magoon in Cuba*, pp. 138–43 (Church property settlement); pp. 117–21, 211 (McGivney-

Rokeby and Havana sewerage system controversies); pp. 94–96, 207–9 (pardons). See also Chapman, *A History of the Cuban Republic*, pp. 237–46.

With the amount of high-level attention (including close examination and final decisions by Roosevelt and Taft) the contractual disputes received, it is little wonder that Cuban historians and American apologists have centered their researches (and charges) upon them. The author is inclined to agree with Lockmiller that the various settlements were legal, fair, and honest, but there is much to the contention that mere legality did not mean that they represented the Cubans' preferences. Moreover, the controversies were and are of peripheral importance in the history of the Second Intervention. See also David A. Lockmiller, "The Settlement of the Church Property Question in Cuba," *Hispanic American Historical Review*, XVII (November, 1937). 488–98. The documentary evidence is ample: R. Floyd Clarke, "Brief on the Havana Paving and Sewer Contract," Crowder Papers; File 035 CC/PGoC, RG 199, on the same subject; File 060, CC/PGoC (Church Property); File 070, CC/PGoC (Marianao Telephone Company concessions); File 115, CC/PGoC (Cienfuegos waterworks).

10. The best way to share Magoon's burial in minutiae is to examine his handiwork: *Republic of Cuba, Under the Provisional Government of the United States: Decrees, 1906–1909* (9 vols., Havana, undated), in the Library of the Bureau of Insular Affairs, National Archives. Hereafter cited as *Decrees* by number and year.

11. Magoon, *Report, 1907–1908*, pp. 1–6.

12. On the state of the Treasury, see Maj. E. F. Ladd's report of October 26, 1906, in Taft-Bacon *Report*, pp. 534–39.

13. Magoon, *Report, 1906–1907*, pp. 38–39.

14. Magoon, *Report, 1907–1908*, p. 114.

15. U.S. Senate, *Supplemental Report of the Provisional Governor of Cuba, December 1, 1908–January 29, 1909*, 61st Cong., 1st Sess., Senate Doc. 80, pp. 12–13. Hereafter cited as Magoon, *Supplemental Report*. See also Lockmiller, *Magoon in Cuba*, pp. 201–2.

Recent Cuban studies still criticize Magoon's profligate spending: Álvarez Díaz, *Estudio sobre Cuba*, p. 367; Portell Vilá, *Historia de Cuba*, IV, 567. Actually the estimated revenues easily covered the fiscal 1909 budget before President Gómez changed it.

16. Magoon, *Report, 1906–1907*, pp. 83–86; Magoon, *Report, 1907–1908*, p. 6.

17. Taft-Bacon *Report*, pp. 461, 506, 508–9.

18. Magoon, *Report, 1906–1907*, pp. 20–21. The best account of the Provisional Government's legal reforms is Lockmiller, *Magoon in Cuba*, pp. 146–73; this chapter also was published as David A. Lockmiller, "The Advisory Law Commission of Cuba," *Hispanic American Historical Review*, XVII (February, 1937), pp. 2–29.

19. Decree 284, December 27, 1906, *Decrees, 1906*.

20. E. V. Morgan to Root, December 31, 1906, Case 1852/59–60, *Num. File 1906–1910*, Vol. CCI, RG 59. The Cuban members were (Liberals) Alfredo Zayas, Juan Gualberto Gómez, Felipe González Sar-

raín, Miguel F. Viondi, Erasmo Regüeiferos Boudet, and (conservatives) Francisco Carrera Justiz, Manuel M. Coronado, Marió Garcia Kohly, and Rafael Montoro. All but Gómez and Coronado (editors) were lawyers; all had political and professional reputations.

21. Lockmiller, *Magoon in Cuba*, pp. 149–50.
22. Crowder to Taft, January 12, 1907, Crowder Papers.
23. "Final Report of the Advisory Law Commission," Magoon, *Supplemental Report*, pp. 16–24.
24. Magoon, *Report, 1906–1907*, pp. 119-39.
25. *Ibid.*, pp. 135–36.
26. *Ibid.*, p. 139. Judge Manuel Landa, acting secretary of the Department of Justice, commented that the Advisory Law Commission had not harmonized "the Substantive with the remedial. . . . If therefore, the Provisional Government is preparing us for public life, why not attend to our private life?" Landa advocated "total revision of the law" under the aegis of "the great American nation which so efficiently intervenes in the destinies of Cuba." Magoon, *Report, 1906–1907*, pp. 207, 236.
27. Magoon, *Report, 1906–1907*, pp. 75–76.
28. *Ibid.*, pp. 20–22.
29. Lockmiller, *Magoon in Cuba*, pp. 150–73. Portell Vilá admits the Advisory Law Commission's work was excellent. Portell Vilá, *Historia de Cuba*, IV, 550.
30. Wright, *Cuba*, p. 196. Aliens, however, did become eligible for election to the municipal councils.
31. Crowder continued to stress American responsibility for change in Cuba throughout his distinguished career as *exofficio* adviser to President Zayas and Ambassador to Cuba. Crowder to Secretary of State Charles Evans Hughes, July 15, 1923; Crowder to President Gerardo Machado, January 26, 1925, Crowder Papers.
32. Magoon, *Report, 1906–1907*, pp. 36–45; U.S. Department of Commerce and Labor, *Monthly Consular and Trade Reports*, November, 1907, pp. 75–78, and January, 1908, pp. 3–12.
33. Magoon, *Report, 1906–1907*, pp. 60–63. The banking problems were complicated because Cubans seldom deposited their savings in banks in the justified fear that these unsupervised institutions would fold. Borrowers, especially the sugar planters, had to seek funds from foreign sources at high interest rates. As for the Panic of 1907, Magoon believed it would bring a healthy readjustment of credit in Cuba.
34. Magoon, *Report, 1907–1908*, p. 8.
35. Magoon to Roosevelt, August 31, 1908, Roosevelt Papers.
36. Louis V. Placé to Magoon, January 5, 1907, File 89, CC/PGoC, RG 199.
37. Root to Magoon, March 2, 1907, File 89, CC/PGoC, RG 199. Magoon did arrange a more expeditious way of settling customs disputes by using the Chamber as a mediary.
38. Maj. Frank MacIntyre, BIA, to Magoon, September 6, 1907, File 178, CC/PGoC; MID to C/S, ACP, February 13 and 14, 1908, File

221, CC/PGoC, RG 199; James H. Wilson to Lt. Col. E. StJ. Greble, November 5, 1906, and July 11, 1908, Wilson Papers.

39. Editorial, *Diario de la Marino* (Havana), October 13, 1907.

40. David A. Lockmiller, "Agriculture in Cuba During the Second United States Intervention," *Agricultural History*, XI (July, 1937), 181–88; Arredonda, *Cuba: tierra indefensa*, pp. 189–90.

41. Magoon, *Report, 1906–1907*, pp. 54–60; Magoon, *Report, 1907–1908*, pp. 10–13

There was no pressure from the Department of Agriculture, Industry, and Commerce (Francisco I. Vildosola, secretary) for such an institution. This department's activities were limited to technical service, data publication and research.

42. Magoon, *Report, 1906–1907*, pp. 63–68.

43. MID to C/S, ACP, December 28 and 30, 1907, File 214, CC/PGoC, RG 199.

44. On the railway strike: Magoon to Taft, October 3, 1907; MID to C/S, ACP, October 2, 7, 8, 1907, File 195–195–12, CC/PGoC. On general labor conditions: MID to C/S, ACP, December 23, 1907, and January 3, 1908, Files 196 and 215, CC/PGoC, RG 199.

45. MID to C/S, ACP, January 18, 1908, File 220; MID to C/S, ACP, January 22, 1908, File 220–2; MID to C/S, ACP, October 16, 1907, File 196–3, all CC/PGoC, RG 199.

46. On the cigar-makers' settlement: "The result does great credit to your tact and judgment." Taft to Magoon, July 31, 1907, File 160, CC/PGoC. On business resentment: Magoon to Taft, October 2, 1907, File 195, CC/PGoC, RG 199.

47. Portell Vilá, *Historia de Cuba*, IV, 548–49.

48. James L. Rodgers, "Report on the Commerce and Industries of the Republic of Cuba for the Calendar Year of 1908," No. 202, *Dispatches*, U.S. Consul-General, Havana, 1909, RG 59.

49. Magoon, *Report, 1906–1907*, pp. 48–68.

50. "The general plan I have in view is to secure connection by wagon roads, for all parts of the Island with the tide water." Magoon to Brig. Gen. C. R. Edwards, June 24, 1907, File 134–1, CC/PGoC, RG 199; Magoon, *Report, 1906–1907*, p. 50; Lockmiller, *Magoon in Cuba*, pp. 99–105.

51. Magoon to Maj. Gen. J. F. Bell, July 21, 1907, File 152, CC/PGoC, RG 199.

52. Wright, *Cuba*, p. 254. See also Irene Wright, "The Cart-Roads of Mister Magoon," *The World To-day*, XVI (June, 1909), 641–48.

53. Bullard manuscript autobiography, Bullard Papers.

54. MID to C/S, ACP, April 20, 1907, File 100–12, CC/PGoC, RG 199.

55. Magoon, *Report, 1907–1908*, pp. 22–25; A. G. Robinson to J. H. Wilson, February 8, 1908, Wilson Papers.

56. *Ibid.*, pp. 24–25.

57. *Ibid.*, p. 22.

58. "Report of D. Lombillo Clark, C. E., Acting Secretary of Public Works," Magoon, *Report, 1906–1907*, pp. 361–400.

59. Magoon, *Report, 1906–1907*, p. 359. Among Black's proposed projects, which the Provisional Government did not undertake, was to modernize Havana's water system with meters, new reservoirs, sewers and plumbing at an estimated cost of $1.5 million.

60. *Ibid.*, pp. 239–85.

61. *Ibid.*, pp. 332–33, 353–54.

62. Bullard diaries, September 22 and 26, 1908, Bullard Papers; Greble to Wilson, August 21, 1908, Wilson Papers. *Cf.* Robert L. Bullard, "Education in Cuba," *Educational Review*, XXXIX (April, 1910), 378–84. In this article, Bullard called Cuba the victim of its "degreed, diplomaed ignoramuses" and deplored the impracticality of Cuban education, which did not develop character or serve as "a weapon in the struggles of life." He admitted that Wood's reforms had been too radical, too democratic for Cuba.

63. The principal source of documentation for this section is the letterbooks and the personal and official correspondence received by Major Kean during his service as adviser to the Department of Sanitation, 1906–9, Kean Papers.

64. Kean to Magoon, August 10, 1908; Maj. J. R. Kean, "Memorandum for the Provisional Governor: Organization of the Sanitary Department," April 8, 1907, Kean Papers.

65. Kean to Magoon, May 29, 1908, Kean Papers. The national tuberculosis sanitarium was in Havana, which explains the high TB mortality rate in that city.

66. Maj. P. C. Fauntleroy to Kean, December 31, 1908, Kean Papers.

67. Maj. J. R. Kean, "Yellow Fever in Cuba," memo submitted to the Secretary of War, December (?), 1907, Kean Papers.

68. E. V. Morgan to Root, August 1–October 1, 1907, Case 1844, *Num. File, 1906–1910*, Vol. CC, RG 59. The number of cases of yellow fever in Cuba from October 1, 1906, to November 1, 1908, was 174, including 47 fatalities. Lockmiller, *Magoon in Cuba*, p. 113.

69. Root to Magoon, January 20, 1908, File 171, CC/PGoC, RG 199.

70. Kean to Magoon, November 10, 1908, Kean Papers, Magoon, *Report, 1907–1908*, pp. 97–100. Magoon agreed with Kean, and the Provisional Government eventually spent $1.1 million on yellow fever control and another $2.2 million on public sanitation. Within Cuba, yellow fever cases were reported to the Provisional Government in coded messages by the local medical officers (examples in Kean Papers).

71. Maj. J. R. Kean, "The Department of Sanitation," manuscript, March 14, 1907, and "Memorandum for the Provisional Governor: Organization of the Sanitation Department," April 8, 1907, Kean Papers.

72. Kean to Maj. M. W. Ireland, January 10, 1907, Kean Papers; Decree 70, November 1, 1906, República de Cuba, *Gaceta oficial* (November–December, 1906), p. 3249.

73. Decree 894, August 26, 1907, *Decrees, 1907*.

74. Magoon, *Report, 1906–1907*, pp. 46–47, 456–57. The Department of Charities (Beneficiencia) from the Department of Government was incorporated into the new agency.

75. Kean manuscript, "The Department of Sanitation," March 14, 1907; Kean to Magoon, August 10, 1908; Maj. J. R. Kean, "A Department of Public Health for Cuba," manuscript dated December (?), 1908, Kean Papers.

76. This attitude is clearly evident in Kean's correspondence with Capt. J. H. Allen, his inspector in the Cienfuegos area. Kean-Allen Correspondence, December 9, 1907—April 4, 1908, Kean Papers. The Cuban attitude toward yellow fever control was less than enthusiastic; after the oiling and fumigation squad left a dwelling, the owners often sued for damages.

77. Kean to Ireland, July 15, 1907, Kean Papers.

78. *Ibid.*

79. Kean to Ireland, December 31, 1907, Kean Papers.

80. Kean to Magoon, February 20, 1908, Kean Papers.

81. *Army and Navy Journal,* January 12, 1907.

# CHAPTER EIGHT

# THE RECONSTRUCTION OF THE CUBAN ARMED FORCES

A T THE BEGINNING of the Second Intervention, the Provisional Government viewed the important and delicate task of reorganizing Cuba's armed forces as simply a matter of increasing the size of the Rural Guard and detailing American officers to it as advisers. Before the occupation ended, however, Cuba had both a Rural Guard and a regular army, and what had begun as a military and administrative reform became a major political issue.

The controversy over Cuba's military establishment united the *políticos* against the Provisional Government, set Magoon against his advisers, and caused a division between the political and military leaders in Washington and the officers in Cuba. Throughout the negotiations, which culminated with the formation of the Permanent Army of Cuba, the American officers and Cuban politicians defended their positions with skill and persistence. They used military and political justifications interchangeably to advocate either a national constabulary or a regular army. When Magoon attempted to mediate the controversy, he found himself allied with the Cubans against the Army officers in his administration. His own position followed Washington's line. The issue finally was decided by Roosevelt and Taft, but their decision stemmed from political conditions in Cuba. During the episode there was never any meaningful public interest in the United States concerning the problem of Cuba's armed forces. Thus, the question, one of significance in Cuban institutional history, was decided by Roosevelt relatively free of domestic political pressure.

To understand the twisted path that led to the creation of the Permanent Army, it is necessary to examine the structure, function, and political orientation of the Rural Guard, to explore its role in the August Revolution, and to follow its regeneration during the Second Intervention.

## The Rural Guard: The Politics of Military Efficiency

In the social and economic wreckage of 1898, the American military governors formed provincial and municipal constabularies, largely recruited from former insurgents, to keep the peace. By 1902 fifteen separate forces existed, and while their jurisdictions were tangled, their function (police) and loyalty (to the Americans) were clear. In Santiago, Leonard Wood, on the advice of a Cuban veteran and over popular protest, consciously modeled his Rural Guard on Mexican President Porfirio Diaz' Guardia Rurale.[1] During his service as Military Governor, Wood completed the nationalization of Cuba's Rural Guard. It was an apolitical national constabulary to enforce the laws of the central government and the decisions of the national courts. Its jurisdiction extended to all areas where there was no urban or municipal police.[2] Officers and men were selected and appointed by the Military Governor, and it can be assumed that while basic soldierly qualities were a prime consideration, Wood also sought men who were "professional," or apolitical in American military usage. In 1905 the Rural Guard manned 244 posts throughout the island, each post averaging around twelve men. Because the Rural Guard devoted its efforts to police work, it lacked the training to carry out even company-sized military operations. After the departure of its American advisers, the Rural Guard's discipline and efficiency deteriorated.[3] Only in the sense that it was armed was the Rural Guard an army.

In 1904 the Cuban government enlarged its Artillery Corps to six hundred men. Ostensibly, the artillerymen were to replace the American garrison of Havana's forts. One Cuban historian suggests that Estrada Palma wanted a palace guard which owed its allegiance strictly to him, for he believed the Rural Guard was too pro-American or, at least, had little loyalty to him personally.[4] Whatever Estrada Palma's motives, the Artillery Corps was armed and trained as infantry, and in 1906 was the nation's only military unit capable of immediately taking offensive action against rebellion.[5]

Discredited and demoralized by its political role in the elections of 1905 and its military defeats of 1906, the Rural Guard badly needed American assistance, just as the Provisional Government needed the Rural Guard if it was to follow a Cubans-fight-Cubans policy. The Rural Guard officers believed they had followed American teachings by supporting the constitutional government, though in doing so they antagonized many of their countrymen. Generally loyal to Estrada Palma, they had failed him and incurred the Liberal's wrath. They were aware that their ineptness contributed to the government's collapse, for the Rural Guard had been unable to produce even the hint of effective resistance, which Estrada Palma might have turned into American support.[6]

Taft, Magoon, and their Army advisers believed the Rural Guard had acted unwillingly in suppressing the Liberals, that it remained true to the principles learned under Wood, and that it longed to return to its legitimate functions.[7] Therefore, the Provisional Government immediately went to work to restore public confidence in the Rural Guard, to return it to its proper duties, and to place it firmly under American control.

The experience of the Rural Guard after the American intervention was influenced most by American efforts to professionalize it and make it an effective counterguerrilla force. Shortly after the intervention Taft publicly announced that the Guard repudiated its past political activities; he then switched detachments to different posts to reduce local tensions.[8] To command the Rural Guard and the Artillery Corps,

Taft decided to retain Alejandro Rodríguez and promoted him to Major General. Magoon might have replaced him with Enrique Loynaz del Castillo, but the volatile Liberal general denounced this possibility with flaming oratory:

> Every time I see an American I have contempt for him, and I cannot bear to look at the Stars and Stripes waving unjustly over Cuba. If some day the Cubans have to fight, it will be with the Americans, and then only will I accept the chieftancy of the Rural Guard.[9]

The Provisional Governor decreed that there would be no partisanship within the Guard itself. In General Order No. 28 (March 11, 1907) General Rodríguez announced that participation in political activity would be henceforth a court-martial offense:

> The members of the Armed Forces will not discuss, either publicly or privately, their political opinions. They are soldiers of the state, and as such have no right to mix in politics. Their duty is to serve their government and take no part in its construction: their duty is to obey its orders. . . . The welfare of the entire force depends upon its being free from political combinations.[10]

Of course, such an order did not restrain the government from using its soldiers to carry out political chores, as the Moderate regime had done in 1905. The order might, however, protect the Rural Guard from public criticism. Professionalization was not really thorough, for political pressure (particularly from the Liberals) still affected the promotion or transfer of Guard personnel.[11]

To inculcate professionalism in the Rural Guard and to improve its readiness, Magoon and Bell detailed an able, experienced group of American officers to advise and train the Cubans. All but one of the original eight advisers had served with the Military Government or in the Philippines. Major Herbert J. Slocum, Wood's supervisor of the Rural Guard, took up his old post at Guard headquarters. His field advisers were Captains Powell Clayton, Jr., James A. Ryan, George C. Barnhardt, Andrew J. Dougherty, Charles F. Crain, C. I. Crockett, and Edmund Wittenmyer. In the course of the occupation this group changed, but there were never more than nine officers in the detail. Though the officers were only to train and advise, both Dougherty and Wittenmyer took part in bandit chases during their tours.[12]

To use the Rural Guard most effectively, the American advisers retained the Guard's pre-revolt deployment. This return to the scattered post system was based on the assumption that the Army of Cuban Pacification served as a ready field force and that the small posts were consistent with the Guard's mission. Nonetheless, a reserve force of one hundred men was planned for each provincial capital, but for lack of troops was not constituted until late in the occupation. The three Guard regiments (each with eight mounted and two foot companies numbering around 1,700 men) handled a two-province area of responsibility. The bulk of the Guard was stationed in sugar growing areas.[13] The First Regiment manned 15 posts in Pinar del Rio and Havana provinces; the Second Regiment, 26 in Matanzas and Santa Clara; the Third Regiment, 101 posts in Camaguey and Oriente. During the winter of 1906–7, training and reorganization progressed rapidly enough to allow each regiment to increase its posts. By September, 1907, the Rural Guard had more than doubled its stations.[14]

A sharp drop in non-effectives and discharges by mid-1907 reflected the Guard's improved morale. Though the pay was low, quarters unappealing, and discipline capricious, the Guard's losses from desertion, court-martials, and discharges for unfitness dropped from 285 in 1906 (including 64 men who defected to the Liberals) to almost half that after six months of tutelage. The American advisers reported that improved morale was due to the Guard officers' increased concern for the men's welfare, and the excellent example set by the Army of Cuban Pacification.[15]

The Guard's readiness was increased by redistributing its weapons and improving its communications. To reduce supply problems, each regiment received one standard weapon, either the Remington–Lee .30 cal. rifle, the Winchester .44 cal. carbine, or the Mauser 7mm. rifle. To offset the widespread location of the Guard posts and to allow a quicker concentration of troops if rebellion threatened, Rodríguez and Slocum pushed the construction of phone lines to all posts. The communications net was completed by the end of 1907. Magoon's road-building program also increased the Guard's coverage.

The Rural Guard's primary tactic for subduing incipient rebellion was active patrolling. Unfortunately its police duties, which included serving and executing court orders and investigating the numerous rural fires and accidents, prevented it from patrolling as much as its advisers would have liked. The Rural Guard, however, used its patrolling procedures to increase its reputation for trustworthiness. To insure that a patrol completed its mission, a post chief assigned every party a specific route. The patrol, as it passed through each property, would then have the owner or manager sign a form to verify the patrol's presence and good behavior. The goal was to increase mutual confidence, and the Americans were satisfied that this was attained.[16]

The Artillery Corps was also placed under American supervision. It was stationed in Havana, received primarily artillery instruction, and served the Provisional Government by providing troops for a show-of-force in the 1906 railway strike. The Americans equipped one company with pack howitzers and also created a machine gun company armed with ten Colts.

The Rural Guard, coaxed and cajoled by its American advisers, served the Provisional Government well in its constabulary role. In terms of military efficiency, it was vastly improved. Some success followed the American attempt to professionalize it, for many of its officers were still committed to the ideals of the Wood regime; some, indeed, wished for the return of the Puritan general.[17] In addition, American supervision of recruiting and commissioning was close.

The political sum of the American reform of the Rural Guard, however, was to model it on American values: the sanctity of person and property, prompt and strict law enforcement without regard to personal influence and station, and political neutrality. These were the ideals toward which the Americans pushed the Rural Guard. If, in fact, its advisers succeeded in Americanizing and increasing the Rural Guard, the Guard would stand even more firmly against the *personalismo* of the Liberal politicians and support the interests of the alien and conservative sectors. In reality, the reform of the Rural Guard marked the beginning of Liberal pressure to create a regular army. The subsequent political controversy ended with a Liberal victory over Washington, Governor Magoon, and the United States Army and the creation of the Permanent Army of Cuba.

## The Permanent Army Issue

Despite all the improvements that were wrought in Cuba's armed forces as they existed in 1906, the Provincial Government concluded that Cuba needed more armed men to keep internal order. The military lesson of the August Revolution was clear, as Tomás Estrada Palma pointed out in his letter of October 10, 1906: Cuba needed "a competent force to suppress insurrection and disperse rebel bands." He had found in August that no force existed "to immediately undertake an active campaign."

Roosevelt, Taft, and Magoon clearly recognized that more Cuban soldiers were needed if the Americans were to pull out; Taft feared that it might be necessary to keep American troops in Cuba even after the government was restored.[18] Magoon's first thought was simply to enlarge the Rural Guard and Artillery Corps to ten thousand men, thus giving General Rodríguez and Major Slocum plenty of provincial reserves. "Of course," Magoon reported, "this . . . will cost more Liberals should not object because the Rural Guard will keep them in power after election."[19]

In October, 1906, General Bell convened a board of officers of the General Staff Corps serving in Cuba to study the possibility of increasing the Rural Guard. The board first considered the Rural Guard's proposals for a manpower increase. The Rodríguez-Slocum plan was simply to increase each Guard regiment by two troops of cavalry, add a machine gun company, and flesh out the Artillery Corps, in all an increase of a thousand men. There would be no change in the Rural Guard's constabulary function.[20]

As a result of its own study, the board decided that as long as American troops remained in Cuba, it was unnecessary to enlarge the Rural Guard, but recommended that after the occupation ended, the Rural Guard be enlarged to four cavalry regiments and two infantry regiments, organized like United States Army units. The Rural Guard's minimum strength would be 7,715, capable of expansion to 9,875. In addition, the board recommended the creation of field artillery batteries, more coast artillery and service troops, bringing the minimum total force to 9,439 men. Neither Rodríguez, Slocum, nor the board believed a militia system to be workable.[21]

With this organization plan in mind, Magoon met with three Liberal military chiefs—Pino Guerra, Carlos García Vélez, and José de Jesus Monteagudo. The three Cubans opposed any increase in the present armed forces and said that their opposition represented the party's position. Magoon stated that reorganization was underway, for, "I appreciate, as I think you do, the necessity of having a force that will give stability to the Government. The problem is to find out how many that is and then make it an agent of the Government and not a political body."[22] Nevertheless, Magoon then promised there would be a chance for public discussion before he acted.

Public reaction there was, but it provided Magoon no comfort and little guidance. The more he considered an enlarged Rural Guard, the more expensive it appeared and the more criticism he heard. Liberals and others, he reported to Taft, opposed the creation of a large armed body "available for enforcement of the desires of a single individual." Magoon had learned that the people

. . . are apprehensive of a recurrence in Cuba of the dangers of militarism and consider it as great a peril to Cuba as it has been in other islands of the West Indies and in the countries of Central and South America. They call attention to the racial characteristics, traditions, etc., which they allege make it impossible for an armed force to be non-political or to assume the attitude of the soldiers of the United States towards political affairs.

Instead, most of the Cubans would rather accept the military weakness of the police rather than have a politically powerful army. Even though the Liberals were confident of victory in the next election, they opposed an enlarged Rural Guard. In all, Magoon concluded, he still favored the General Staff board's proposals.[23]

Roosevelt, after digesting the problem, directed Magoon to begin reorganizing the Rural Guard and other services into the ten-thousand-man force recommended by the board, Magoon, and General Bell.[24] This news brought political uproar in Cuba to a new pitch; all the Havana press opposed the government, the Moderates being more critical than the Liberals.[25] The Spanish *La Lucha* best presented the conservative argument. Although it did not doubt the military wisdom of the General Staff officers' plans, *La Lucha* worried about the political factors. First, the September, 1906, law which placed the legal size of the Cuban armed forces at ten thousand men was an expedient passed by a discredited government in panic. The law did not represent the wishes of the Cuban people. Rather, there must be more public discussion. A plan of reorganization of the Rural Guard in Cuba could be dictated not only by military technicism. There were "a great many factors which must be taken into consideration. . . . The economic, the administrative, and the political aspect cannot be disdained in a matter of this kind."[26]

While Magoon weighed Cuban criticism, the Liberal Committee took the initiative and suggested the creation of an entirely new force, a Permanent Army of Cuba. To accomplish its goal, it put together arguments blending political expediency, fiscal policy, and military theory. The Liberals used North America rhetoric to convince Washington and to outreason the American officers who opposed the Permanent Army. Much of their purpose was undoubtedly to reward their followers and strengthen their leadership. In all respects they were stunningly successful.

On February 6, 1907, Zayas, Juan Gualberto Gómez, Monteagudo, García Vélez, Recio, and Asbert (a majority of the Liberal Committee) called on Magoon to present an alternative armed forces plan. They first pointed out that police work was a civil function, whereas national security was a military function. Therefore, the Rural Guard, a constabulary close to the people, could not function as a regular army, which should be isolated from the people for training and discipline. A militia would not serve because it would lack the military training for modern warfare. In addition, the army, as the embodiment of the nation's honor, must be beyond reproach, and the Rural Guard was associated with the repression of the old regime. The Liberals stated they did not want the tainted Guard officers involved in forming a new army. Moreover, the Liberals said they feared more civil oppression by the Guard, which an army might check. Then, as the clincher, they pointed out that a mounted Rural Guard would be more expensive to maintain than a similar number of foot soldiers.[27]

Major Slocum defended the Rural Guard with a sharp attack on the Liberals' motives. They opposed the Rural Guard, Slocum said, because they had failed to subvert it with their own cronies, and the commissioning and enlistment laws would continue to protect the Guard. The Permanent Army, Slocum candidly pointed out, was nothing more than a giant political payoff.[28]

Magoon cabled Washington that the proposal to increase the Rural Guard had stirred up a hornet's nest: "Much opposition from all parties. Every newspaper here opposes plan. Liberal papers respectfully, Moderates fiercely." He urged a postponement of the reorganization decree to allow him to give the problem more consideration. Taft granted the request, but wanted "no unreasonable delay."[29]

With the proposal of a new regular army now introduced into the debate, the battle lines of the controversy underwent a rapid shift. Suddenly, Cubans of almost all political persuasions found a regular army attractive. There were many reasons, not the least of which was suspicion of the Americanized Rural Guard. On the other hand, Americans and other aliens in Cuba (soldiers and civilians) backed the Rural Guard increase and opposed the creation of a regular army. *El Mundo,* speaking for the Liberals, and *La Discusión,* of the conservative press, hailed the Permanent Army as the guarantor of stability, adding, with perhaps double meaning, that a new army precluded other American interventions.[30] In a conference with Magoon on February 19, Pino Guerra told the governor that Cuba needed a regular army, not more Guards. The weak response of the Rural Guard gave his guerrillas the illusion of victory, Guerra said, which rallied the people to his cause. A determined, trained force would have scattered the Constitutional Army in forty-eight hours.[31] The *Army and Navy Journal* reported that the "ignorant and radical classes" wanted only an enlarged Rural Guard; the Permanent Army was the Cuban conservatives' idea. General Bell further elaborated that conservatives found conscription and a universal military liability extremely distasteful.[32] In the face of such confusing evidence, it is little wonder that Roosevelt wanted to go slow on the problem, though Taft said the President was more worried about economy than militarism.[33]

The American opposition to the creation of the Permanent Army was focused on three arguments: the Army would be a giant swindle economically, it would be worthless militarily, and it would be political and social disaster for Cuba. The *Havana Post* believed the army would not only be wasteful, but dangerous to Cuba's domestic tranquillity.

The proposition of an increase to 10,000 of the army of Cuba will be as full of peril to Cuba today as it would be to arm the Moros of the Philippines with modern firearms. It will mean war and bloody riot. It will mean not the survival of the fittest as some contend, but it will mean, if it means anything, an empire of arms. If they undertook to increase the Army of the United States in proportion it would make an army in the United States of 240,000; would the people stand for such a thing? Let the Congress try it and see.[34]

The American officers attached to the Rural Guard adamantly opposed the creation of a regular army on sound political and military grounds. Major Slocum and Captain Wittenmyer sent memos of protest to the Provisional Governor. The most forceful and closely reasoned objections were made in an essay by Captain James A. Ryan, who was soon to become Magoon's personal aide. Ryan's study, which was forwarded to Magoon, pointed out that the Permanent Army was primarily a Liberal political device to reward present followers and to win new faithfuls. The Liberal attack on the Rural Guard stemmed from its loyalty to the constitutional government in 1906. Ryan particularly opposed the creation of a regular army at that moment because, in essence, such an act would produce a force dominated by the former insurgents. It would be a political army and "an army dominated by politics is ruined. In proportion to its freedom from interference by politicians is proficiency proclaimed. History repeats itself from Rome to South America and the use of politics has ruined every army, every military force, with which it has been connected."

Switching to more immediate military considerations, Ryan stressed that the Platt Amendment already guaranteed Cuba against foreign invasion. The only need for an army was to keep internal order. For this Cuba needed a loyal, professional constabulary. The military requirements of suppressing revolt demanded direct contact with the people and an intimate knowledge of local society and geography. Only the Rural Guard would have this information, and because it was largely mounted, it made a more effective counterguerrilla force than foot soldiers. Hitting at what he knew was a tender spot in Washington's policy, Ryan unequivocally stated that a Cuban army offered little security to the sugar business. "Which kind of force does Cuba need?" Ryan concluded. "Is it an Army? No."[35]

Within the staff of the Army of Cuban Pacification, there were officers who opposed the Permanent Army, because, in view of Cuba's limited resources, they thought it a poor investment on political, economic, and military grounds. Let the funds instead be used for road-building, which would bring general economic improvement, essential for internal peace. Improve Cuba's transportation system and farm produce would come in from the countryside, thus underwriting a rejuvenated freeholding class. As for internal security, an enlarged Rural Guard would suffice.[36]

A sincere objection to the Permanent Army reached Washington from an American planter in Cuba, Mr. H. E. Havens. Havens' analysis went more deeply into political problems such as economic backwardness and the social acceptability of violence in Cuba than did most American criticism. In thinking over the proposed plan for a regular Cuban army, Havens believed

. . . that such a measure could do no good and would have in it the greatest peril to the people of this Island. The politicians are divided into hostile factions of the most bitter and vicious character, all stimulated by a consuming desire for the opportunity to make appropriations and operate the various forms of graft peculiar to the Cuban Government, and animated by no trace of genuine patriotism. Some one of these factions would succeed to the control of the proposed Army upon the withdrawal of the United States troops; and that control would inevitably be used to protect against their rascalities; and also to control elections and maintain themselves in power.

It now seems probable that those politicians who call themselves the Liberal Party will carry the elections and obtain control. Those men are not of as high character as those who surrounded Palma and are more desperate, reckless and ravenous, and under any conditions would prove dangerous to the peace and safety of the people of Cuba. But to place Fifteen Thousand armed men under their authority, and then withdraw the United States troops would create an alarming condition

But if the so-called Liberals fail to obtain control some other faction will, and there is not enough difference between them to make any material differences as to consequences.

The maintenance of an appearance of peace by suppressing the people with an armed force in the hands of a gang of professional looters and grafters is not the sort of peace the United States should wish to be responsible for. If the United States is to withdraw from Cuba it would be far better to leave the people the remedy of revolution against the inevitable abuses of the factions in the ascendency, than to place them at the mercy of a corrupt despotism, and call it established peace.

In any case the placing of any more guns in the hands of these people is a dangerous experiment. It would be far better if every gun and machete now in the Island were thrown into the sea.[37]

The Liberal Committee, however, did not surrender the initiative and promptly came up with a specific reorganization plan of their own. They proposed to separate the Rural Guard and the new army, the latter to be a mixed brigade (infantry, cavalry, and artillery) of four thousand men. Again they emphasized the importance of segregating the national constabulary from the army and the army from the people. They stressed that Cuba need not fear military oppression. The August Revolution succeeded not, they argued, because the government had been weak but because it was unpopular: "When the government has the country against it, the number of bayonets of which it may dispose matters little; the result is always the same, since no people worthy of unity fails to throw off the yoke that it deems insupportable."[38]

During Secretary Taft's April, 1907, visit to Cuba, the Permanent Army issue was discussed and the Liberal Committee restated its regular army plan. While its arguments of February and March were repeated, it further elaborated on the economic and political benefits (in terms of American policy) of its proposal. The Liberal Committee's soldiers would cost only $500,000 annually, much less than a like number of Rural Guards, for the soldiers would not need mounts or expensive police training. The Committee also made it clear to Taft that the Provisional Government could not expect its full co-operation if Magoon favored the Rural Guard, for the Rural Guard menaced the Liberal party. Juan Gualberto Gómez, the Negro orator and editor, stated that an army was needed to protect the next Cuban government from the Rural Guard:

. . . In my memorandum I mentioned a gentleman, who was well known in France, M. Prud'homme, who had a sword and who said that sword would serve as well to destroy the Government as to defend it, and the present Rural Guard reminds me very much of the sword of M. Prud'homme.[39]

Whatever his inclination to settle the Permanent Army question, Taft made no public decision in Havana, for he was waiting for what Washington considered a compromise solution. Although General Bell had approached the General Staff board which had mapped the Rural Guard reorganization, he found it reluctant to approve the Liberal plan. Therefore another scheme, drafted by Major Frank MacIntyre of the Bureau of Insular Affairs, was submitted. This plan incorporated the separation of the army and the Rural Guard, as the Liberals desired, while adopting the organizational structure advocated by the General Staff board, including a seven hundred man increase in the Guard. Again citing the Cuban law of September 15, 1906, MacIntyre placed the strength of the armed forces at ten thousand.[40] General Bell approved of this plan. Magoon and Taft were to have discussed the compromise plan in Havana, but did not because the staff papers were mishandled and did not reach the Secretary until the end of his trip.

In the meantime President Roosevelt acted on his own to get a reading of public feeling in Cuba on the proposed army. He asked William E. Curtis, noted Latin American correspondent of the Chicago *Record-Herald* and former official of the Pan American Union, to sound out opinion during a trip to Cuba. Curtis' report could hardly have reassured the President of the wisdom of the War Department's compromise. Everyone he talked to, Curtis said, opposed the Permanent Army, except its potential officers. Curtis viewed the army as a reward to the insurgents, who told him they had too much prestige to work. He told Roosevelt that "if you could see the men who will command the proposed army, and the men who would compose the rank and file it would not be necessary to discuss this subject." In all, Curtis concluded, the Cuban army, which would cost $5 million annually, would waste money better used on roads and schools.[41]

When Magoon again (April 23, 1907) asked to postpone announcing any decision on the Permanent Army, the delay was promptly approved. Roosevelt and Taft, however, could not find any other alternative. Six months later, on October 16,

Magoon asked Taft's permission to go ahead with the creation of the Permanent Army; two days later Taft told him to act.[42] Although Magoon's specific reasons for proceeding with the Cuban army are unclear it is reasonable to assume that from the April discussions Washington had accepted the principle of a Cuban army and was concerned thereafter only with the timing. The other influences on the October request were most probably the Liberal's continued insistence on a regular army, the emergence of the Conservative party in the summer of 1907, the prospect of national elections and American withdrawal, and the relative peace following the Masso Parra conspiracy.

The final formal consideration of the Permanent Army plan took place in an hour-and-a-half session of the Advisory Law Commission. The Army law appeared on the agenda because Magoon wanted the Commission's opinion before his trip to Washington in February, 1908. Secretary Taft, Magoon told the Commission, wanted final action on the matter before he went to the Philippines. A subcommittee had already considered all the plans. Interestingly enough, it categorized as "Cuban" the Liberal Committee proposal drafted by Monteagudo and as "American" the Rural Guard plan, the General Staff board recommendations, and the War Department compromise plan.

The full Commission, considering the subcommittee's recommendation that the War Department's plan be accepted, realized that the central issue was the creation of a Permanent Army separate from the Rural Guard. Still the discussions had little originality. Alfredo Zayas presented the Liberal arguments *una vez más*, emphasizing that the suggested law was truly eclectic and represented everyone's best interests because it incorporated Washington's structural recommendations. In the final vote the Commission approved the compromise plan, 6-3, with one abstention. The two Americans voting (Crowder was in Washington) voted against acceptance. The six votes "for" came from four Liberals, a Conservative, and an independent.[43]

In decrees on April 4, 1908, Magoon published the laws establishing the Armed Forces of Cuba, consisting of a

Permanent Army, the Rural Guard, and a militia. No missions were assigned the different forces, and the militia clause meant only that males from 21–45 had some vague military obligation. General Rodríguez continued as commander of the Rural Guard. The Zayista Liberal and hero of 1906, General Pino Guerra, took command of the Permanent Army.[44]

In assessing the political impact of the decrees, Magoon wrote Taft that the compromise plan had "given general—I might say, universal—satisfaction." Rodríguez, his officers and advisers, and the conservatives were happy with the strengthened Rural Guard, while the Liberals were satisfied with the Permanent Army. Public opinion and the press were equally pleased. Magoon, looking back over the controversy, believed that the need for more troops was obvious from the start and that the Rural Guard's partisan taint made it inexpedient to continue it as the sole armed force. Magoon was quite optimistic about Guerra's appointment, for Pino had been out of politics for a whole year. His appointment had won Liberal plaudits and the conservatives recognized his military prowess. "This puts an end to insurrections; nobody will want 'Pino' to go after them; he would not bring in prisoners—he served to [*sic*] long with Maceo for that"—such were the comments Magoon said he heard. In any event, the Provisional Governor pointed out, the character of the new armed forces hinged on the way the laws were executed.[45]

*La Discusión*, in a representative editorial, extolled the new army as a keeper of the peace and the embodiment of modernity and patriotism· "What the country demands is a military machine, disciplined, scientific, robust, ready at all times at the defense of the constituted power." *La Discusión* (whose editor voted against the law in the Advisory Law Commission) added, however, that it would be a good idea if the army had American advisers, since they had been so successful with the Rural Guard.[46]

Viewed from the perspective of the Military Information Division, the Governor's decrees cast a different shadow. Guerra's appointment, Captain Furlong reported, was viewed as a Zayista triumph and a stunning setback for the Miguelistas. The latter had already stepped up their efforts to subvert the Rural Guard, but if the Guard could remain intact, the army would be no political threat.[47]

The importance of the settlement to the Provisional Government was clearly recognized by the Grupo Cubano de Investigaciones Económicas, when, writing some fifty years after the fact, they stated: "After having organized the Cuban Army under the command of General Pino Guerra, Magoon held elections. . . . "[48] The Provisional Government had pragmatically solved the Cuban army "problem" through the time-tested devices of compromise and public discussion. Cuba now had a force adequate to crush insurrection, a force which filled the military void of 1906 so annoying to Roosevelt.

In developments that reached beyond 1909, however, the American officers in Cuba more clearly saw the future than did Washington. The Cuban army, despite its few American advisers, became the fiscally rapacious and politically potent institution the American officers predicted. José Miguel Gómez first removed General Rodríguez from the command of the Rural Guard, replacing him with his old crony, José de Jesus Monteagudo. Gómez then coerced Pino Guerra from his post (with the help of a would-be assassin's wounding bullet) and merged the Permanent Army with the Rural Guard under Monteagudo. Gómez also purged the Rural Guard officers he considered politically unreliable. To the dismay of his generals, Gómez broke up the Army's camps and ordered the troops to garrison Cuba's major cities. Like Topsy, the Army continued to grow; it was joined by a navy and by a Department of War and Navy. Militarily the Army performed well in the Race War of 1912, but it could hardly be called apolitical. Despite the efforts of the officers of the United States Army, the Cuban armed forces were once again Cubanized.

The reconstruction of the Cuban armed forces created another perplexing political morass for the Roosevelt administration because American policy remained the captive of its political assumptions. At a loss as to who represented the Cuban people, Washington found itself again dealing almost entirely with the Liberal Committee. On the other hand, the administration (including Magoon) chose to override the advice of American officers serving with the Provisional Government because it believed that their position was too rooted in institutional interest and favored a minority of the Cuban people. Certainly the administration did not acquiesce in the formation of the Permanent Army because it believed it would protect only the economic and social position of the alien commercial class. Instead, it approved the Permanent Army as a politically acceptable solution to what it believed were the basic military requirements for the withdrawal of American troops. In its deliberations its concern was to please its constituents, the Cuban politicians. To have ignored them, to have decided on a strengthened Rural Guard alone, would have denied the American way in foreign affairs: that matters being negotiated, regardless of the social and economic environment, may be settled by a peaceful adjustment of power between the negotiators.

In Cuba the Roosevelt administration clearly followed the path of least resistance to please those whom it thought spoke for Cuba. The Cuban armed forces controversy ended with a compromise which was in substance no compromise at all for the United States. On the basic issue—the creation of a separate regular army—the Liberals were the outright victors. However spurious their arguments, however bogus their pretensions as spokesmen for the Cuban people, however harmful their army in terms of Cuba's future welfare, the Liberals were the only popular politicians the United States could find. In its futile effort to foster a stable party system, the United States served as midwife for another institution with which Cuba's politicians could exploit their nation's weaknesses.

1. Johnson, *Cuba*, IV, 144–45; Hagedorn, *Leonard Wood*, I, 214.

2. Order No. 114, Military Government of Cuba, July 5, 1901, *Civil Report, 1901*, II, 172–91.

3. Capt. Matthew E. Hanna, USA, "The Necessity of Increasing the Efficiency of the Cuban Army," *Journal of the Military Service Institution*, XXXV (July, 1904), 28–36.

4. Portell Vilá, *Historia de Cuba*, IV, 388–89.

5. Magoon, *Report, 1906–1907*, p. 110.

6. Estrada Palma letter of October 10, 1906, in Magoon, *Report, 1906–1907*, pp. 12–15.

7. Magoon, *Report, 1906–1907*, pp. 17–18; Maj. H. J. Slocum to Brig. Gen. H. L. Scott, December 15, 1906, Scott Papers; Maj. Gen. Leonard Wood to Maj. Gen. A. Rodríguez, January 13, 1907, Wood Papers.

Part of the Rural Guard's failure, Magoon reported, came from Palma's instructions "to avoid armed conflict with resulting loss of life and arousing passion and animosities which battles engender."

8. Magoon, *Report, 1906–1907*, p. 18; *New York Times*, October 11, 1906.

9. *Havana Post*, February 8, 1907.

10. República de Cuba, Decree 281, December 14, 1906, *Gaceta oficial* (November–December, 1906), pp. 4594–95. General Order 28, March 11, 1907, Republic of Cuba, Headquarters of the Armed Forces, copy in File 206–1, CC/PGoC, RG 199.

11. Capt. E. Wittenmyer to Maj. H. J. Slocum, December 5, 1907; Capt. A. J. Dougherty to Capt. J. A. Ryan, August 8, 1907, both in File 206, CC/PGoC, RG 199.

Wittenmyer's comment on the requested transfer of Capt. Ramon Martín sheds light on his own political values; Martín, he reported, had "queer ideas about government. . . . He is no friend of property," having "anarchistic views."

12. Magoon, *Report, 1906–1907*, pp. 19, 112; Dougherty to Slocum, October 25, 1907, File 146–21, CC/PGoC, RG 199.

13. Magoon to Taft, November 16, 1906, File 005, CC/PGoC, RG 199.

14. "Report of the Rural Guard Corps of the Republic of Cuba . . . September 29, 1906 . . . September 30, 1907," in Magoon, *Report, 1906–1907*, pp. 493–551.

15. *Ibid.*, pp. 498–500.

16. *Ibid.*, p. 501.

17. Slocum to McCoy, June 6, 1907, Wood Papers. "Cubans should not lose confidence in the future and, above all, in their friends." Wood to Rodríguez, January 13, 1907, Wood Papers.

18. Taft to Roosevelt, October 10, 1906, Roosevelt Papers.

19. Magoon to Taft, October 26 and 30 and November 16, 1906, File 005, CC/PGoC, RG 199.

20. Memorandum of October 26, 1906, to the Provisional Governor from Maj. H. J. Slocum; Maj. Gen. A. Rodríguez to the Provisional Governor, December 27, 1906, both in File 15984, General Classified Files, BIA, RG 350.

The best sources of documentary evidence on Rural Guard affairs and the creation of the Permanent Army are Files 866, 931, and 15984 in the General Classified Files of the Bureau of Insular Affairs and Files 062 and 064 in the Confidential Correspondence, Provisional Governor of Cuba.

21. Transcript, "Proceedings of a Board of Officers Convened to Consider the Proposed Plan of Rural Guard Reorganization." File 15984, General Classified Files, BIA. The members of the board were Lt. Col. W. W. Wotherspoon (C/S, ACP), Maj. W. A. Mann (Ass't C/S, ACP), and Maj. D. D. Gaillard (MID, ACP); Maj. F. S. Foltz to Capt. F. R. McCoy, December 22, 1906, McCoy Papers.

22. Transcript, "Report of Conference of the Provisional Governor with Generals Faustino Guerra, Carlos García Vélez and José de Jesus Monteagudo, November 28, 1906," File 012, CC/PGoC.

23. Magoon to Taft, December 31, 1906, File 062, CC/PGoC. One cause of Liberal concern may have been the position of the old Moderates. At the convention abolishing that party, General Ríus Rivera called for a five-thousand man regular army as part of the platform of the conservative party he hoped to form. *Independent*, LXI (November 8, 1906), 1078–79.

24. Taft to Magoon, February 2, 1907, File 062, CC/PGoC, RG 199.

25. Magoon to Taft, February 6, 1907, File 062, CC/PGoC, RG 199.

26. Editorial, *La Lucha* (Havana), February 4, 1907.

27. Stenographic record, "Conference between the Provisional Governor and Liberal Directorate, February 6, 1907," File 062, CC/PGoC, RG 199.

28. Memo, Maj. H. J. Slocum to the Provisional Governor, February 7, 1907, File 062, CC/PGoC, RG 199.

29. Magoon to Taft, February 7, 1907, and Taft to Magoon, February 8, 1907, File 062, CC/PGoC, RG 199.

30. *El Mundo* (Havana), February 10, 1907; *La Discusión* (Havana), February 9, 1907.

31. Notes, conference of the Provisional Governor with General Faustino Guerra, February 8, 1907, File 062, CC/PGoC, RG 199.

32. *Army and Navy Journal*, April 20 and May 11, 1907.

33. Taft to Magoon, February 15, 1907, File 062, CC/PGoC, RG 199.

34. Editorial, *Havana Post*, reprinted in the *Army and Navy Journal*, February 23, 1907.

35. Memorandum, "The Political Aspect of a Cuban Army," Capt. J. A. Ryan to Maj. H. J. Slocum, February 25, 1907, File 15984, General Classified Files, BIA, RG 350.

36. Brig. Gen. W. W. Wotherspoon to Capt. Frank Parker, October 10, 1910, Frank Parker Papers, Southern Historical Manuscripts Collection, Library of the University of North Carolina (Chapel Hill).

37. H. E. Havens to Taft, February 19, 1907, File 15984, General Classified Files, BIA, RG 350.

38. Position paper from the Liberal Committee to the Provisional Governor, March 14, 1907, File 15984, General Classified Files, BIA, RG 350.

39. Transcript, "Meeting of the Secretary of War William Howard Taft with the Liberal Committee, April 8, 1907," File 15984, General Classified Files, BIA, RG 350.

40. Brig. Gen. C. R. Edwards, Chief, Bureau of Insular Affairs, to Taft, April 3, 1907; Memorandum to Brig. Gen. J. F. Bell from Maj. Frank MacIntyre, April 2, 1907, both File 15984, General Classified Files, BIA, RG 350.

41. William E. Curtis to Roosevelt, April 17, 1907, Taft-Roosevelt Correspondence, Taft Papers.

42. Magoon to Taft, October 16, 1907; Taft to Magoon, October 18, 1907, both 15984, General Classified Files, BIA, RG 350.

43. República de Cuba, *Diario de sesiones de la Comisión Consultiva,* Tomo III, numero 212, 31 enero 1908 (Havana, 1908), pp. 141–52. Voting for the Permanent Army: Garcia Kohly, Zayas, González Sarraín, Carrera Justiz, Juan Gualberto Gómez, Regüeiferos Bodet; voting against: Viondi, Winship, Coronado, Schoenrich; Montoro, abstaining. Later Zayas proposed to create the cabinet post of Secretary of War and Navy (Cuba had no Navy), but Crowder squelched him.

44. República de Cuba, Decrees 365 and 366, April 4, 1908, *Gaceta oficial* (April-May, 1908), pp. 3393–3405.

45. Magoon to Taft, April 9, 1908, File 15984, General Classified Files, BIA, RG 350. To keep Guerra out of the country until after the 1908 elections and to broaden his formal military education, Magoon shipped him off to the Army schools in the United States and then to France. Pino took it all philosophically. There was little, he said, for a military man to do in Cuba with the United States troops on hand. Magoon, *Report, 1907–1908,* p. 77; Lockmiller, *Magoon in Cuba,* p. 145; Capt. J. A. Ryan to Maj. Gen. Faustino Guerra, November 3, 1907, File 247, CC/PGoC, RG 199.

46. *La Discusión* (Havana), April 6, 1908.

47. MID to C/S, ACP, April 7, 1908, File 229, CC/PGoC, RG 199.

48. Álvarez Díaz *et al., Estudio sobre Cuba,* p. 368.

# CHAPTER NINE

# RESTORATION AND WITHDRAWAL

ALTHOUGH no date had yet been set for the first round of elections, the Cuban *políticos* were campaigning in earnest by the fall of 1907. Their speeches, as analyzed by the Military Information Division, had made Havana indifferent, the provincial towns excited, the peasants fearful, and the whole situation unpredictable: "Politics are becoming more and more complicated every day; the pretensions of the politicians are changing from hour to hour. The enthusiasm of the populace for the Presidential candidates of today is constantly diminishing, and none of them are able to count upon victory."[1] The reaction of the Havana bankers and merchants to this situation was to send a memorial to Roosevelt asking him to postpone all but the municipal elections until all the political factions requested them.[2]

The style and content of José Miguel Gómez' campaign for the presidency were characteristic. Gómez, accompanied by compadres like Loynaz del Castillo and Morúa Delgado, made speeches for strong government, national unity, and patriotism to small crowds around Havana.[3] He then shifted his base back to Santa Clara where he continued to campaign with discretion and moderation. On one occasion, when a man shouted "Viva José Miguel Gómez, Abajo los americanos," Gómez shook his head and said, "No, we need the Americans." He then added that he hoped the American Army would remain to back the government.[4] Gómez stumped around the province, banqueting, laying a wreath on the grave of Enrique Villuendas in Cienfuegos, and listening to his orators speak for Law, Order, Patriotism, Independence, and Gómez. (They also had plenty of unpleasant things to say about the Zayistas.) Popular response, however, was luke-warm. The crowds (from 500 to 3,000) were well-behaved. The only development of interest was that Gómez was trying to get Mario Menocal to be his running mate.[5]

In April, 1908, the Miguelistas found in Oriente that the only way to whip up a crowd was to denounce the Americans; therefore Gómez allowed Loynaz del Castillo, Enrique Collazo, and Orestes Ferrara to berate the United States. Their speeches (to American ears) were full of hints of violence, anarchism, and demagoguery.[6] As the Gómez entourage moved up the island, the crowds grew, the speeches became more violent, and the choice of speakers varied. Gerardo Machado and Nicanor Lopez, representing the Spanish Board of Trade of Havana, joined the Gómez partisans, which added another insurgent officer and a representative of "commercial or industrial character" to the platform. The oratory continued to run heavily to anti-Americanism and threats of violence, but Gómez preached that the elections must be peaceful. He explained away the inconsistencies to a Marine officer by saying that there "must be some pepper in the food."[7] The Military Information Division believed Gómez was pitching his campaign away from the common people to win more influential backers. As the August 1 elections approached, the single most controversial issue was American policy in Cuba.[8]

The Zayistas' canvas differed in few respects from the Miguelistas' except that they were less cautious in their criticism of the United States. The general line of the Zayistas' appeal was summarized by Captain John W. Furlong:

> On all sides can be seen the signs of general discontent coming from the political and economic condition through which the Island is passing, and for which the American government is responsible.
>
> It has been asserted in private conversation that the United States government is exercising a policy very much akin to the one it saw fit to apply to California and Texas in days gone by. As a result, Cuba finds itself in a disorganized political and social state in order to please

American interests that have placed the country where it is now, and which makes it feel the lack of government that is responsible for its actions.[9]

The Conservatives, in the meantime, were having a difficult time shaking their image as "men of books and laws who wished to deceive the Liberals" and only the Liberal split encouraged them to campaign. The Junta Patriotica (old-time conservative patriots) and the Independent Party of Color were making little headway. Still, despite the talk of violence, Magoon was satisfied that the municipal elections would be orderly though the vote close.[10]

## American-Cuban Relations and the Restoration

In his annual message to Congress on December 7, 1907, Theodore Roosevelt expressed his pleasure over the Provisional Government's work. He announced that elections were in the offing to turn Cuba over to a government "chosen by the people." Once more he emphasized what he considered the irreducible elements of the United States relations with Cuba:

Cuba is at our doors. It is not possible that this Nation should permit Cuba again to sink into the condition from which we rescued it. All that we ask of the Cuban people is that they be prosperous, that they govern themselves so as to bring content, order and progress to their island . . . and our only interference has been and will be to help them achieve these results.[11]

To formally begin the restoration of self-government, Roosevelt set the date of the American withdrawal as no later than February 1, 1909.[12]

In the wake of Roosevelt's announcement, the British Foreign Office attempted to find out just how the United States was going to give Cuba both independence and stability. The chargé in Havana, A. C. Grant-Duff, thought that the political situation did not promise tranquillity or any lessening of antiforeign sentiment in Cuba; he suggested that the Foreign Office get concrete guarantees of protection of

British property before the Americans withdrew.[13] Opinions in London were divided; one official observed that the problem was entirely in Washington's hands:

> If the U.S. government wants to come back to Cuba, they will create disturbances in the island in order to provide a pretext for annexation or the American capitalists will do so.
> If, on the other hand, it is to their interest that things should remain quiet, they will take steps in that direction and as their troops are to remain after political evacuation, they can easily do this.[14]

Ambassador Bryce had already been investigating the future of Cuban-American relations and found "singularly little interest" in the subject within or without the government. Roosevelt seldom mentioned Cuba, and any impulse toward extending American control in the Spanish American republics seemed to have been "damped down among the people" for the time being.[15] Bryce had learned, however, through a conversation between Robert Bacon and an officer in the British embassy, that Roosevelt's latest public statement did not mean American troops would be brought home. When the British official observed that Cuba would then be like Egypt, Bacon agreed.[16] After reading Grant-Duff's letter, Bryce observed that the Platt Amendment morally bound the United States to see that order was maintained. In any event, the size of American investment in Cuba and the number of American companies doing business there were in themselves guarantees of intervention. Troops stationed at Guantanamo Bay would quite likely be enough to deter revolt. Bryce did report that Roosevelt told him he would probably withdraw all troops before his term expired.[17]

In late January, Roosevelt, at Root's urging, called Magoon and Crowder to Washington to discuss Cuban affairs. The purpose of the meeting, so Magoon understood, was "to devise [a] plan for exercising [the] power of the United States in Cuba after withdrawal in such [a] way as to make it less difficult and less expensive to discharge our obligations."[18] The State Department, since Cuba soon would become its worry again, wanted to study how this could be accomplished.

Steinhart cabled Magoon that if the United States wanted to influence Cuban domestic affairs in the future, the government should leave Magoon as minister, create an extraterritorial enclave near Havana garrisoned by three thousand American troops, and detail Army officers to both the Cuban army and Rural Guard as "instructors."[19]

The Washington conference, however, became involved in settling public works problems and the administrative control of Cuba's sanitation services. The participants did agree that "some sort of potential supervision" should be established over the Cuban government, but the talks on details proved inconclusive.[20]

Again, in April, Roosevelt asked Magoon's views on leaving troops in Cuba and on a plan to police the Cuban government suggested by the German ambassador and the President's friend, Baron Herman Speck von Sternberg. It was time, Roosevelt wrote, to plan the kind of Cuban government the United States wanted to restore. The President was doubtful that leaving troops would be wise. What then did the Governor think of Speck von Sternberg's proposal: to leave three American officers as advisers to the Cuban government? One would work to professionalize the Rural Guard, the second would insure that the Department of Justice administered the law without regard to wealth and influence, and the third would protect the Treasury from corruption.[21]

Magoon's reply on April 16 was an assessment of American policy, an analysis of Cuban politics, and a forthright interpretation of Cuba's national development.[22] The Provisional Governor reaffirmed the American commitment to an independent Cuba, and did not approve of any measure that compromised Root's strict interpretation of the Platt Amendment. He believed that occupation policy since 1906 had been within the framework of Cuba's constitution; the Provisional Government had, in fact, improved it with administrative reforms, despite the uncertainty about the length of the occupation. Magoon believed the legal reforms were fundamental changes, for the "Cuban Government was unstable because it lacked even the ordinary means and agencies by which stability is secured." The Provisional Government had enacted many laws "adapted to the government of a Republic and in harmony with modern thought . . . to give stability to the government of the Republic of Cuba, or any other Republic." In addition, Cuba now had an armed force, "a reasonable and necessary agency for the stability of the Government," adequate for the nation's needs and organized so as to reduce "the danger of militarism." Moreover, the government was now committed to an ambitious public-works program to offset seasonal unemployment, reduce unrest, and assist in economic development. Although the governmental reforms were by no means completed, the new Cuban administration would start off "well equipped with the ordinary means and agencies of stability."

After examining the various proposals to increase American supervision over the next Cuban government, Magoon rejected most of them. He feared that to leave American troops would disturb rather than keep the "moral peace," for such a force did not scare the Cubans and the occupation would disrupt Cuban-American relations. Speck von Sternberg's adviser plan, designed to insure that the government performed on American standards, was feasible, but not, in Magoon's opinion, likely to be very effective. Nonetheless, he agreed that advisers to the armed forces and Department of Justice be left behind if they were acceptable to the Cuban government.

Magoon made his own policy recommendations. He believed that the Provisional Government should go on with its legal reforms, public works, and administrative reorganization. After withdrawal, he urged both Cuba and the United States to reduce their tariffs for their mutual benefit. His most interesting proposal was that a "high joint commission" of respected Cubans and Americans be established to settle "contested elections or other controversies involving the relations of an administration and any large portion of the population." Magoon thought that such a "Tribunal" would be an effective substitute for military intervention as the Cubans could take their grievances to it rather than rise in revolt.

The Provisional Governor readily admitted that, for several reasons, neither party politics nor Americanization contributed to governmental stability. One reason was "the racial characteristics of the inhabitants of the Island." Magoon described the Cubans as "like all other people of Spanish origin . . . hot blooded, high strung, nervous, excitable and pessimistic . . . suspicious of every one." Cuba's colonial past had "intensified" these characteristics, particularly the war against Spain when antisocial behavior was to a large degree the key to survival. Magoon wrote:

> We cannot change these racial characteristics by administering their Government for two or twenty years, nor would they be changed by a military occupation. The changes, if made, will be effected by forces and influences of altogether different kind and character. All we can do is wait the progress of events, doing what is practicable to keep the progress orderly.

Magoon believed two developments "would make the Government of Cuba stable" and change the nature of party politics. The first would be the "cessation of the constant, senseless and trouble-breeding criticism with which the Government is surrounded as by a circle of perpetual fire." Any governmental act was criticized as favoritism, and there was no public confidence or desire to participate in "good government." "The second great accomplishment would be to induce the property owning and commercial classes to engage in active politics, assume and discharge the obligations of Cuban citizenship." Magoon was disheartened that the private associations and businesses did not "exercise their political influence." "With a modicum of interest and organization," they "could absolutely control the political situation." He realized that the "non-politicos" looked to the United States to protect their interests. Yet the participation of the business elite was essential:

> The stability of all governments comes from the business element and property owners and if those of Cuba would overcome their present inertia and go into politics, not to hold office, but establish good government, the question of further guarantees would be solved. How to

get them to do it, is a question I have vainly attempted to answer for the past year.

Magoon recognized the dilemma American policy faced: the Cuban economy was controlled by people divorced from the country's political life. Survival in Cuba thus pitted what were two "nations" against each other with the United States often protecting the economically privileged. He urged that the United States restore some impartiality to its attitude. First, it must "make known, in no uncertain way," that it supported the next legitimate government. "If abuses exist or arise," they must be corrected at the polls under law. If foreign lives and property were lost through violence, the United States "will call for indemnity from the Cuban Treasury instead of taking over the administration. . . . " Only by withdrawing the protection of the Platt Amendment would the "non-politicos" be assimilated into Cuba's political life. Otherwise the present "perilous" situation would continue. "The authority granted by the Platt Amendment should not be perverted into a menace to the object it was intended to conserve."

If Magoon's April 16 letter revealed the Governor's economic naïveté, it also was a forceful protest against the effect of American intervention on Cuba's internal development. Although Magoon believed his occupation government had made lasting reform, he was clearly worried that the 1906 occupation had done even more to increase the likelihood of future interventions. He wanted Cuba to be free again to cope with its internal problems. It was Magoon's views which prevailed, at least in the waning days of the Roosevelt administration.

Roosevelt's immediate reaction to Magoon's lengthy analysis of Cuba's problems and the United States responsibility for assisting Cuba to conquer them was to consider leaving Magoon as minister to Cuba and Crowder as military adviser. He also accepted the Provisional Governor's advice not to leave troops or press beyond requesting that the Provisional Government's work be continued.[23] Two months later, Roosevelt had retreated even further from the Speck von Sternberg plan. In a letter to Elihu Root, he set forth the United States demands on Cuba, " . . . that finances be kept straight, that order be maintained; and that fair elections be guaranteed." The United States would interfere only if Cuba's independence was endangered, the President wrote in an effort to restore the Platt Amendment to its original (Root's) interpretation. A significant point of Roosevelt's letter, however, was that advisers would be left behind only if the Cuban government requested them, but that it must carry on the Provisional Government's programs. As for the Provisional Governor, Roosevelt had cooled on his ability to promote order in Cuba: "Magoon gets on beautifully with the Cuban; he has done his work well, but he is not a man of masterful type or, indeed, of great force, and he shrinks from following any course to which he thinks any considerable number of Cubans would object, whether rightly or wrongly."[24]

In late August, Magoon again went to Washington to settle the details of the national election and the withdrawal. Upon his return to Havana, he wrote Roosevelt on Cuba's economic condition.[25] His major concern was to secure funds to continue the public works projects by floating another loan. He felt that only another bond issue was a sure source of money to attack the seasonal unemployment problem. The larger questions of Cuba's economic instability he left unstated, and it was just as well, for Roosevelt had accepted his earlier advice not to exercise more control over the Cuban government. Without the security of American-imposed stability, there would have been little inclination in Congress to lower the tariff.

Roosevelt was no longer optimistic about the United States ability to influence other nations' development without exploitation and antagonism. As he told editor-diplomat Whitelaw Reid, he could see many difficulties in "the control of thickly peopled tropical regions by self-governing northern democracies . . . "—not the least of which was that legislatures seldom understood the conditions in such lands and the measures necessary to develop them. Then Roosevelt put the Cuban occupation in its broad historical and political context:

> We have passed the time when a nation with even an imperfectly developed conscience is content simply to exploit for its own benefit a country that it has conquered; and the effort to govern such a country in its own interest without falling into mawkish sentimentality implies some mighty difficult steering.[26]

Close to the end of his administration, when his thoughts were far from Kettle Hill and his Corollary, Roosevelt, in a conversation with his military aide and Cuban veteran Captain Archibald Butt, gave his (and his nation's) eulogy to the Second Intervention. "I do not think about Cuba now," he said. "It is not our fault if things go badly there. . . . "[27]

Cuba was still very much on the mind of Leonard Wood's friends in the Provisional Government as the end of the occupation neared. After Roosevelt ordered elections, Steinhart wrote the General that everyone was working with restoration in mind; he, for example, was putting Wood's friends in the government where possible. Steinhart was unhappy with Roosevelt's policy, but reconciled that withdrawal would come.[28] Lieutenant Colonel Bullard was convinced that peaceful elections under American aegis were a poor way to test Cuba's capacity for self-government: "The question here is one of men and slow change which can come only in time and so we may not expect to see any appreciable results from an election."[29]

The *políticos'* triumph in the national elections further discouraged Wood's partisans. As Steinhart wrote McCoy: "Within a few weeks the second intervention will be a thing of the past and the Lord only knows what the future may have in store for this misfortunate island, in which I am informed bullfights, cock fights and lotteries are the new elements of contentment to be introduced."[30] Major Slocum hoped the new government would last, but, despite the accomplishments of the Provisional Government, feared it would not.[31] Captain John W. Wright of the Military Information Division wrote Wood that the "better classes" of

Cubans and his old officers hoped that at the next intervention Wood would return to Cuba and continue his work. Wright was sure such an opportunity would arise, and then perhaps the Army could get on with its nation-building:

> I see no hope for the new Cuban Government not only on account of the character of these people, but because I am afraid our policy was a mistaken one from the start. It was unfortunate for Cuba that our elections were so near when our policy was dictated. It was the policy to avoid trouble at any price and have everybody satisfied—or at least quiet—by the time our presidential votes were cast. In other words, our policy was directed not by the situation in Cuba, but by the American political status.
>
> I will return here and I hope for the sake of Cuba that you will be sent down here and allowed to remain at least ten years to continue your old policy, and only then, will this rich little Island come into her own.[32]

In view of the coming withdrawal, General Bell asked Captain John W. Furlong of the Military Information Division to study the character of Cuba's political leaders and report who were "the best men" or those most suited for "being used by Americans."[33] Furlong's criteria for a "good" public figure were that he be honest and have some resemblance to Porfirio Díaz of Mexico. Except for the "rascals" of which Alfredo Zayas ("who lived modestly on graft") was the archetype, most Cubans, he believed, lacked sufficient aggressiveness and self-confidence to be political leaders.

Furlong's "best men" were a curious group with but one common characteristic, the meaninglessness of their party affiliation. They were the conservative Manuel Sobrado, acting secretary of the Department of Justice; Ernesto Asbert, Liberal and next governor of Havana province; the conservative Domingo Lecuona, former governor of Matanzas; Tomás Recio, Liberal boss in Camaguey; Major Eduardo F. Lores of the Rural Guard; José Miguel Gómez' henchman José de Jesus Monteagudo; and Liberal *políticos* Demetrio Castillo Duany and Juan Gualberto Gómez. If there was any common denominator in these men's pasts, there was certainly none in their political futures except that their loyalties seemed to have been always negotiable. Perhaps they were selected as possible collaborators in a future military government, for in Army circles it was generally assumed that there would be other interventions.[34]

Lieutenant Colonel Bullard probably summed up the Army position when he observed that Cuba was pacified but not changed, that there could be no lasting government or peace there. The flaws in the Cuban body politic were so deep that the people would have to overthrow the government again, for "with the domineering, grandee spirit of Spanish blood, no Cuban in power can abstain from squeezing his fellows, from making them feel his power and authority. . . . The U. S. will have to go back. It is only a question of time."[35]

## Cuban Elections American Style

Pacified, enumerated, registered and administratively re-formed, the Cubans went to the polls in August, 1908, to begin to elect away the American occupation. Governor Magoon cautioned them that on their behavior at the polls rested the restoration of their own government and the future happiness and stability of their Republic.[36] On August 1, the Cubans elected provincial governors and councilmen and mayors and municipal councilors.[37] The elections went off with only minor problems as 269,132 of Cuba's 451,677 registered voters cast ballots.

The result was a stunning victory for the Conservatives over the still split Liberal factions of Gómez and Zayas. Conservative governors won in Pinar del Rio, Matanzas, and Santa Clara, and the party elected twenty-eight mayors. The potential Liberal strength was obvious, however, for the factions elected three governors and fifty-three mayors, and if their votes had been combined, they would have elected all their gubernatorial candidates and sixty-one of eighty-two mayors. Of the two factions, the Miguelistas were the stronger. Prominent among the Liberal victors were eight generals of the Constitutional Army: Enrique Loynaz del Castillo, Ernesto Asbert, Andres Paez, Baldermo Acosta, José Rumán Montero, Gerardo Machado, Adriano Galano, and Eduardo Guzmán.

Elated by the effectiveness of the electoral law and by the tranquillity of the elections, Magoon recommended that there be no delay of the national elections.[38] After his August trip to Washington, the Governor set November 14 as their date.

In the meantime, the *políticos* were busy repairing their alliances. The Liberals, seeing defeat in continued division, reunited and nominated Gómez and Zayas, a repeat of the slate of 1905; the fusion itself was artfully managed by three "Heroes of 1906," Pino Guerra, Julian Betancourt, and Loynaz del Castillo.[39] The Conservatives nominated Mario Menocal and Rafael Montoro. A "third force" movement in opposition to the historic parties was almost launched. If formed, this coalition would have been most interesting, for it spanned in social class, race, and region most of the Cuban body politic. The interested parties were José Manuel Govín (a Nuñezista) of the Agrupación Nacional Independiente, Tomás Recio (a Liberal who eventually supported Menocal) of the Partido Liberal Camagueyano, Salvador Cisneros Betancourt of the Junta Patriotica, Juan Gualberto Gómez of the "independent" Liberals, and Evaristo Estenoz of the Independent Party of Color.[40]

In November, after a noisy campaign, Gómez and Zayas won a majority of 70,943 votes and all 107 electors. In addition, all the newly elected senators were Liberals and, under proportional representation, fifty-one of the eighty three representatives. The election was orderly and fair, although Menocal thought the United States favored the Liberals.[41] Satisfied by the results, Roosevelt, on December 8, said that withdrawal would soon begin. As for the United States, it had only one desire, that the Cubans should "govern themselves with justice, so that peace and order may be secure."

To avoid being governed by others, they must prove their ability and desire to govern themselves.[42]

## Restoration and Withdrawal

The new year, 1909, found the Army of Cuban Pacification packing for home. In a gala round of banquets, the Provisional Government prepared to turn over power to José Miguel Gómez and his friends. The first American soldiers (the Twenty-eighth Infantry) sailed on New Year's Day and the Eleventh Infantry and Fifteenth Cavalry followed shortly thereafter.[43]

While there was still talk of the permanency of a future intervention, the Havana correspondent of the *Times* (London) reported that the Americans were satisfied that Cuba was better off for the occupation, but that the British interests were skeptical.[44] One American visitor to Havana, editor-publisher Henry Watterson went to the heart of Cuba's immediate political future. "The Cubans," he wrote, "are presently to be freed from the despotism which has flung around their political cradle the spell of a prospering but to them an oppressive ministration." The Provisional Government had given "benevolence galore without finding the least assimilation." The Cubans preferred Spain to the United States as a ruler, and the mass of the people resented Americans. What the future held for Cuban-American relations, one could not say:

The Havanese hate us, but would not fight us. The "rurales" do not hate us, but would fight for the republic we promised them. But the riff-raff, Lord, the riff-raff; injin, nigger, beggarman, thief—"both mongrel, puppy, whelp and hound and cur of low degree." . . . When the pie is cut, when the offices are all filled, what of the rejected ones? Will each turn conspirator? [45]

As the Army of Cuban Pacification folded its tents and packed its haversacks, it received praise from the President and the Havana press for its conduct of the occupation. Roosevelt sent, "on behalf of the whole American people," his thanks for a job well done.[46] The Havana press was equally laudatory, though no Cuban journal suggested the Army remain. *La Discusión* complimented the Army on being businesslike and mannerly and for not insulting the people by parading about. Considering the Cubans' excitability and the Americans' tendency to drink too much, *La Discusión* marveled at the lack of incidents. The civil government had been inferior to Wood's regime, it concluded, but the Army was just as effective as it had been in the earlier occupation.[47] In April, as the last soldiers left, *El Triunfo* echoed the same thought:

> The second intervention . . . has been the object of eulogies and censure, which it is not necessary to discuss at this moment; but we readily recognize and declare with sincere loyalty that the part of the intervention assigned to the American army merits only applause and congratulations from the Cubans.[48]

Magoon worked hard to order the government's affairs, primarily issuing decrees that made Gómez responsible for unfinished business in claims and public works. On January 28, the birthday of José Martí, Magoon ceremoniously transferred the Cuban government to the newly inaugurated Gómez on the balcony of the palace. Inside, Magoon, in a formal message, asked the new President's assurances that he would continue the Provisional Government's programs and uphold the Platt Amendment and the laws passed since 1906.[49] Gómez replied that he would, opened the palace doors, and shook hands with the crowd until his fingers became swollen. Cuba's new president, American readers were told, was a man of the people, not a doctor or lawyer, but "a soldierly inclined man of the Porfirio Díaz type, beloved by the country-people . . . whose mailed fist will command much more respect than the rather meek and forebearing patriotism of Estrada Palma."[50]

That afternoon, Magoon and his aides rode between cheering crowds to Caballeria Wharf. There José Miguel Gómez gave the ex-governor a warm *abrazo,* and the Americans went by launch to the battleship "Maine" and the transport "McClellan." The harbor swarmed with lighters and bumboats flying the Cuban colors, and from the city's rooftops handkerchiefs waved and whistles shrieked. As the United States warships, including the battleship "Mississippi," left the harbor, a Cuban military band (at Magoon's request) began to play "Bayamo," the national anthem. As one reporter described the scene:

It was a brilliant picture, made more perfect by a God given January day, by the tropic sun and the dark smoothness of the sea. At Morro, the khaki clad Artillery band struck up the strains of the Cuban hymn. Every head was uncovered. The governor could be seen to uncover . . . and the din of the whistles redoubled. In a saturnalia of noise, which drowned the efforts of the band, the Maine turned her nose north, as sedately as an old maid in a lavendar dress walking primly to church on an Easter morning. . . .

From Morro, whose signal tower was a galaxy of the flags of many nations . . . the lookout with his telescope followed the gray warships far out to sea. It was he who saw the last of the provisional governor that was.[51]

By mutual agreement, the United States Army stayed on in Cuba to insure a peaceful transition. The Army of Cuban Pacification headquarters, the Twenty-seventh Infantry, and the Engineers occupied Camp Columbia until March 31. On that day they turned over the post to the Cuban Army. With bands playing the two national anthems, the Republic's banner went up the staff. That night the American officers were honored by a banquet at the Hotel Miramor with much toasting and good cheer. At ten o'clock the next morning, the last troops left Havana aboard the transports "Sumner" and "McClellan."[52] The second American military occupation of Cuba was over.

Although the military occupation of Cuba was little more than an annoying necessity to the Roosevelt administration, it had a lasting impact on Cuba's political history and a negative but important influence on American foreign policy in the Caribbean.

The act of intervention, Manuel Márquez Sterling wrote in 1906, demonstrated once more that despite the United States great moral and material progress, Roosevelt had not learned that partisan politics, "good" and "educating" from a North American's point of view, had been in Latin America a source of criminality:

> Liberty is invoked in order to establish tyrannies; in its name grafters fight one another to divide precious resources; administrative honesty, free elections, and true suffrage are promised by those who proceed in the opposite manner, and sensitive people have seen with sadness in Colombia, in Mexico, in Paraguay or in Cuba, that the triumph of the evil ones has not been over the good, but, in most cases, over the poor. Politics in our unfortunate lands consists of alternating between two different, demoralizing systems, under tyranny or under chaos, under the rapacious power of reactionaries or under the anarchistic power of equally rapacious demagogues. Politicians, in the step from colony to independence, have made reform a deformation of social character.[53]

Cuba's war of liberation had placed political power in the hands of men who knew how to use violence as a political weapon, but who knew little else. They could hardly have been less prepared for constitutional government. As one Cuban conservative reflected: "When the last soldier of the war of independence is dead . . . when there is no longer left any soldier or General of the rebellion of . . . 1906, then and not until then, will it be wise for the United States to trust us with a second experiment in self-government."[54]

Of equal consequence was the fact that free Cuba retained its colonial economy. The economic and social destruction of the war of 1895–98 sped the trend to sugar monoculture, the heart of Cuba's economic instability. For Enrique José Varona, the lack of domestic capital was a more important problem than foreign ownership, and he urged the government to assume a positive role in economic development. If the economic situation did not change, Varona wrote in 1906, the Cuban people would be in an increasingly weak and desperate position. "If this is so, the resulting irreconcilable confusion of mind will sustain the sordid agitation I see everywhere, the budding anarchy becoming evident in so many places, the malevolence and mad hostility with which we persecute one another, as if each Cuban was the natural enemy of all other Cubans."⁵⁵

Varona thought the remedy "for our evils" should be sought in "a change in our internal political organization," rather than in a "change in the form of our relations with the United States. . . . ." Whatever Roosevelt's good intentions, he could not alter the basic facts of Cuban-American relations, for the only way to do that "would be to push the island several thousand leagues out in the Atlantic and outside the radius of the influence of the United States." Varona's interpretation of the United States duty under these circumstances reflected the characteristic ambivalency of the Cuban-American dialogue: Roosevelt must "guarantee in a permanent manner . . . peace on the island, and the right to labor undisturbed and acquire wealth by all licit means."⁵⁶

The intervention, as Enrique Barbarrosa saw it, was to a large degree the fault of the United States, whose economic policy was to dominate Cuba. In the resulting social disintegration, "the force of circumstances . . . made Uncle Sam give the disconsolate virgin of America, full on the face, the kiss of intervention." The occupation that followed proved but one thing: "One cannot establish a rich and free government with a nation of beggars."⁵⁷

The thrust of Cuban criticism was well aimed, for it was not so critical of the intervention itself as of the occupation that followed. Disregarding the annexationists and the xenophobes, the Cuban nationalist interpretation of the occupation is best summarized by Herminio Portell Vilá. Writing in the first period of the Batista dictatorship, Portell Vilá criticized the Magoon government for ignoring the impact of American policy on Cuba's economic growth, while it wrongly attributed Cuban apathy toward the nation's problems to a fundamental lack of national character. Portell Vilá believed this apathy was a result of American policy which had frustrated the Cuban Revolution.⁵⁸ Magoon's administration had done nothing to dispel the notion that government was the foremost national industry. By dealing sympathetically with the *políticos*, rather than using Cubans who were "able, progressive, and dedicated to service in the cause of national regeneration," Magoon paved the way for the *políticos'* final conquest of the Republic of Cuba. After 1909, "administrative corruption, violence and incapacity" increasingly dominated Cuban government and were an insurmountable barrier to reform.[59]

A perceptive contemporary assessment of the American occupation came from Dr. Juan Guiteras in a letter to Major Jefferson R. Kean. The United States, Doctor Guiteras wrote, had the best intentions and Cuba was grateful to be rescued from the violence of 1906. The problem was that American policy-makers failed to use their power to provide for the long range conditions which would insure the United States security and trade and Cuba's development. The expedient acts of the occupation brought only temporary improvement:

> A rather remarkable group of well-meaning, intelligent men, with a great power behind them, have come down here, and with much tact, hard work, self sacrifice and kindness, have managed things very well. They have maintained peace and order, and have much improved the administration; they have opened up new lines in the way of progress; but that they have made us better fit for self-government, I cannot believe.
>
> . . . In Cuba there are no parties, and the Intervention has done nothing towards teaching us to construct and maintain two great political parties. It has, on the contrary, fostered our natural bent for individual or boss following. When this second Intervention came upon the scene the people appeared to be divided into two great political parties . . . worthy rivals to contend for the control of the future Republic. But the conglomerate that made up the so-called parties began to disgregate [*sic*], and the Government proceeded to cultivate the several factions into which they divided. The result was a most luxurious multiplication of parties, in the shape of three or more independent followings in every Province, and perhaps in every municipality. This is exactly what was done in the days of the Republic and the procedure must likewise lead to revolution so soon as you withdraw the big stick of Uncle Sam that makes everything go.[60]

Fearing a costly and politically unjustifiable war, the Roosevelt administration reluctantly assumed the responsibility of governing Cuba in 1906. Caught between its hesitancy to incur domestic criticism and its sensitivity to Cuban resistance, the Provincial Government was unable to take advantage of the security given it by the Army of Cuban Pacification to work basic social and economic changes in Cuba. To a large degree, Magoon and his advisers were limited in their policy choices by Roosevelt, Taft, and Root who guided policy under two basic assumptions: that Cuba should not be annexed and that there was no chance of altering the two nations' economic relationship. The Provisional Government's mission was to hold elections and withdraw. In order to do this, to restore some order in Cuba, it did improve transportation, government services, and, by its stability and fiscal policy, the economy. The laws drafted by the Advisory Law Commission and put into effect by Magoon were badly needed, but more related to establishing the machinery for American withdrawal than to promoting long-term reforms.

Governments, however, are built on men as well as laws, and the political program of the Provisional Governor and the administrative reforms initiated by the Army officers on his staff contributed to Cuba's problems rather than solved them. Magoon, Taft, and Roosevelt believed that political parties were an expression of popular will and necessary to representative government; their faith in the American experience was obvious. Beyond their ideological commitment to party government, they recognized that parties were essential to the elections which would return Cuba to its own government. Ironically, while the Provisional Government's constitutional reforms were in accordance with the Cuban conservatives' suggestions for cleansing the government, the United States, through elections, turned the whole apparatus over to men whose political values did not include belief in a division and balance of power, limited government, efficiency, honesty, and public interest, as Americans prized them.

Within the Provisional Government, the greatest impulse for change in Cuba came from the officers of the United States Army. Their experiences with Leonard Wood and in the other insular possessions convinced them that the former Spanish colonies needed long periods of tutelage and control if they were not to slip into anarchy or absolutism. They saw the native political class as unprincipled exploiters of the people, men whose influence must be checked. They blamed Cuban antisocial behavior as much on ignorance and the Hispanic cultural heritage (which could be overcome) as on poverty and biological inferiority, the characteristics that most repulsed their civilian contemporaries. They believed some important American values (such as justice, fair play, honesty, and community co-operation) were transferable and offered the only real hope of stability. For the moment, however, American political institutions had best be left at home. An American military government, on the other hand, the officers thought, was an appropriate instrument for inculcating the attitudes of a peaceful citizenry. Since the Army would have to police the violent societies for which the United States had assumed responsibility, the officers were anxious to reshape these societies to their own liking. This is what they attempted to do, without much satisfaction, in Cuba from 1906 to 1909.

To a large degree, the Army was responsible for the Provisional Government's successes and had little to do with its more obvious shortcomings. The Army of Cuban Pacification kept the peace and thwarted the annexationists, while the officers of the Provisional Government administered the government, however restively, under Magoon and his civil superiors. But in their more far-reaching developmental plans, the officers were disappointed. Colonel Crowder did not get the reformed legal codes; Lieutenant Colonel Bullard did not get a chance to rebuild the educational system; Lieutenant Colonel Black did not get the better roads and waterworks he wanted to construct; Lieutenant Colonel Greble did not have enough time to purge the incompetents from the Department of Government; Major Kean had to leave the epidemic disease problem relatively untouched; Major Slocum did not get the Rural Guard thoroughly professionalized. Paradoxically, the major institutional change sponsored by the Provisional Government, the establishment of the Permanent Army of Cuba, was opposed by the officers because of its political and economic implications. They were overruled by their superiors in Washington and the civil authorities, who were willing to follow a more expedient course: to give the *políticos* the armed forces they wanted for internal security.

The officers could see no constructive purpose in stimulating party politics and establishing the governmental machinery of a working democracy for an undemocratic society, and they said so. They did not, however, argue their case outside their own circle of Army associates and the official channels of the government. To a large degree, they accepted limitations on their reforms because they could see few possible political allies in either American or Cuban civil society.

There were other inhibitive influences besides their political isolation. The most important was the attitude of the Army itself. In 1906 the new colonial possessions, pacified or not, presented the United States Army with demanding strategic problems it did not have before 1898. Confronted with new tasks, the Army rapidly lost its interest in constabulary duties and colonial administration. By 1909, it had become thoroughly involved in planning and organizing for war with one or another of the major world powers. This was its own inevitable adjustment to the United States new stature as an international force. As the Army redefined its missions and professional interests, it placed a lower priority on the skills of maintaining internal security and nation-building. The officers who had made careers in Cuba and the Philippines had to refashion them at the Army War College and on the General Staff within a decade. For the Army, as well as for the nation, there was little time for unpopular occupations in the Caribbean and the reform of Latin republics.

Throughout the occupation the Army officers consistently found themselves thwarted by the central tenet of American policy: the Provisional Government's function was to liquidate the intervention of September, 1906. While the officers saw their tasks as eliminating the causes of insurrection and of continuing the Americanizing, reformist work of Wood's military government, Roosevelt, Taft, and Root viewed occupation policy only in relation to restoring a Cuban political balance which would allow the United States to withdraw.

The United States government was more concerned with concluding the historical act of military occupation rather than changing the conditions which brought it about. For both countries, the withdrawal marked a restoration of Cuban self-government at the expense of Cuba's political development.

The impact of the Second Intervention on American policy in the Caribbean has been underestimated. The occupation of Cuba coincided with the development of fiscal supervision in the Dominican Republic, and it was the tool of fiscal supervision perfected in the latter country which seemed best suited and was subsequently most applied to influence the lives of the Caribbean republics. In a sense, the Roosevelt administration had two experiments underway at the same time, and it bequeathed the results of both to Taft and Woodrow Wilson. Recognizing the unique circumstances of each of the United States Caribbean interventions, the Cuban model, military occupation and direct governmental control sanctioned by treaty, was not willingly used again elsewhere. The Dominican model, financial supervision and indirect control, seemed a handier way to bring stability while reducing the political risks.

There were some obvious factors in the increasing reluctance to use military occupations elsewhere: no other Caribbean island was as strategically and economically important to the United States as Cuba, nor did any other hold the same historic and emotional relationship. Armed intervention and outright military occupation in Cuba might be rationally and emotionally acceptable to the Americans, but these measures might not be so easily justifiable in another republic.

In the broadest sense, the Second Intervention reminded American policy-makers that outright control and military occupation, as in Cuba, brought the United States government face to face with the problem of political and social change in the former Spanish colonies. The United States government was unwilling to assume the responsibility for making any institutional changes which it would have to supervise over a long and indefinite period. Undoubtedly this disavowal represented the prevailing sentiments of the American people.

Ironically, the attempts to achieve stability in the Caribbean through a variety of indirect controls often became the bloody and unproductive military affairs the policy was designed to avoid. Again there were military interventions and occupations, sometimes against native resistance, and the same problems of institutional change was forced upon the United States.

William Howard Taft did not forget that intervention was a poor remedy for Caribbean instability, a lesson Cuba may easily have taught him. As heavy-handed and, in the long run, unprofitable as Dollar Diplomacy was, it was Taft's clumsy alternative to reformist military occupations. By "substituting dollars for bullets," or capital investment and financial supervision for Army occupation, and (hopefully) prosperity for rebellion, Taft looked for a more politically acceptable answer to Caribbean instability than the Army could provide. Dollar Diplomacy was the idiom of the bank, not the drill field. It reflected the ideals of middle-class, productive, civilian America: social peace, profits, progress, and the spread of civilization.

Dollar Diplomacy's political component was also a rejection of the Cuban experience, for the support of *de jure* native governments became increasingly preferable to outright American political control. In practice, this diplomatic stance did not make the United States reaction to civil war less ambiguous, nor did it reduce the likelihood of intervention; an established government's ability to defend itself (and foreign property) continued to be an important criterion for winning or losing American support.

Although Dollar Diplomacy cut the domestic political risks of intervention, it was unable to correct the economic conditions which helped insure that the United States would be drawn into the Caribbean civil wars of the next thirty years. Here the Cuban experience was ignored at two levels. The growth of American businesses, as in Cuba, provided perfect political hostages when a faction wanted to coerce the United States government. Not to intervene, to allow American lives and property to be destroyed, was to risk widespread criticism at home and economic collapse in the affected Caribbean country. The problem had another dimension. The employment habits, the marketing risks, and the patterns of wealth distribution that characterized the Cuban economy in 1906 (the result of the increasing dominance of industrialized, cash-crop agriculture) were in themselves a cause of political instability. The Provisional Government became increasingly aware of this, yet, except for temporary palliatives, it could not change Cuba's economic structure. Among the restraints were the direct limitations imposed by the United States government and the economic preconceptions of the Americans serving in Cuba. The causes of Cuba's economic instability were clear enough. Yet this understanding of Cuba's economic vulnerability did not prevent the Taft administration from encouraging American investors to create similar problems in other Caribbean nations by introducing or expanding economic institutions similar to Cuba's. If the economic phase of Dollar Diplomacy was based on the impact of foreign capital on the Cuban political system, it was an unwise precedent to follow. The Cuban experience demonstrated that the politics of violence were part of the cost of a certain form of economic development.

The social and political insecurity of Cuba's type of economic growth far outweighed the stabilizing effect brought about by a simple increase of the nation's wealth. However imperfectly stated, this was the argument the officers of the United States Army serving in Cuba wanted to present, that stability without reform and institutional change brought no peace at all. In retrospect, the authoritarian American government the officers wished to establish for Cuba, in order to reshape the Cuban way of life, might have been a humanitarian, just, and effective alternative to the indigenous, self-determined Cuban government created in the image but not the spirit of American economic and political liberalism.

1. MID to C/S, ACP, October 31, 1907, File 203, CC/PGoC, RG 199.

2. MID to C/S, ACP, December 18, 1907, File 196–6, CC/PGoC, RG 199.

3. Reports of Miguelista meetings by MID, September 15 to October 27, 1907, File 191, CC/PGoC, RG 199.

4. Maj. W. D. Beach to Adj. Gen., ACP, November 20, 1907, File 191, CC/PGoC, RG 199.

5. MID to C/S, ACP, November 25, 1907, to January 5, 1908, File 191–3 to File 191–9 and File 196–9, CC/PGoC, RG 199.

6. MID to C/S, ACP, April 25 to June 8, 1908, File 191–10 to File 191–14, CC/PGoC, RG 199.

One orator, José L. Castellanos, called Christ the first Liberal, which drew a few hisses.

7. Memo, Capt. H. J. Hirshinger to Adj. Gen., ACP, June 28, 1908, File 191–17, CC/PGoC; MID to C/S, ACP, June 30 to July 8, 1908, File 191–16 to 191–19, CC/PGoC, RG 199.

8. MID to C/S, ACP, July 8 and 14, 1908, File 191–19 and 20, CC/PGoC. Collazo described Cuban-American relations: "Cuba was in the position of a man strung up by the neck with his toes barely touching the ground and then counseled affectionately by his lynchers to enjoy himself."

Magoon reported the Miguelistas might revolt if not victorious in the election. Magoon to Taft, May 26, 1908, File 017–44, CC/PGoC, RG 199.

9. MID to C/S, ACP, June 13, 1908, File 017–45, CC/PGoC, RG 199.

10. Magoon to Taft, June 4, 1908, File 017–46, CC/PGoC; A. Waldo Stevenson to Brig. Gen. T. H. Barry, July 29, 1908, File 194–2, CC/PGoC, RG 199; A. C. Grant-Duff, chargé, to Sir Edward Grey, April 20, 1908, FO 371–446, PRO. On the Independent Party of Color, see G. Cornell Tarler, chargé, to Secretary of State, October 5, 1908, Case 1943/164, *Num. File, 1906–1910*, Vol. CCV, RG 59.

11. Richardson (ed.), *Messages and Papers of the Presidents*, X, 7501.

12. Roosevelt to Taft, January 13, 1908, Roosevelt Papers.

13. Grant-Duff to Grey, February 4, 1908, FO 371–446, PRO.

14. Memo by Louis Mallet appended to Grant-Duff letter of February 4, 1908, FO 371–446, PRO.

15. James Bryce to Grey, January 15, 1908, FO 371–446, PRO.

16. Bryce to Grey, January 22, 1908, FO 371–446, PRO.

17. Bryce to Grey, March 9, 1908, FO 371–446, PRO.

18. Magoon to Steinhart, February 3, 1908, File 222, CC/PGoC, RG 199.

19. Steinhart to Magoon, February 4, 1908, File 222, CC/PGoC, RG 199.

20. Magoon to Barry, February 8, 1908, File 219, CC/PGoC; cable-grams and memoranda, Provisional Governor's conferences with Roose-

velt, Root, and Taft, January 21 to February 20, 1908, File 219, CC/PGoC, RG 199; Taft to Roosevelt, June 30, 1908, Roosevelt Papers.

21. Roosevelt to Magoon, April 4, 1908, Roosevelt Papers.

22. Magoon to Roosevelt, April 16, 1908, Roosevelt Papers.

23. Roosevelt to Root, April 27, 1908, Roosevelt Papers.

24. Roosevelt to Root, July 20, 1908, Roosevelt Papers.

25. Magoon to Roosevelt, August 31, 1908, Roosevelt Papers.

26. Roosevelt to Whitelaw Reid, September 3, 1908, Roosevelt Papers.

27. Capt. Archibald Butt to Mrs. Lewis F. Butt, February 3, 1909, in Lawrence F. Abbott (ed.), *The Letters of Archie Butt* (New York, 1924), p. 325.

28. Steinhart to Wood, May 8, 1908, Wood Papers.

29. Entries of May 31 and July 19, 1908, Bullard diaries, Bullard Papers.

30. Steinhart to McCoy, November 23, 1908, Scott Papers.

31. Slocum to Wood, November 25, 1907, Wood Papers.

32. Two letters, Capt. J. W. Wright to Wood, December (?), and 31, 1908, Wood Papers.

33. Capt. J. W. Furlong, "Memorandum for General Bell," November 16, 1908, AWC Doc. File 5399, RG 165.

34. *Army and Navy Journal,* June 27 and July 25, 1908.

35. Entry for February 13, 1909, Bullard diaries, Bullard Papers. Greble and Winship thought the new government had some chance of lasting four years. Capt. A. Butt to Mrs. L. F. Butt, February 3, 1909, in Abbott, *The Letters of Archie Butt,* p. 325.

36. República de Cuba, Proclamation of July 24, 1908, *Gaceta oficial* (July–August, 1908), pp. 645–46.

37. On the elections: Magoon, *Report, 1907–1908,* pp. 34–36, 42–44; Marió Riera Hernández, *Cuba política, 1899–1955* (Havana, 1955), pp. 121–49; Lockmiller, *Magoon in Cuba,* pp. 177–85.

38. Magoon to Root, August 1, 1908, Case 1943/112, *Num. File, 1906–1910,* Vol. CCV, RG 59.

39. Riera Hernández, *Cuba política,* p. 135.

40. *Ibid.,* p. 136.

41. Lockmiller, *Magoon in Cuba,* p. 183. Seventy-one per cent of the registered voters balloted.

42. Richardson (ed.), *Messages and Papers of the Presidents,* X, 7614.

43. "Report of the Army of Cuban Pacification," U.S. War Department, *Annual Reports, 1908–1909* (Washington, 1909), III, 235.

44. *Times* (London), January 2, 1909.

45. Editorial, "Again Cuba Libre," January 29, 1909, reprinted in Arthur Krock (comp.), *The Editorials of Henry Watterson* (Louisville, Ky., 1923), pp. 277–82.

46. "Report of the Army of Cuban Pacification," U.S. War Department, *Annual Reports, 1908–1909,* III, 270.

47. *La Discusión,* January 20, 1909.

48. *El Triunfo,* April 2, 1909.

49. Magoon, *Supplemental Report,* pp. 9–10.

50. Carmela Nieto de Durland, "Home Rule in Cuba Once More," *The World To-Day,* XVI (March, 1909), 285–88. In a similar description, Gómez was characterized as a patriot, a commoner, and an ardent nationalist who "measures up to the standard of Porfirio Díaz." William Hemmingway, "To-morrow in Cuba," *Harper's Weekly,* LIII (March 20, 1909), 24–25.

51. *Havana Post,* January 29, 1909. Magoon never again held office, presumably because of ill health. Living frugally in Washington, he was on cordial social terms with the Roosevelts, Tafts, and Wilsons. Though there was some talk of his appointment to Taft's cabinet, he would not have been a political asset. He died on January 14, 1920, following an appendix operation.

52. "Report of the Army of Cuban Pacification," U.S. War Department, *Annual Reports, 1908–1909,* III, 240. Three captains remained behind to train the Cuban army.

53. Márquez Sterling, *Alrededor de nuestra psicologia,* pp. 170–72.

54. Alexander González to Wood, November 19, 1906, Wood Papers.

55. Enrique José Varona, "¿ Abriremos Los Ojos?" October 17, 1906, in *Mirando en torno,* pp. 35–36.

56. Enrique José Varona, letter to *El Comercio,* December 3, 1906, in Case 1943/40, *Num. File, 1906–1910,* Vol. CCL, RG 59.

57. Enrique Barbarrosa, *El proceso de la república, analisis de la situación económica de Cuba bajo el gobierno presidencial de Tomás Estrada Palma y José Miguel Gómez* (Havana, 1911), pp. 25–30, 67.

58. Portell Vilá, *Historia de Cuba,* IV, 561.

59. *Ibid.,* pp. 535–36, 570. *Los responsables* marked the occupation as the end of the conservative influence in the Cuban government, Wright, *Cuba,* p. 189.

60. Dr. Juan Guiteras to Maj. J. R. Kean, March 6, 1908, Kean Papers.

# Bibliography

*Archival Material and Manuscripts*

*Public Records.*—The records of the agencies of the United States government involved in the intervention and occupation of Cuba held by the National Archives of the United States, Washington, D.C., are numerous. Of first importance are the Records of the Provisional Government of Cuba (Record Group 199), which include the Confidential Correspondence of the Provisional Governor of Cuba, public health and fiscal reports, and cartographic records. These documents run heavily to reports of political and administrative affairs and economic conditions. Additional materials concerning the Provisional Government are located in the case files in the General Classified Files, 1898–1945, of the Bureau of Insular Affairs, War Department (Record Group 350). The diplomatic correspondence, including private letters, post reports, newspaper clippings, and other documents, is part of the *Numerical File, 1906–1910* (1,172 volumes) and consular *Dispatches* in the General Records of the Department of State (Record Group 59). The military records are voluminous. The most useful source is the Records of the War Department General Staff (Record Group 165), which include reports from the Army of Cuban Pacification in the papers of the Military Information Division, and the documents in the Army War College Document File, 1903–19, in the records of the Army War College Division. Of almost equal value are the Records of the Adjutant-General's Office (Record Group 94), for the Adjutant-General was the custodian of the Army's correspondence. Another good source is the Records of the Office of the Inspector General (Record Group 159), containing "Inspection Reports, Department of Cuba and Cuban Posts, 1903–1912." The naval records are preserved in the Naval Records Collection of the Office of Naval Records and Library (Record Group 45), particularly the geographic Area 8 File (Caribbean, 1775–1910), and the General Records of the Navy Department (Record Group 80).

In addition, selected documents from the records of the British Foreign Office, the Public Record Office, London, England, were used.

*Private Papers.*—The private correspondence, diaries, and manuscripts of American political leaders and Army officers are essential for interpreting the Second Intervention. From the civil policy–making side, the papers of Theodore Roosevelt, William Howard Taft, Elihu Root, and Charles J. Bonaparte, held by the Manuscript Division, Library of Congress, are basic; the Taft-Roosevelt Correspondence in the Taft Papers is the most significant single group of letters. The Library of Congress also holds the papers of American officers whose careers were inextricably tied to Cuba. A major source is the papers of General Leonard Wood, which contain many letters from Cubans and Army officers written in 1906–9. A collection of equal interest is the papers of General Robert L. Bullard, containing diaries, notebooks, a manuscript autobiography, letters, and article manuscripts. Another collection of value is the papers of General James Harrison Wilson, a critic of American policy; the Wilson Papers include letters from Lieutenant Colonel E. St.J. Greble and journalist Albert G. Robinson. The papers of Generals Hugh L. Scott, Tasker H. Bliss, and Frank R. McCoy have varied Cuban materials, and those of Generals Henry T. Allen, James G. Harbord, and John J. Pershing shed light on the problems of pacification. The Library of Congress holds the papers of Admiral William F. Fullam, which include two Cuban subject files of great value for the reconstruction of the naval intervention.

The papers of General Enoch H. Crowder (Western Historical Manuscript Collection, University of Missouri, Columbia, Missouri) and General Jefferson Randolph Kean (Manuscripts Division, University of Virginia Library, Charlottesville, Virginia) are invaluable. Other collections add intertesting insights: the papers of Generals Frank Parker and William P. Upshur, USMC (Southern Historical Collection, University of North Carolina Library, Chapel Hill, North Carolina), and General William G. Haan (State Historical Society of Wisconsin Collections, Madison, Wisconsin).

## Printed Public Documents

### Cuba

*Diario de Sesiones de la Comisión Consultiva de la República de Cuba bajo la administración provisional de los Estados Unidos.* 4 Vols. Habana: Imp. Rambla, Bouza y Ca, 1908 y 1916.

*Gaceta oficial de la república de Cuba, 1902.* Habana: Administración de la Imprenta, mayo, 1906–febrero, 1909.

MAGOON, CHARLES E. *Republic of Cuba: Report of the Provisional Administration, October 13, 1906—December 1, 1907.* Havana: Rambla & Bouza, 1908.

*Presidente. Mensajes presidenciales, remitodos al congreso . . . 1903–1906.* Habana: Administración de la Imprenta, 1903–6.

*Republic of Cuba, Under the Provisional Government of the United States, Decrees, 1906–1909.* 9 Vols. Havana: Rambla & Bouza, 1907–9.

### United States

*Congressional Record.* Vols. XL, XLI.

*Cuba: General Orders, Circulars and Special Orders, Headquarters, Army of Cuban Pacification 1906 and General*

*Orders, Circulars and Special Orders Headquarters, First Expeditionary Brigade, 1906.*

*Cuba: General Orders, Special Orders and Circulars Headquarters, Army of Cuban Pacification, 1907–1909.* 5 Vols. Havana: n.p., 1908–9.

DEPARTMENT OF COMMERCE AND LABOR, BUREAU OF MANUFACTURERS. *Monthly Consular and Trade Reports, 1906–1909.* Washington: Government Printing Office, 1906–9.

DEPARTMENT OF THE NAVY. *Annual Report of the Colonel Commandant of the United States Marine Corps to the Secretary of the Navy, 1893–1906.* Washington: Government Printing Office, 1906.

DEPARTMENT OF STATE. *Papers Relating to the Foreign Relations of the United States, 1903, 1906–1909.* Washington: Government Printing Office, 1904–1911.

GANNETT, HENRY AND OLMSTEAD, VICTOR H. (comp.). *Cuba: Population, History and Resources, 1907.* Washington: U.S. Bureau of the Census, 1909.

HOUSE OF REPRESENTATIVES. *Documents.* "Report of the Provisional Governor of Cuba, December 1, 1907—December 1, 1908," Vol. 147, House Document No. 1457. 60th Cong., 2d Sess., 1908.

MAGOON, CHARLES E. *Report on the Law of Civil Government in Territory Subject to Military Occupation by the Military Forces of the United States.* 3d edition. Washington: Government Printing Office, 1903.

QUESADA, GONZALO DE. *Cuba.* (Handbook of the International Bureau of the American Republics.) Washington: Government Printing Office, 1905.

RICHARDSON, JAMES D. (ed.). *A Compilation of the Messages and Papers of the Presidents, 1789–1908.* 11 Vols. Washington: Government Printing Office, 1908.

*Speeches Incident to the Visit of Secretary Root to South America.* (July 4 to September 30, 1906) Washington: Government Printing Office, 1906.

SENATE, COMMITTEE ON THE PHILIPPINES. *Hearings.* "Charges of Cruelty, Etc., to the Natives of the Philippines," Vol. XV, Senate Document No. 205. 57th Cong., 1st Sess., 1902.

SENATE COMMITTEE ON THE PHILIPPINES. *Hearings.* "Affairs in the Philippines," 3 vols., Senate Document No. 331. 57th Cong., 1st Sess., 1902.

SENATE *Documents.* "Supplemental Report of the Provisional Governor of Cuba, December 1, 1908—January 29, 1909," Vol. 9, Senate Document No. 80.

*United States Statutes at Large.* Vol. XXXI.

WAR DEPARTMENT. *Annual Reports, 1899, 1905–1909.* Washington: Government Printing Office, 1899, 1906–9.

———. *Civil Report of Major General Leonard Wood, Military Governor of Cuba, for the Period from December 20, 1899, to December 31, 1900.* 12 Vols. Washington: Government Printing Office, 1901.

———. *Civil Report of Brigadier General Leonard Wood, Military Governor of Cuba, for the Period January 1 to December 31, 1901.* 15 Vols. Washington: Government Printing Office, 1902.

———. *Civil Report of Brigadier General Leonard Wood, Military Governor of Cuba, for the Period from January 1 to May 20, 1902.* 6 Vols. Washington: Government Printing Office, 1902.

———. (Adjutant General's Office). *Correspondence Relating to the War with Spain, April 15, 1898—July 30, 1902.* Washington: Government Printing Office, 1902.

———. *Five Years of the War Department Following the War with Spain, 1899–1903, As Shown in the Annual Reports of the Secretary of War.* Washington: Government Printing Office, 1904.

———. Office of the Chief of Staff. *Military Notes on Cuba, 1909.* (Study No. 15, Second Section, General Staff, compiled by Capt. John W. Furlong, Military Information Division, Army of Cuban Pacification.) Washington: Government Printing Office, 1909.

————. The Adjutant General's Office. *Official Army Register, 1906, 1907*. Washington: Government Printing Office, 1905, 1906.

————. Office Director Census of Cuba. *Report on the Census of Cuba, 1899*. Washington: Government Printing Office, 1900.

————. Office of the Chief of Staff. *Road Notes, Cuba, 1909*. (Study No. 16, Second Section, General Staff.) Washington: Government Printing Office, 1909.


*Newspapers, 1906–1909*

> *Army and Navy Journal*
> *Diario Español* (Havana)
> *Diario de la Marina* (Havana)
> *El Comercio* (Havana)
> *El Liberal* (Havana)
> *El Mundo* (Havana)
> *El Triunfo* (Havana)
> *Havana Daily Telegraph*
> *Havana Post*
> *La Discusión* (Havana)
> *La Lucha* (Havana)
> *New York Times*
> *New York Tribune*
> *Times* (London)
> *Washington Evening Star*
> *Washington Post*
> *World* (New York)


*Magazines, 1906–1909*

> *American Magazine*
> *Arena*
> *Graphic* (London)
> *Harper's Weekly*

*Independent*
*Journal of the Military Service Institution*
*Leslie's Weekly*
*Nation*
*North American Review*
*Outlook*
*Review of Reviews*


*Memoirs, Letters, Other Printed Materials*

ABBOTT, LAWRENCE F. (ed.). *The Letters of Archie Butt.* Garden City, New York: Doubleday, Page & Co. 1924.

ARCHER, WILLIAM. *Through Afro-America.* London: Chapman & Hall Ltd., 1910.

ATKINS, EDWIN F. *Sixty Years in Cuba.* Cambridge, Mass.: Riverside Press, 1926.

BACON, ROBERT, and SCOTT, JAMES BROWN, (eds.). *Latin America and the United States.* (Addresses by Elihu Root.) Cambridge, Mass.: Harvard University Press, 1917.

————. *The Military and Colonial Policy of the United States.* (Addresses and Reports by Elihu Root.) Cambridge, Mass.: Harvard University Press, 1916.

BISBEE, WILLIAM HAYMOND. *Through Four American Wars: The Impressions and Experiences of Brigadier General William Henry Bisbee.* Boston: Meador Publishing Co., 1931.

CULLOM, SHELBY M. *Fifty Years of Public Service.* Chicago: A. C. McClurg & Co., 1911.

FERRER, HORACIO. *Con el rifle al hombro.* Habana: Imprenta "El Siglo XX," 1950.

FORAKER, JOSEPH B. *Notes on a Busy Life.* 2 vols. Cincinnati: Steward & Kidd Co., 1917.

FUNSTON, FREDERICK, Brig. Gen. U.S.A. *Memories of Two Wars.* New York: Charles Scribner's Sons, 1911.

HEVIA, AURELIO. *Colección de artículos y documentos referentes a la condición actual de Cuba.* Habana: Imprenta de Rambla y Bouza, 1909.

KROCK, ARTHUR (comp.) *The Editorials of Henry Watterson.* Louisville, Ky.: Louisville Courier-Journal Co., 1923.

*La República de Cuba en 1909, Septiembre.* (Articles from *El Mundo* in Spanish and English.) Habana: Imprenta de Rambla y Bouza, 1909.

LODGE, HENRY CABOT. *Selections from the Correspondence of Theodore Roosevelt and Henry Cabot Lodge.* 2 Vols. New York: Charles Scribner's Sons, 1925.

MILES, NELSON A. *Personal Recollections and Observations of General Nelson A. Miles.* Chicago and New York: Werner Co., 1897.

————. *Serving the Republic.* New York and London: Harper & Bros., 1911.

MONTERO, TOMÁS. *Grandezas y miserias, el libro de un reporter.* Habana: Ed. Alfa., 1944.

MOORE, J. HAMPTON. *With Speaker Cannon Through the Tropics.* Philadelphia: Book Print, 1907.

MORISON, E. E. (ed.). *The Letters of Theodore Roosevelt.* 8 Vols. Cambridge, Mass.: Harvard University Press, 1952.

PARKER, JAMES. *The Old Army: Memories, 1872–1918.* Philadelphia: Dorrance & Co., 1929.

PÉREZ, MARINO LUIS (comp.). *Newspaper Clippings Relative to the Period of the Administration of Cuba by the United States, September, 1906, to January, 1909.* 15 Vols. (Available in the Library of Congress, Washington, D.C.)

PURI, MANUEL C. (ed.). *La revolución de agosto: historia de corresponsal por Arture F. Sainz de la Peña.* Habana: Imprenta "La Prueba," 1909.

SECADES Y JAPÓN, MANUEL, and DÍAZ PARDO, HORACIO (eds.). *La justicia en Cuba: los veteranos y los indultos.* Habana: Imprenta "La Prueba," 1908.

————. *La justicia en Cuba: patriotas y traidores.* 2 vols. Habana: Imprenta P. Fernandez y Ca., 1912, 1914.

SCOTT, HUGH LENOX. Maj. Gen. USA (Ret.). *Some Memories of a Soldier.* New York and London: Century Co., 1928.

WHITE, WILLIAM ALLEN. *Autobiography of William Allen White*. New York: Macmillan Co., 1946.

WILSON, JAMES HARRISON. *Under the Old Flag*. 2 vols. New York and London: D. Appleton & Co., 1912.

WRIGHT, IRENE. *Cuba*. New York: Macmillan Co., 1010.


SECONDARY SOURCES


*Bibliography and Historiography*

CORBITT, DUVON C. "Cuban Revisionist Interpretations of Cuba's Struggle for Independence," *Hispanic American Historical Review*, XLIII (August, 1963), 395–404.

HANKE, LEWIS (ed.) and the Hispanic Foundation in the Library of Congress. *Handbook of Latin American Studies, 1935–1965*. Cambridge, Mass.: Harvard University Press, 1936–51; and Gainesville, Fla.: University of Florida Press, 1951–65.

HILTON, RONALD (ed.). *Handbook of Hispanic Source Materials and Research Organizations in the United States*. Toronto, Canada: University of Toronto Press, 1942.

HUMPHREYS, R. A. (ed.). *Latin American History: A Guide to the Literature in English*. London: Oxford University Press, 1958.

PAN AMERICAN UNION. *Index to Latin American Periodical Literature, 1929–1960*. Compiled in the Columbus Memorial Library. Boston: G. K. Hall & Co., 1962.

PERAZA Y SARAUSA, FERMÍN. *Anuario bibliografico cubano, 1937–1964*. 28 vols. Habana: Ediciones anuario bibliografico cubana, 1938–59; and Gainesville, Florida: Fermín Peraza, 1961–64.

———. *Bibliograficas cubanas*. Washington: Library of Congress Hispanic Foundation, 1945.

SMITH, ROBERT F. "Twentieth-Century Cuban Historiography, *Hispanic American Historical Review*, XLIV, (February, 1964), 44–73.

TRELLES Y GOVÍN, CARLOS MANUEL. *Biblioteca historica cubana*. 3 vols. Matanzas: Imprenta de Andres Estrada, 1922, 1924, 1926.

## Books

ALGER, R. A. *The Spanish-American War*. New York and London: Harper & Bros., 1901.

ÁLVAREZ DÍAZ, JOSÉ R., *et al*. *Un estudio sobre Cuba: colonia-república-experimento socialista*. Miami, Florida: University of Miami Press, 1963.

ARREODONDO, ALBERTO. *Cuba: tierra indefensa*. Habana: Editorial Lex, 1945.

BACLAGON, ULDARICO S. *Philippine Campaigns*. Manila: Graphic House, 1952.

BARBARROSA, ENRIQUE. *El proceso de la república, analisis de la situación politica y económica de Cuba bajo el gobierno presidencial de Tomás Estrada Palma y José Miguel Gómez*. Habana: Imprenta Militar de A. Perez Sierra, 1911.

BANGS, JOHN KENDRICK. *Uncle Sam Trustee*. New York: Riggs Publishing Co., 1902.

BEALE, HOWARD K. *Theodore Roosevelt and the Rise of America to World Power*. Baltimore: Johns Hopkins Press, 1956.

BEALS, CARLETON. *The Crime of Cuba*. Philadelphia and London: J. B. Lippincott, 1933.

BEMIS, SAMUEL FLAGG (ed.). *The American Secretaries of State and Their Diplomacy*. 10 Vols. New York: Alfred A. Knopf, 1927–29.

———. *The Latin American Policy of the United States*. New York: Harcourt, Brace & Co., 1943.

BLUM, JOHN MORTON. *The Republican Roosevelt.* Cambridge, Mass.: Harvard University Press, 1954.

BOWERS, CLAUDE G. *Beveridge and the Progressive Era.* New York: Literary Guild, 1932.

BUELL, RAYMOND LESLIE, et al. *Problems of the New Cuba.* Report of the Commission on Cuban Affairs. New York: Foreign Policy Association, Inc., 1935.

CAMACHO, PÁNFILO D. *Estrada Palma, el Gobernante Honrado.* Habana: Editorial Trópico, 1938.

CARABALLO SOTOLONGO, F. *El Imperialismo Norte-Americano.* Habana: Imprenta "El Siglo XX," 1914.

CARBALLAL, RODOLFO Z. *El General José Miguel Gómez.* Habana: Imprenta Rambla y Bouza y Ca., 1913.

CARBONELL, JOSÉ M. *Cuba Independiente.* Vol. XI of *Historia de America.* Edited by RICARDO LEVENE. 14 Vols. Buenos Aires: Imprenta Lopez, 1941.

CÁRDENAS, RAÚL DE. *La política de los Estados Unidos en al continente americano.* Habana: Sociedad Editorial Cuba Contemporanea, 1921.

CARTER, WILLIAM HARDING. Maj. Gen. U.S.A. *The American Army.* Indianapolis, Ind.: Bobbs-Merrill Co., 1915.

————. *The Life of Lieutenant General Chaffee.* Chicago: University of Chicago Press, 1917.

CATÁ, ALVARO. *De guerra á guerra.* Habana: La Razon, 1906.

CHADWICK, FRENCH ENSOR. *The Relations of the United States and Spain: The Spanish-American War.* 2 vols. New York: Charles Scribner's Sons, 1911.

CHAPMAN, CHARLES E. *A History of the Cuban Republic.* New York: Macmillan Co., 1927.

COLLAZO, ENRIQUE. *Cuba intervenida.* Habana: C. Martinez y Ca., 1910.

————. *La Revolución de agosto de 1906.* Habana: C. Martinez y Ca., 1907.

————. *Los Americanos en Cuba.* 2 vols. Habana: C. Martinez y Ca., 1905.

Córdova, Federico. *Manuel Sanguily*. Habana: Seoane, Fernandez y Ca., impresores, 1942.

Deutrich, Mabel E. *Struggle for Supremacy: The Career of General Fred C. Ainsworth*. Washington: Public Affairs Press, 1962.

Duffy, Herbert S. *William Howard Taft*. New York: Minton, Balch & Co., 1930.

Dupuy, R. Ernest. *The Compact History of the United States Army*. New York: Hawthorne Books Inc., 1956.

Ekirch, Arthur A., Jr. *The Civilian and the Military*. New York: Oxford University Press, 1956.

Ferguson, Erna. *Cuba*. New York: Alfred A. Knopf, 1946.

Figueras, Francisco. *La intervención y su política*. Habana: Avisador Commercial, 1906.

Fitzgibbon, Russell H. *Cuba and the United States, 1900–1935*. Menasha, Wisconsin: George Banta Publishing Co., 1935.

Foner, Philip S. *A History of Cuba and Its Relations With the United States*. 2 vols. New York: International Publishers, 1962, 1964.

Forbes, W. Cameron. *The Philippine Islands*. 2 vols. Boston and New York: Houghton Mifflin Co., 1928.

Forbes–Lindsay, C. H. A. *Cuba and Her People of To-day*. Boston: L. C. Page and Company, 1911.

Ganoe, William Addleman. *The History of the United States Army*. 2d ed. revised. New York and London: D. Appleton–Century Company, 1942.

Garrigó, Roque E. *La convulsión cubana*. Habana: Imprenta "La Razon," 1906.

Guerra y Sánchez, Ramiro. *Sugar and Society in the Caribbean: An Economic History of Cuban Agriculture*. New Haven, Conn.: Yale University Press, 1964.

Guerra y Sánchez, Ramiro, *et al. Historia de la Nación Cubana*. 7 vols. Habana: Editorial Historia de la Nacion Cubana, S. A., 1952.

GUGGENHEIM, HARRY F. *The United States and Cuba.* New York: Macmillan Co., 1934.

GUTIÉRREZ Y SÁNCHEZ, GUSTAVO. *El desarrolo económico de Cuba.* Habana: Publicaciones de la Junta Nacional de Económica, 1952.

GRUNDER, GAREL A. and William E. Livezey. *The Philippines and the United States.* Norman, Oklahoma: University of Oklahoma Press, 1951.

HAGEDORN, HERMANN. *Leonard Wood: A Biography.* 2 vols. New York and London: Harper & Bros., 1931.

HARBAUGH, WILLIAM HENRY. *Power and Responsibility: The Life and Times of Theodore Roosevelt.* New York: Farrar, Straus & Cudahy, 1961.

HEALY, DAVID F. *The United States in Cuba, 1898–1902.* Madison: University of Wisconsin Press, 1963.

HILL, HOWARD C. *Roosevelt and the Caribbean.* Chicago: University of Chicago Press, 1927.

HOLDEN, EDWARD S. and ROBINSON, WIRT (eds.). *General Cullum's Biographical Register of the Officers and Graduates of the U. S. Military Academy: Supplements, 1890–1900 and 1900–1910.* Vols. IV and V. Cambridge, Mass.: Riverside Press, 1901; and Saginaw, Michigan: Seeman & Peters, 1910.

HORREGO ESTUCH, LEOPOLDO. *Juan Gualberto Gómez.* Habana: Editorial Lex, 1954.

HUNTINGTON, SAMUEL P. *The Soldier and the State.* Cambridge, Mass.: Harvard University Press, 1957.

INFIESTA, RAMON. *Historia constitucional de Cuba.* 2d ed. Habana: Cultural, S. A., 1951.

JENKS, LELAND H. *Our Cuban Colony: A Study in Sugar.* New York: Vanguard Press, 1928.

JEREZ VILLAREAL, JUAN. *Oriente: biografía de una provincia.* Habana: Imprenta "El Siglo XX," 1960.

JESSUP, PHILIP C. *Elihu Root.* 2 vols. New York: Dodd, Mead & Co., 1938.

JOHNSON, WILLIS FLETCHER. *The History of Cuba.* 5 vols. New York: B. F. Buck and Company, Inc., 1920.

JONES, CHESTER LLOYD. *The Caribbean Since 1900.* New York: Prentice–Hall, Inc., 1936.

LOCKMILLER, DAVID A. *Enoch H. Crowder: Soldier, Lawyer, Statesman.* (University of Missouri Studies, No. 27.) Columbia, Missouri: University of Missouri Press, 1955.

——. *Magoon in Cuba: A History of the Second Intervention, 1906–1909.* Chapel Hill, North Carolina: University of North Carolina Press, 1938.

LEOPOLD, RICHARD W. *Elihu Root and the Conservative Tradition.* Boston: Little, Brown & Co., 1954.

LORENZO, RAÚL. *El empleo en Cuba.* Habana: Seoane, Fernandez, impresores, 1955.

LOVEIRA, CARLOS. *Generales y doctores.* Edited by Shasta M. Bryant and J. Riis Owre. New York: Oxford University Press, 1965.

MACGAFFEY, WYATT and BARNETT, CLIFFORD R. *Cuba.* New Haven, Connecticut: Human Relations Area Files, Inc., 1962.

MARTÍNEZ ORTIZ, RAFAEL. *Cuba: los primeros años de independencia.* 2 vols., 2d ed. Paris: Le Livre Libre, 1921.

MÁRQUEZ STERLING, CARLOS. *Alrededor de nuestra psicologia.* Habana: Imprenta Avisador Comercial, 1906.

——. *Don Tomas: biografia de una epoca.* Habana: Editorial Lex, 1953.

——. *Proceso histórico de la Enmienda Platt, 1897–1934.* Habana: Imprenta "El Siglo XX," 1941.

MECHAM, J. LLOYD. *Church and State in Latin America.* Chapel Hill, N.C.: University of North Carolina Press, 1934.

MEDEL, JOSÉ ANTONIO. *The Spanish–American War and Its Results.* Habana: P. Funandez y Ca., 1932.

MILLIS, WALTER. *The Martial Spirit.* Boston and New York: Houghton Mifflin Co., 1931.

MORGAN, H. WAYNE. *William McKinley and His America.* Syracuse, New York: Syracuse University Press, 1963.

MOWRY, GEORGE E. *The Era of Theodore Roosevelt and the Birth of Modern America.* New York: Harper & Row, 1958.

MUNRO, DANA G. *Intervention and Dollar Diplomacy in the Caribbean, 1900–1921.* Princeton, New Jersey: Princeton University Press, 1964.

――――. *The United States and the Caribbean Area.* Boston. World Peace Foundation, 1934.

NEARING, SCOTT and FREEMAN, JOSEPH. *Dollar Diplomacy: A Study in American Imperialism.* New York: Viking Press, 1925.

NELSON, LOWRY. *Rural Cuba.* Minneapolis: University of Minnesota Press, 1950.

NELSON, OTTO L., JR. Maj. Gen., U.S.A. *National Security and the General Staff.* Washington: Infantry Journal Press, 1946.

ORTIZ FERNÁNDEZ, FERNANDO. *Cuban Counterpoint: Tobacco and Sugar.* Trans. by HARRIET DE ONÍS. New York: Alfred A. Knopf, 1947.

PARDO SUAREZ, VICENTE. *La elección presidencial en Cuba.* Habana: Rambla, Bouza y Ca., 1923.

PARKER, WILLIAM B. (ed.). *Cubans of To-Day.* New York and London: G. P. Putnam's Sons, 1919.

PÉREZ CABRERA, JOSÉ MANUEL. *Estrada Palma y el alba de la República.* Habana: Cuadernos de la Universidad del Aire, 1952.

PERKINS, DEXTER. *Hands Off! A History of the Monroe Doctrine.* Boston: Little, Brown & Co., 1941.

――――. *The Monroe Doctrine, 1867–1907.* Baltimore: Johns Hopkins Press, 1937.

――――. *The United States and the Caribbean.* Cambridge, Mass.: Harvard University Press, 1947.

PORTELL VILÁ, HERMINO. *Historia de Cuba en sus relaciones con los Estados Unidos y España.* 4 vols. Habana: J. Montero, 1938–41.

PORTER, ROBERT P. *Industrial Cuba.* New York: Knickerbocker Press, 1899.

PORTUONDO DEL PRADO, FERNANDO. *Historia de Cuba*. 4th ed. Habana: Ed. Minerva, 1950.

PRATT, JULIUS. *America's Colonial Experiment*. New York: Prentice–Hall, Inc., 1950.

PRINGLE, HENRY F. *The Life and Times of William Howard Taft*. 2 vols. New York and Toronto: Farrar & Rinehart, Inc., 1939.

———. *Theodore Roosevelt*. New York: Harcourt, Brace & Co., 1931.

REA, GEORGE BRONSON. *Facts and Fakes About Cuba*. New York: George Munro's Sons, 1897.

RHODES, JAMES FORD. *The McKinley and Roosevelt Administrations, 1897–1909*. New York: Macmillan Co., 1922.

RIERA HERNÁNDEZ, MARIO. *Bayamo política, 1898–1956*. Habana: Imprenta Modelo, 1957.

———. *Cuba política, 1899–1955*. Habana: Imprenta Modelo, 1955.

———. *Cincuenta y dos años de política, Oriente, 1900–1952*. Habana: Llinas esq. A. Belascoain, 1953.

ROBINSON, ALBERT GARDNER. *Cuba and the Intervention*. New York, London, and Bombay: Longmans, Green & Co., 1905.

———. *Cuba Old and New*. New York, London and Bombay: Longmans, Green & Co., 1915.

ROIG DE LEUCHSENRING, EMILIO. *El intervencionismo, mal de males de Cuba republicana*. San Jose de Costa Rica: A. C., Ediciones del "Repertorio Americano," 1931.

———. *Historia de la Enmienda Platt*. 2 vols. Habana: Cultural, S. A., 1935.

———. *La colonia superviva: Cuba a los veintidós años de república*. Habana: Imprenta "El Siglo XX," 1925.

———. *La enmienda Platt: su interpretación primitiva y sus aplicaciones posteriores*. Anuario de 1922, Sociedad Cubana de Derecho Internacional. Habana: Imprenta "El Siglo XX," 1922.

————. *Males y vicios de Cuba republicana, sus causas y sus remedios.* Habana: Oficina del Historiador de la Ciudad de la Habana, 1959.

ROOSEVELT, THEODORE. *Autobiography.* Vol. XXII of *The Works of Theodore Roosevelt.* Edited by HERMANN HAGEDORN. New York: Charles Scribner's Sons, 1926.

————. *State Papers.* Vol. XV of *The Works of Theodore Roosevelt.* Edited by HERMANN HAGEDORN. New York: Charles Scribner's Sons, 1926.

————. *The Rough Riders.* Vol. XIII of *The Works of Theodore Roosevelt.* Edited by HERMANN HAGEDORN. New York: Charles Scribner's Sons, 1924.

RUBENS, HORATIO S. *Liberty: The Story of Cuba.* New York: Brewer, Warren & Putnam, Inc., 1932.

SANTOVENIA Y ECHAIDE, EMETERIO S. *Huellas de gloria: frases historicas cubanas.* Habana: Ed. Trópico, 1944.

————. *Los presidentes de Cuba libre.* Habana: Seoane y Fernandez, 1930.

————. *Un dia como hoy: 366 fechas en la historia de Cuba.* Habana: Ed. Trópico, 1946.

SCOTT, JAMES BROWN. *Robert Bacon: Life and Letters.* New York: Doubleday, Page & Co., 1923.

SEXTON, WILLIAM T. *Soldiers in the Sun.* Harrisburg, Pa.: Military Service Publishing Co., 1939.

SMITH, ROBERT F. (ed.). *Background to Revolution: The Development of Modern Cuba.* New York: Alfred A. Knopf, 1966.

SMITH, ROBERT F. *The United States and Cuba.* New York: Bookman Associates, 1960.

SPAULDING, OLIVER LYMAN. *The United States Army in War and Peace.* New York: G. P. Putnam's Sons, 1937.

STOREY, MOORFIELD and LICHAUCO, MARCIAL. *The Conquest of the Philippines by the United States, 1898–1925.* New York and London: G. P. Putnam's Sons, 1926.

STRODE, HUDSON. *The Pageant of Cuba*. New York: Harrison Smith & Robert Haas, 1934.

STUART, GRAHAM H. *Cuba and Its International Relations*. New York: Institute of International Education, 1923.

SUÁREZ VERA, LUIS. *General Emilio Núñez: su historia revolucionaria y su actuación en la vida publica*. Habana: Imprenta Pi y Margall, 1915.

SULLIVAN, MARK. *The Turn of the Century*. Vol. I in *Our Times*. New York and London: Charles Scribner's Sons, 1934.

———. *America Finding Herself*. Vol. II in *Our Times*. New York and London: Charles Scribner's Sons, 1927.

———. *Pre-War America*. Vol. III in *Our Times*. New York and London: Charles Scribner's Sons, 1930.

TRELLES Y GOVÍN, CARLOS MANUEL. *El progreso (1902–1905) y el retroceso (1906–1922) de la República de Cuba*. Habana: Imprenta el Score, 1923.

VARELA ZEQUEIRA, EDUARDO. *La política en 1905*. Habana: Rambla y Bouza, 1905.

VARONA, ENRIQUE JOSÉ. *De la colonia a la república: selección de trabajos politicos ordenada por sus autor*. Habana: Sociedad Editorial Cuba Contemporanea, 1919.

———. *Mirando en torno*. Habana: Rambla y Bouza, 1910.

VAUGHAN, WALTER. *The Life and Work of Sir William Van Horne*. New York: Century Co., 1920.

VELASCO, CARLOS DE. *Aspectos nacionales*. Habana: Libreria "Studium," 1915.

———. *Estrada Palma: contribución historica*. Habana: "La Universal," 1911.

WAGENKNECHT, EDWARD. *The Seven Worlds of Theodore Roosevelt*. New York, London, Toronto: Longmans, Green & Co., 1958.

WEIGLEY, RUSSELL F. *Towards an American Army*. New York and London: Columbia University Press, 1962.

WEINBERG, ALBERT K. *Manifest Destiny: A Study of Nationalist Expansion in American History*. Baltimore: Johns Hopkins Press, 1935.

Wisan, Joseph E. *The Cuban Crisis as Reflected in the New York Press, 1895–1898*. New York: Columbia University Press, 1934.

Wolff, Leon. *Little Brown Brother*. Garden City, New York: Doubleday & Co., 1961.

Worcester, Dean C. *The Philippines Past and Present*. 2 vols. New York: Macmillan Co., 1914.

Wright, Philip G. *Sugar in Relation to the Tariff*. New York: McGraw-Hill Book Co., 1924.

————. *The Cuban Situation and Our Treaty Relations*. Washington: Brookings Institution, 1931.

*Articles*

Adams, Frederick Upham. "Cuba, Its Condition and Outlook," *World's Work*, XIII (November, 1906), 8237–42.

Aquirre, Charles M. "A Struggle for Cuban Liberty" *Independent*, LXI (September 20, 1906), 664.

Atkins, Edwin F. "Tariff Relations with Cuba—Actual and Desirable," *Annals of the American Academy of Political and Social Science*, XXXII (September, 1908), 321–29.

Baker, Ray Stannard. "General Leonard Wood," *McClure's Magazine*, XIV (February, 1900), 368–79.

Bieberstein, Rogalla von. "Die Intervention der Vereignigten Staaten auf Kuba," *Historische Blaetter*, CXXXIX (1907), 614–27.

Brooks, Sydney. "Cuba," *Fortnightly Review*, LXXXVIII (November, 1910), 796–806.

Brownell, Atherton. "The Cuban Republic on Trial," *Review of Reviews*, XXXIV (October, 1906), 424–25.

————. "The Commercial Annexation of Cuba," *Appleton's Magazine*, VII (October, 1906), 406–11.

Bryce, James. "Some Reflections on the State of Cuba," *North American Review*, CLXXIV (March, 1902), 449–56.

BULLARD, ROBERT L. Lt. Col., U.S.A. "Education in Cuba," *Educational Review*, XXXIX (April, 1910), 378–84.

———. "How Cubans Differ from Us," *North American Review*, CLXXXVI (November 11, 1907), 416–21.

———. "The Army in Cuba," *Journal of the Military Service Institution*, XLI (September, 1907), 152–57.

———. "The Cuban Negro," *North American Review*, CLXXXIV (March 15, 1907), 623–30.

CARRILLO ALDAMA, M. "The Cuban Government's Side," *Independent*, LXI (September 20, 1906), 664.

COLETTA, PAOLO E. "McKinley, the Peace Negotiations and the Acquisition of the Philippines," *Pacific Historical Review*, XXX (November, 1961), 341–50.

CONANT, CHARLES A. "Our Duty in Cuba," *North American Review*, CLXXXV May 17, 1907), 141–46.

DUPUY, WILLIAM A. "Road Building by the United States in Cuba," *Scientific American*, C (February 13, 1909), 136–38.

EARLE, F. S. "Agricultural Cuba," *World To-Day*, XI (November, 1906), 1175–84.

FORBES–LINDSAY, C. H. "Cuba: The Land of Promise," *World To-Day*, XIV (February, 1908), 141–50.

FOSTER, JOHN W. "The Annexation of Cuba," *Independent*, LXI (October 25, 1906), 965–68.

GANNETT, HENRY. "Conditions in Cuba Revealed by the Census," *National Geographic Magazine*, XX (February, 1909), 200–202.

GREENE, FRED. "The Military View of American National Policy, 1904–1940," *American Historical Review*, LXVI (January, 1961), 354–77.

GUERRA, FAUSTINO. "Causes of the Cuban Insurrection," *North American Review*, CLXXXIII (September 21, 1906), 538–40.

GUIRAL MORENO, MARIO. "Nuestros problemas políticos, economicos y sociales," *Cuba contemporanea*, V (August, 1914), 401–24.

HANNA, MATTHEW E. Capt., U.S.A. "The Necessity of Increasing the Efficiency of the Cuban Army," *Journal of the Military Service Institution,* XXXV (July, 1904), 28–36.

HEMMINGWAY, WILLIAM. "To-morrow in Cuba," *Harper's Weekly,* LIII (March 20, 1909), 24–25.

HENNESSY, C. A. M "The Roots of Cuban Nationalism," *International Affairs,* XXXIX (July, 1963), 345–59.

HOWLAND, HAROLD F. "Saving a People from Themselves," *Outlook,* LXXXIV (October 27, 1906), 455–64.

HUGHES, RUPERT. "Shall We Meddle with Cuba?" *Harper's Weekly,* L (September 8, 1906), 1277–78.

INGLIS, WILLIAM. "The Armed Struggle for Control of Cuba," *Harper's Weekly,* L (September 22, 1906), 1344–47, 1363.

———. "With the Rebel Leader in the Cuban Hills," *Harper's Weekly,* L (September 29, 1906), 1380–83.

———. "How Cubans Fight Cubans," *Harper's Weekly,* L (October 6, 1906), 1416–18, 1434–35.

———. "The Disappointed Rebels in Wait About Havana," *Harper's Weekly,* L (October 13, 1906), 1454–56.

———. "The Collapse of the Cuban House of Cards," *Harper's Weekly,* L (October 20, 1906), 1488–91, 1505.

———. "The Last Act of Cuba's Tragi-Comedy of Insurrection," *Harper's Weekly,* L (October 27, 1906), 1524–26, 1541.

———. "How the 'Warlike' Cubans Gave Up Their Arms," *Harper's Weekly,* L (November 3, 1906), 1564–66.

———. "The Rain-Coat of Rodriguez," *Harper's Weekly,* LI (July 27, 1907), 1092–93.

JOHNSON, SIR HARRY. "An Englishman's Impression of American Rule in Cuba," *McClure's Magazine,* XXXIII (September, 1909), 496–504.

LEUCHTENBURG, WILLIAM E. "Progressivism and Imperialism: The Progressive Movement and American Foreign Policy, 1898–1916," *Mississippi Valley Historical Review,* XXXIX (December, 1952), 483–504.

LOCKMILLER, DAVID A. "Agriculture in Cuba During the Second United States Intervention, 1906–1909," *Agricultural History*, XI (July, 1937), 181–88.

———. "La base legal de la intervención de los Estados Unidos en Cuba en 1906," *Revista bimestre cubana*, XXXVIII (September–December, 1936), 268–81.

———. "The Advisory Law Commission of Cuba," *Hispanic American Historical Review*, XVII (February, 1937), 2–29.

———. "The Settlement of the Church Property Question in Cuba," *Hispanic American Historical Review*, XVII (November, 1937), 488–98.

McCLERNAND, E. J. MAJ., U.S.A. "Our Philippine Problem," *Journal of the Military Service Institution*, XXIX (November, 1901), 327–32.

MAGOON, CHARLES E. "The War Department: Administration of Civil Government," *Scribner's Magazine*, XXXIV (July, 1903), 85–95.

MAÑACH, JORGE. "Revolution in Cuba," *Foreign Affairs*, XII (October 1933), 46–56.

MINGER, RALPH ELDIN. "Taft, MacArthur and the Establishment of Civil Government in the Philippines," *Ohio Historical Quarterly*, LXX (October, 1961), 308–31.

———. "William Howard Taft and the United States Intervention in Cuba in 1906," *Hispanic American Historical Review*, XLI (February, 1961), 75–89.

"The Nature of the Government in Cuba." Editorial in *American Journal of International Law*, I (January, 1907), 149–50.

NIETO DE DURLAND, CARMELA. "Home Rule in Cuba Once More," *The World To-day*, XVI (March, 1909), 285–88.

ORTIZ, FERNANDO. "La decadencia cubana," *Revista bimestre cubana*, XIX (January–February, 1924), 17–45.

PATRICK, MASON M. LT. COL., CE. "Notes on Road Building in Cuba," *Professional Memoirs*, II (July–September, 1910), 263–84.

POMEROY, EARL S. "The American Colonial Office," *Mississippi Valley Historical Review*, XXX (March, 1944), 521–32.

"The Restoration of the Cuban Government." Editorial in *American Journal of International Law*, III (April, 1909), 431–34.

ROCKWOOD, JOHN G. "Rescuing Cuba from the Cubans," *World To-day*, XI (November, 1906), 1199–1203.

ROWE, LEO STANTON. "The Reorganization of Local Government in Cuba," *Annals of the American Academy of Political and Social Science*, XXV (March, 1905), 311–21.

SEMSCH, PHILIP L. "Elihu Root and the General Staff," *Military Affairs*, XXVII (Spring, 1963), 16–27.

SHEPARDSON, FRANCIS W. "American Guardianship of Cuba," *The World To-day*, XI (November, 1906), 1197–99.

SMITH, ROBERT F. "Cuba: Laboratory for Dollar Diplomacy, 1898–1917," *The Historian*, XXVIII (August, 1966), 586–609.

TWAIN, MARK. "A Defense of General Funston," *North American Review*, CLXXIV (May, 1902), 611–24.

WARD, L. B. "The Economical Surface Mining Operations of Cuba," *Scientific American*, XCVII (July 6, 1907), 11.

WEIGHTMAN, RICHARD C. "Cuba's American Governor," *Review of Reviews*, XXXIV (November, 1906), 556–59.

WILDMAN, EUGENE. "From Bowery Boy to General," *World To-day*, XVI (March, 1909), 281–85.

WILLIAMS, TALCOTT. "The Causes of the Cuban Insurrection," *Outlook*, LXXXIV (September 15, 1906), 111–14.

WOOD, LEONARD. "The Existing Conditions and Needs in Cuba," *North American Review*, CLXVIII (May, 1899), 593–601.

———. "The Military Government of Cuba," *Annals of the American Academy of Political and Social Science*, XXI (March, 1903), 153–82.

WRIGHT, IRENE A. "The Cart-Roads of Mister Magoon," *World To-day*, XVI (June, 1909), 641–48.

*Unpublished Works*

BROWN, RICHARD C. "Social Attitudes of American Generals, 1898–1940." Unpublished Ph.D. dissertation, University of Wisconsin, 1951.

CUMMINS, LEJEUNE. "The Origin and Development of Elihu Root's Latin American Diplomacy." Unpublished Ph.D. dissertation, The University of California, Berkeley, 1964.

DAVIS, JACK. "The Latin American Policy of Elihu Root." Unpublished Ph.D. dissertation, University of Illinois, 1956.

ELLSWORTH, HARRY ALANSON, CAPT. USMC. *One Hundred Eighty Landings of the United States Marines, 1800–1934.* 2 vols. Washington, 1934. Mimeographed. Copy in the Marine Corps Museum, Quantico, Virginia.

HITCHMAN, JAMES HAROLD. "Leonard Wood and the Cuban Question, 1898–1902." Unpublished Ph.D. dissertation, The University of California, Berkeley, 1965.

MEYER, LEO J. "Relations Between the United States and Cuba, 1898–1917." Unpublished Ph.D. dissertation, Clark University, 1928.

NICHOLS, LAWRENCE R. "The Bronze Titan: The Mulatto Hero of Cuban Independence, Antonio Maceo." Unpublished Ph.D. dissertation, Duke University, 1954.

THACKER, JOEL D. "Interventions in Cuba under the Platt Amendment." Unpublished manuscript, Cuba Subject File, Historical Reference Section, Historical Branch, G–3, Headquarters Marine Corps, Washington, D.C.

# Index

Acosta, Baldermo, 255

Acton, Lord, 98

Adee, Alvey A., 64

Advisory Law Commission, 197–201, 213, 236, 262; membership of, 197; working procedures of, 197–98

Agriculture, 24, 25, 35, 39; development of, 202–3; need for credit in, 35, 38–39, 203; and soil, 21; United States aid to, 32

Aguinaldo, captured by Gen. Funston, 4, 9

Aguirre, Col. Charles, 61

Ainsworth, Gen. Fred C., 64, 89

Alemán, Gen. José B., 45

Alger, Russell A., 30

Aliens, 23, 25; business community of, 39

American-Cuban relations: American carpetbaggers, effect of, 28, 169; and American opinions of Cubans, 27–29; and Army's pacification policy, 12–16, 133–39; and Cuban independence, promised by Root, 36; and Military Government of Cuba, 29–44; occupation of Cuba, effect of, 256–57 (see Occupation of Cuba); and pacification programs, 12–16, 133–39; and Platt Amendment, 40–42; and Provisional Government (see Provisional Government); and reciprocity treaty, 48, 175, 202; and restoration and withdrawal, 245–54; and United States Cuban policy, 33, 40, 65–67, 79–80

American Journal of International Law, 148

American public opinion: on anti-imperialism, 36; on Philippine insurrection, 10–12; and reaction to pacification, 111

American Tobacco Company, 179

Americanization policy, 34–35, 38–39, 43

Anarchists, 203

Annexation of Cuba, 49, 52–53, 139, 169–89, 262–63

—American debate on: and opposition by Magoon, 170; and opposition by Root, 147; and support by Wood, 32, 34; and U.S. policy, 32, 34, 36, 39, 43, 147, 162, 169–70

—Cuban support of: by alien and conservative business groups, 169–71; and annexationists, 164, 169–89; in Havana, 171; by Moderate party, 108; and Masso Parra conspiracy, 178–85, 205; and occupation, efforts to prolong, 180, 183–84

Anti-Americanism, 244–45

Armas, José de, 170, 176

Army and Navy Journal, 134, 213, 231

Army of Cuban Pacification, 121–43, 225, 232; and American goals in Cuba, 133–39; marches by, 129–30; garrisons of, 126–27, 129; health programs of, 136; indoctrination program of, 123; and influence on American policy, 138–39; and mapping the island, 131; Military Information Division of, 130–31 (see also Military Information Division); occupation duty of, 133–39; and